# Lecture Notes in Computer Science　11550

Commenced Publication in 1973
Founding and Former Series Editors:
Gerhard Goos, Juris Hartmanis, and Jan van Leeuwen

More information about this series at http://www.springer.com/series/7409

Seraphin Calo · Elisa Bertino ·
Dinesh Verma (Eds.)

# Policy-Based Autonomic
# Data Governance

 Springer

*Editors*
Seraphin Calo 🆔
IBM Research
Yorktown Heights, NY, USA

Elisa Bertino 🆔
Purdue University
West Lafayette, IN, USA

Dinesh Verma 🆔
IBM Research
Yorktown Heights, NY, USA

ISSN 0302-9743          ISSN 1611-3349   (electronic)
Lecture Notes in Computer Science
ISBN 978-3-030-17276-3          ISBN 978-3-030-17277-0   (eBook)
https://doi.org/10.1007/978-3-030-17277-0

LNCS Sublibrary: SL3 – Information Systems and Applications, incl. Internet/Web, and HCI

This Springer imprint is published by the registered company Springer Nature Switzerland AG
The registered company address is: Gewerbestrasse 11, 6330 Cham, Switzerland

# Preface

## Introduction

As data volumes increase and devices start getting imbued with artificial intelligence, allowing for increased autonomy, managing them, especially managing their security challenges, becomes increasingly difficult. Policy-based management has proven itself useful in simplifying the complexity of management in domains like networking, security, and storage, and it is expected that many of those benefits would carry over to the task of managing big data and autonomous systems. However, the design of suitable policy management systems requires addressing many research challenges. This book aims at providing an overview of recent work that identifies and addresses such challenges.

Most of the chapters in this book are based on extended versions of the papers that were presented at the Second International Workshop on Policy-based Autonomic Data Governance (PADG 2018), held on September 6, 2018 in Barcelona, Spain, in conjunction with the 23rd European Symposium on Research in Computer Security (ESORICS 2018). The workshop was partly sponsored by the UK-US Distributed Analytics and Information Science International Technology Alliance (DAIS ITA) research program. It brought together researchers active in policy-based management to share results, works in progress, and identify new avenues of collaborative research. In addition to the papers that were presented at the workshop, additional papers have been included by well-known researchers in the areas covered by the volume. The book chapters cover a range of topics in the management of data integrity, security, and privacy in autonomous systems, as well as associated analytics, and the autonomic generation and evolution of governance policies.

## Autonomic Systems and Data Governance

The proliferation of IoT devices has led to the production of large volumes of data that can be used to characterize and potentially optimize real world processes. At the same time, the influence of edge computing is leading to more distributed architectures incorporating more autonomous elements. The flow of information is critical in such environments, but the real-time, distributed nature of the system components complicates the mechanisms for protecting and controlling access to data.

In distributed collections of autonomous devices, perimeter-based approaches to security are less effective. Security and privacy mechanisms must take a data-centric approach to make certain that data is protected as it travels within the system. This would include: data access governance, providing mechanisms to manage data access permissions and identify sensitive data; consent/data subject rights management, enforcing privacy over shared data and allowing organizations to search, identify, segment, and amend sensitive data as necessary; and, providing platforms that help operationalize privacy processes and practices.

One promising direction for the management of complex distributed environments is to make the major elements of the system self-describing and self-managing [1]. This would lead to an architecture where policy mechanisms are tightly coupled with the system elements. In such integrated architectures, we need to create new models for information assurance, providing traceability of information and allowing better provenance on information flows. In addition, when dealing with devices that have actuation capabilities and are thus able to make changes to physical spaces, safety is also critical. With an emphasis on policy-based mechanisms for governance of data security and privacy, and for safety assurance, the papers in this volume follow three broad themes.

The first theme is that of ensuring safety in the context of autonomous systems. As devices become more autonomous, and bridge the gap between physical systems and information systems, leveraging the technologies being developed for the Internet of Things, safety and security become of paramount importance. Policies can play an important role in improving the safety and security of distributed, autonomic, cyber-physical systems. Anomaly detection techniques are also critical in order to ensure that data is not stolen or misused by malicious insiders or attackers masquerading as legitimate data users. Such malicious parties may use such data for undermining organizational processes, information theft, and worse for carrying out sabotage activities that may have disastrous consequences, including loss of human life.

The second theme is that of autonomy in collaborative, federated systems. In such systems, operational tasks may be executed across several different organizations. This occurs, for example, in military coalitions, or a complex supply-chain-based retail system, or a network of financial companies working together. These federated systems may interconnect to each other using client–server protocols, or a distributed architecture such as block chain. Several of the papers submitted to the workshop addressed papers in this area.

The third broad theme is that of self-generation of policies. The concept of generative policies, where the policies influencing the behavior of an autonomous system are not provided by humans, but instead are inferred and generated by the system itself based on context and higher-level loose guidance provided by humans, is relatively new. Technologies for the formulation and application of generative policies are presented in this volume, along with motivating use cases.

## Chapters in the Volume

The first three chapters in the book look at systems, use-cases, and foundational principles underlying generative policies:

"AGENP: An ASGrammar-based GENerative Policy Framework," by Seraphin Calo, Irene Manotas, Geeth de Mel, Daniel Cunnington, Mark Law, Dinesh Verma,

Alessandra Russo, and Elisa Bertino, describes an architecture for the autonomic generation of policies based on symbolic learning mechanisms [2]. It introduces a general methodology for creating and adapting policies for dynamic, collaborating, autonomous systems, wherein it is not reasonable to expect that the necessary inputs can be provided by direct human interaction due to the scope and complexity of the environment. A detailed architecture is presented to support the various components of the methodology. The chapter also includes an example of the use of generative policies for connected and autonomous vehicles.

"Value of Information: Quantification and Application to Coalition Machine Learning," by Gavin Pearson, Dinesh Verma, and Geeth de Mel, presents the concept of value of information (VoI), provides a quantitative measure for it, and shows how this can be used to determine the policies for information fusion in a coalition machine learning environment.

"Self-Generating Policies for Machine Learning in Coalition Environments," by Dinesh Verma, Seraphin Calo, Shonda Witherspoon, Elisa Bertino, Amani Abu Jabal, Gregory Cirincione, Ananthram Swami, Gavin Pearson, Geeth de Mel, and Irene Manotas, proposes an architecture for generating the policies required for building a machine learning model in a coalition environment. It addresses the problem of deciding when to accept training data from the different coalition sources. The generated policies provide a mechanism for making these decisions given the variability of the environment and with minimal human input.

The next four chapters in this book explore various aspects related to the subject of safe autonomy:

"Can N-version Decision-Making Prevent the Rebirth of HAL 9000 in Military Camo? Using a "Golden Rule" Threshold to Prevent AI Mission Individuation," by Sorin Matei and Elisa Bertino, addresses the difficult problem of how to prevent autonomous artificial intelligence (AI) systems from misbehaving. Examples of AI systems that end up refusing to obey their human creators are often presented in science fiction books and movies, such as the famous *2001: A Space Odyssey* movie. However, the enormous progress in AI technologies, sensor computing, and intelligent robots is making such scenarios possible. This chapter introduces the idea that one possible reason for an AI system to misbehave is mission individuation; that is, given a specific mission to carry out, the AI system replaces the original mission with its own defined mission, which may be similar to the original one but with some crucial differences. The chapter then discusses two possible approaches to address the problem of mission individuation by AI systems: decision hybridization, by which humans are involved in all decisions made by the AI system, and N-version decision making, by which multiple independent AI systems are involved in decisions. The chapter then outlines a broad research agenda concerning the latter approach, including metrics for assessing the "quality" of decisions and how to build different versions of AI systems.

"Simulating User Activity for Assessing Effect of Sampling on DB Activity Monitoring Anomaly Detection," by Hagit Grushka, Ofer Biller, Oded Sofer, Lior Rokach, and Bracha Shapira, focuses on the use of anomaly monitoring techniques for detecting unusual activities in database accesses. The chapter addresses scalability as it is often difficult to track and monitor every transaction being executed in the system. To address scalability the chapter proposes using a data-driven policy for deciding which transactions to monitor. An interesting aspect of the proposed approach is that such a policy does not need to be crafted manually and can be inferred from past data. The chapter also reports experimental results obtained from a simulation-based system.

"FADa-CPS Faults and Attacks Discrimination in Cyber-Physical Systems," by Pierpaolo Bo, Alessandro Granato, Marco Ernesto Mancuso, Claudio Ciccotelli, and Leonardo Querzoni, deals with the problem of analyzing faults and attacks in cyber-physical systems. Such systems are and will be increasingly pervasive in many different application domains, including energy grids, intelligent transportation, smart cities, and smart civil infrastructures. Their security and safety are thus critical. This chapter addresses the problem of finding the root cause of faults and attacks. For the latter, such diagnosis typically requires identifying the initial step of the attack, at which point it was possible for the attacker to gain entrance to the attacked system. The chapter presents a comprehensive framework supporting such a root cause analysis and then discusses in depth the various components of the framework. It also describes a prototype implementation and reports experimental results from the use of the prototype.

"Techniques and Systems for Anomaly Detection in Database Systems," by Asma Sallam and Elisa Bertino, focuses on using anomaly detection techniques for protecting databases from data theft. The chapter presents a comprehensive survey of approaches proposed for the monitoring of accesses to relational database systems. These approaches monitor database queries issued by users and/or applications and detect queries that are anomalous. Such anomalous queries can be indicative of possible data exfiltration attempts or data misuse. In most cases such indications are combined with other information, such as authentication and network activity. The chapter then describes several prominent anomaly detection systems for database accesses and outlines directions for future work based on the current state of the art.

The last four chapters deal with the subject of policies and autonomy in federated and distributed environments. Federated environments pose a more complex set of challenges because there is no central authority, and it may be that not all parties in a federated environment trust each other.

"Towards Enabling Trusted Artificial Intelligence via Blockchain," by Kanthi Sarpatwar, Roman Vaculin, Hong Min, Gong Su, Terry Heath, Giridhar Ganapavarapu, and Donna Dillenberger, looks at the challenge of trusting data and models when AI solutions are built in a federated environment where machine learning and AI models are created, trained, and used by different entities. The groups that create the models are very often different from the groups that train the models, which are in turn different from the end users of the trained models. This chapter describes how block chain technologies can be used to provide provenance information concerning how models are created, trained, used, and reused, leading to a more trusted process of the application of artificial intelligence in autonomous organizations. Block chain technologies allow the entity that provides bad data or bad models to be determined. Their approach eliminates the need for a trusted server, and allows the solution to work in a peer-to-peer manner.

"Secure Model Fusion for Distributed Learning Using Partial Homomorphic Encryption" by Changchang Liu, Supriyo Chakraborty, and Dinesh Verma looks at a similar problem in a federated environment, where training data is split across several partners, and each is reluctant to share training data or even model parameters with each other. They discuss approaches for building an AI model where all model parameters are encrypted whenever they move between parties that do not trust each other. Partial homomorphic encryption techniques are proposed to protect model parameters, and the training process is modified so that it can work when parameters are encrypted. Because encryption comes with a significant overhead, the paper also examines approaches to improve the performance of federated learning in the presence of encryption.

"Policy-Based Identification of IoT Devices' Vendor and Type by DNS Traffic Analysis," by Franck Le, Jorge Ortiz, Dinesh Verma, and Dilip Kandlur, looks at a challenge in enterprise networks introduced by the growing prevalence of IoT devices. New techniques are required to detect such IoT devices, which may not support the traditional network discovery mechanisms found in network routers, servers, and computers. They propose analyzing domain name service (DNS) traffic to detect the manufacturer and model number of an IoT device in a networked environment. The DNS requests are converted to a virtual text document, and document processing algorithms are shown to be effective in detecting IoT devices. The caveat is that such algorithms need to be used in specific contexts to work effectively, and they propose the use of policies to ensure that the right algorithms are invoked in the right sequence to provide an effective detection.

"Redundancy as a Measure of Fault-Tolerance for the Internet of Things: A Review," by Antonino Rullo, Edoardo Serra, and Jorge Lobo, reviews and analyzes redundancy-based fault-tolerant techniques for the IoT. It shows how the implementation of fault-tolerance for each of the three main tasks performed by the nodes of an IoT network—sensing, routing, and control—is of primary importance for the correct operation of the entire system. As fault-tolerance is less developed in the area of control, the chapter then looks at methods that have been used for the replication of the state machines modelling control devices. This leads to a consideration of consensus protocols and their limitations for the IoT. New directions for consensus algorithms based on the concept of block chains are then presented. Standard block chain based protocols cannot be applied without modification to support fault-tolerance in the IoT.

Results dealing with this class of algorithms are presented and it is shown how they can provide the flexibility required to support implementations of fault-tolerance in control devices to overcome some of the limitations of the traditional consensus protocols.

Overall, the different chapters in this volume cover a wide range of topics, all dealing with aspects of the management of autonomous systems. A key underlying concept is that of self-management using policy-based technologies. All the information required by the system for its management is incorporated in it or can be directly obtained or derived by the system itself without the need for any external control mechanisms. Our conception of policies is thus rather broad and encompasses dynamic, evolving control structures incorporating AI and machine learning models.

We hope you will find many interesting research directions in the book.

February 2019

Seraphin Calo
Dinesh Verma
Elisa Bertino

# References

1. Bertino, E., Calo, S., Touma, M., Verma, D., Williams, C., Rivera, B.: A cognitive policy framework for next-generation distributed federated systems: concepts and research directions. In: Distributed Computing Systems (ICDCS), 2017 IEEE 37th International Conference on, pp. 1876–1886. IEEE (2017)
2. Law, M., Russo, A., Bertino, E., Broda, K., Lobo, J.: Representing and learning grammars in answer set programming. In: 2019 AAAI Conference, to appear

# Contributors

| | |
|---|---|
| Amani M. Abu Jabal | Purdue University, USA |
| Elisa Bertino | Purdue University, USA |
| Ofer Biller | IBM Guardium Security Division, Israel |
| Pierpaolo Bo | Sapienza University of Rome, Italy |
| Seraphin Calo | IBM Research, USA |
| Supriyo Chakraborty | IBM Research, USA |
| Claudio Ciccotelli | Sapienza University of Rome, Italy |
| Greg Cirincione | Army Research Labs, USA |
| Daniel Cunnington | IBM Research, UK |
| Geeth de Mel | IBM Research, UK |
| Donna Dillenberger | IBM Research, USA |
| Giridhar Ganapavarapu | IBM Research, USA |
| Alessandro Granato | Sapienza University of Rome, Italy |
| Hagit Grushka-Cohen | Ben-Gurion University of the Negev, Israel |
| Terry Heath | IBM Research, USA |
| Dilip Kandlur | Google, USA |
| Mark Law | Imperial College London, UK |
| Franck Le | IBM Research, USA |
| Changchang Liu | IBM Research, USA |
| Jorge Lobo | Universitat Pompeu Fabra, Spain |
| Marco Ernesto Mancuso | Sapienza University of Rome, Italy |
| Irene Manotas | IBM Research, USA |
| Sorin Adam Matei | Purdue University, USA |
| Hong Min | IBM Research, USA |
| Jorge Ortiz | Rutgers University, USA |
| Gavin Pearson | Defence Science & Technology Laboratory, UK |
| Leonardo Querzoni | Sapienza University of Rome, Italy |
| Lior Rokach | Ben-Gurion University of the Negev, Israel |
| Antonino Rullo | University of Calabria, Italy |
| Alessandra Russo | Imperial College London, UK |
| Asmaa Sallam | Purdue University, USA |
| Kanthi Sarpatwar | IBM Research, USA |
| Edoardo Serra | Boise State University, USA |
| Bracha Shapira | Ben-Gurion University of the Negev, Israel |
| Oded Sofer | IBM Guardium Security Division, Israel |
| Gong Su | IBM Research, Yorktown Heights, USA |
| Ananthram Swami | Army Research Labs, USA |
| Roman Vaculin | IBM Research, USA |
| Dinesh Verma | IBM Research, USA |
| Shonda Witherspoon | IBM Research, USA |

# Contents

# Systems, Use-Cases and Foundational Principles Underlying Generative Policies

# AGENP: An ASGrammar-based GENerative Policy Framework

Seraphin Calo[1], Irene Manotas[1(✉)], Geeth de Mel[3], Daniel Cunnington[4],
Mark Law[5], Dinesh Verma[1], Alessandra Russo[5], and Elisa Bertino[2]

[1] Distributed AI Department, IBM TJ Watson Research Center, Yorktown Heights,
NY 10549, USA
scalo@us.ibm.com, irene.manotas@ibm.com
[2] Computer Science Department, Purdue University, West Lafayette, IN 47907, USA
bertino@purdue.edu
[3] IBM Research UK, Hartree Center, Warrington, UK
geeth.demel@uk.ibm.com
[4] IBM Research UK, Emerging Technology, Hursley Park, Hursley, UK
DanCunnington@uk.ibm.com
[5] Imperial College London, South Kensington Campus, London, UK
{mark.law09,a.russo}@imperial.ac.uk

**Abstract.** Generative policies have been proposed as a mechanism to
learn the constraints and preferences of a system—especially complex systems such as the ones found in coalitions—in a given context so that the
system can adapt to unexpected changes seamlessly, thus achieving the
system goals with minimal human intervention. Generative policies can
help a coalition system to be more effective when working in a distributed,
continuously transforming environment with a diverse set of members,
resources, and tasks. Learning mechanisms based on logic programming,
e.g., Inductive Logic Programming (ILP), have several properties that
make them suitable and attractive for the creation and adaptation of
generative policies, such as the ability to learn a general model from a
small number of examples, and being able to incorporate existing background knowledge. ILP has recently been extended with the introduction
of systems for Inductive Learning of Answer Set Programs (ILASP) which
are capable of supporting automated acquisition of complex knowledge
such as constraints, preferences and rule-based models. Motivated by the
capabilities of ILASP, we present AGENP, an Answer Set Grammar-based
Generative Policy Framework for Autonomous Managed Systems (AMS)
that aims to support the creation and evolution of generative policies by
leveraging ILASP. We describe the framework components, i.e., inputs,
data structures, mechanisms to support the refinement and instantiation
of policies, identification of policy violations, monitoring of policies, and
policy adaptation according to changes in the AMS and its context. Additionally, we present the main work-flow for the global and local refinement
of policies and their adaptation based on Answer Set Programming (ASP)
for policy representation and reasoning using ILASP. We then discuss an
application of the AGENP framework and present preliminary results.

© Springer Nature Switzerland AG 2019
S. Calo et al. (Eds.): PADG 2018, LNCS 11550, pp. 3–20, 2019.
https://doi.org/10.1007/978-3-030-17277-0_1

# 1    Introduction

With the recent advances in Artificial Intelligence (AI), Autonomous Systems (AS) composed of intelligent, self-managed devices are on the rise [6,18]. In order for these ASs to function as expected, their interactions, both internal and among themselves, need to be governed. This is typically done with the use of policies. However, traditional policy management tools need to be evolved in this regard, since ASs need to manage a myriad of complex situations (e.g., operating in isolation or in a collaborative manner) while ensuring that they assist in making secure and appropriate decisions. Enabling policies to be autonomously created and adapted according to dynamic contexts, where resource availability and conditions change over time, could help autonomous managed systems to take timely decisions while maintaining consistency and compliance with the overall system objectives.

Policy-based Management Systems (PBMSs) usually work with predefined policies that are provided by administrators or experts with knowledge of the system's operations to ensure proper system functionality. Policy definitions are usually not modified unless a human analyzes them and pinpoints corrections or improvements, and new policies are only provided to the system by end users when new business objectives are identified. This manual approach for policy creation and modification is tedious and error prone [14]; hence, approaches for guided and automatic policy generation have been proposed [14,16,20]. However, these approaches are either focused on static policies (i.e., predefined policies that do not change over time) or they rely on large amounts of data to be able to identify new policies, or required policy transformations. To the best of our knowledge, there are no approaches that attempt to learn a policy model to self-generate policies that capture common and optimal policy decisions for a managed system.

The Generative Policy-based Model (GPM), recently proposed in [17], defines the concept of *generative policies*—i.e., policies that are self-generated by the managed system (e.g., devices) to enable systems to determine their own behavior, allowing flexible policy definitions. A generative policy model could be learned from an initial specification of policies for the managed system, and from the analysis of the system's operations, resource usage, and previous policy decisions. One approach that can be used for learning generative policy models is ILASP. ILASP is a learning approach that has been successful at learning representative models (e.g., programs) from examples and background knowledge [7]. ILASP is an appealing symbolic learning approach because, contrary to other popular supervised learning approaches, it is a white-box or knowledge oriented method that provides easy to understand models [10], and does not require large amounts of labeled data to generate a good model of the underlying system's behavior. This paper presents the ASGrammar-based GENerative Policy Framework (AGENP), a PBMS framework based on GPM that is designed to learn a generative policy model via ILASP with the goal of supporting autonomous management systems in self-generating and selecting optimal policies based on the system's operation and history of policy decisions.

The rest of the document is structured as follows: In Sect. 2 we present two scenarios that motivate the need for a generative architecture for policies. We then provide a comparative analysis of a traditional PBMS to that of a generative model in Sect. 3, and in Sect. 4 we discuss means to learn policies, especially following an inductive learning paradigm. In Sect. 5, we present our GPM architecture and discuss its key components, and in Sect. 6 we discuss the AGENP instantiation in more detail. In Sect. 7, we apply the AGENP implementation to the Connected and Autonomous Vehicles (CAVs) domain to evaluate the approach, and we conclude the document in Sect. 8 by providing a discussion and then make final remarks in Sect. 9.

## 2 Generative Policy Scenarios

Various scenarios involving Autonomous Managed Systems (AMSs) could take advantage of the concept of generative policies and a framework instantiation like AGENP. This section highlights some scenarios that we think would benefit from instantiations of the GPM.

### 2.1 Policies for Federated Learning Environments

Federated systems, i.e., systems where multiple organizations work together to share resources and collaborate to achieve common tasks, could benefit from using generative policies to manage their operations as shown in [1]. In the same way, a Federated Learning (FL) system, where the main objective is to learn a common Machine Learning (ML) model, requires the definition and management of policies for distributed learning and data/model fusion. These systems can use generative policies to ensure the correct operation of the FL system. FL-related policies need to consider different characteristics of the FL system and its environment [19], such as the quality of the data and communications, the data arrangements among the different nodes, the type of ML algorithm, and the performance of different participating nodes, to decide how to distribute the data and learn a federated ML model. Given the wide diversity of learning environments and algorithms that can exist in FL systems, a framework like AGENP that helps to self-generate policies could provide great advantages for the proper functionality of the FL system by identifying over time which policies are optimal, and how policies can evolve to handle operations between different AMSs working together.

### 2.2 Policies for Autonomous Vehicle Operations

Autonomous transportation and systems for CAVs are becoming of increasing interest [5]. Policies that help to improve the user experience (e.g., by focusing on personalization and context awareness) enable such vehicles to adapt to the behavior and desires of the users—and the environment—in a safe and secure way, and are an important aspect of CAVs. The GPM in this context can help

CAVs to identify which personalization policies to generate—or instantiate—based on the vehicle's contextual information (e.g., operating environment or user status) and user preferences. Additionally, generative policies can be used to identify policies that define how complex autonomous systems interact—for instance, in situations where multiple CAVs are operating at the same time, interacting with each other to navigate a space [15].

Given the above scenarios, it is apparent that we need a system that supports generative policies so that the interacting entities can adapt in context to the constraints of the environment while executing the tasks that are entrusted to them. In the next section, we present how traditional PBMS have evolved to support the notion of GPM.

## 3  Evolution of Policy-Based Management Systems

Below we compare and contrast traditional policy-based management systems with that of next generation PBMSs, especially generative policy management systems.

### 3.1  Standard Policy-Based Management Systems

Figure 1(a) shows a standard PBMS, such as the one defined by IETF/DMTF[1], standards where policy-based management tools create, edit, and control policies stored in a persistent policy repository. When the system under management requires a decision to be made regarding its operation, a Policy Decision Point (PDP) interprets predefined policies in the policy repository and sends decisions to a Policy Enforcement Point (PEP) using an appropriate format. Then, the PEP executes an action, or set of actions, according to the decisions obtained from the PDP. Policies used in these systems are usually provided by administrators or experts on the system's functionality. In these PBMS, new policies are provided by a domain expert to the managed system when new business goals are identified, and changes to policies do not occur unless an admin user analyzes the current policies and identifies those that need to be corrected or improved.

### 3.2  Evolved Policy-Based Management Systems

Changes in the internal and external conditions of the managed system can create scenarios where the initial predefined policies cannot be used because situations arise that represent events and conditions not foreseen initially in the creation of the policies provided to the PBMS. Learning from the history of actions taken by the managed system, analyzing the decisions taken and the structure of the policies applicable to those decisions (i.e., events, conditions, actions), and improving policy definitions, would make it possible for the managed system to

---

[1] https://tools.ietf.org/html/rfc2753.

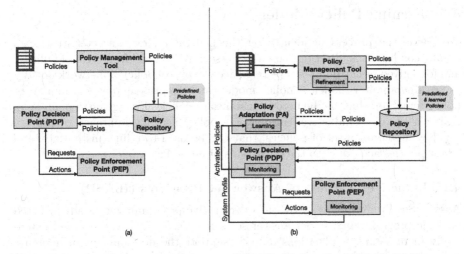

**Fig. 1.** Policy-based management systems (PBMS): (a) Standard PBMS, (b) New generation of PBMS.

make decisions for situations that were not initially anticipated, thus enabling its autonomous operation. Contrary to the standard policy-based management system, a new generation of policy-based management systems would include support for *policy refinement* and *policy learning* to enable both learning from past experiences and the continuous evolution of policies. Figure 1(b) shows an overview of a new generation policy-based management system that includes policy refinement and policy learning processes—described in brief below and in detail in Sects. 5 and 6.

**Policy Refinement:** The refinement process finds the best instantiation of policies used by the managed system. The policy refinement process continuously consolidates the set of policies and their instantiations, according to the policy constraints initially established for the system, and the previous decisions made by the managed system during its operation.

**Policy Learning:** Learning from previous policy decisions allows the managed system to identify new policies that can be used to handle unforeseen situations while complying with the system objectives and constraints, and without waiting for policies to be discovered and provided by an end user. The policy learning process learns a policy model that considers the current set of refined policies and the historical decisions made by the system. The policy model is used to instantiate new policies that are predicted to be useful for managing immediate and future system operations.

In the next section, we provide our intuition for a GPM that is designed to support the operations of autonomous managed systems, and we introduce ILASP, the learning approach used in our GPM instantiation.

## 4    Learning Policy Models

We define the process of identifying the general policy characteristics (e.g., events, conditions, and actions, and their associated values) from a set of policies, and for a given policy domain type (e.g., access-control policy or network policy), as learning a policy model. A policy model can be represented as a grammar, or policy template, that can be used to instantiate policies for a given domain of an AMS. We propose inductive learning as a policy learning approach to capture a policy model for a set of policies, that can be used to refine, instantiate, and adapt policies according to the operations of an AMS.

### 4.1    Inductive Learning of Answer Set Programs (ILASP)

Answer Set Programming (ASP) is a declarative programming paradigm based on logic programming, under answer set semantics, that has been used extensively in reasoning applications, and to support the development of inference engines. ASP is a highly declarative paradigm for knowledge representation and reasoning, and it allows us to specify policy constraints at the attribute level, enabling more flexible and dynamic policy specifications. Its characteristics make it suitable for representing generative policies. Hence, we propose to leverage Answer Set Programs (ASPs), more specifically Answer Set Grammars (ASGs) which are written in the language of ASPs, as a low-level representation of policies.

In Inductive Logic Programming (ILP) [7], the main task is to find a hypothesis that together with given background knowledge, explains a set of observations (i.e., positive examples). Recently, an ILP approach for ASP called ILASP was proposed [11], which learns inductive solutions as ASPs. ILASP extends traditional ILP by supporting the automated acquisition of complex knowledge structures in the language of Answer Set Programming (ASP). The learning framework underpinning ILASP enables the learning of constraints and preferences as well as rule-based models. For instance, ILASP can learn the concept that a coin may non-deterministically land on either heads or tails, but never both; this is appealing for learning tasks mainly because it has the ability to learn a general model with a small number of examples utilizing an existing background knowledge base [11], and also because the learned model (or hypothesis) can be expressed in plain English making it easier for a human user to understand [13].

In the next section, we present a review of the GPM, and then describe the design of the ASGrammar-based GENerative Policy Framework (AGENP) that uses ASP and ILP techniques to learn a generative policy model to instantiate policies according to the GPM model.

## 5    The Generative Policy Model (GPM)

This section presents a more detailed description of the GPM [17], including inputs and outputs of the model, and the components of the management system and the managed system. Figure 2 shows an overview of the GPM architecture for the policy-based management of AMSs.

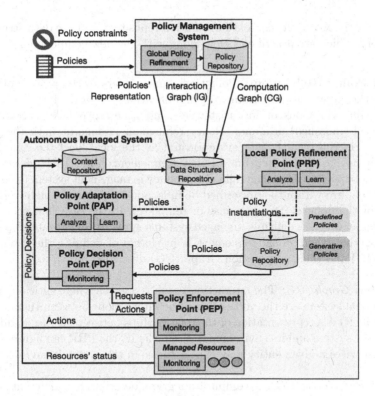

**Fig. 2.** Overview of the generative policy model architecture

## 5.1 Inputs and Outputs

The GPM takes as inputs *policy definitions* and *policy constraints*. Policy definitions are provided by admin users to reflect the correct actions to take for different conditions of the managed system's operation. Policy constraints allow the AMS to establish bounds within which policies can be defined, and they can be seen as a specification of the regions of the search space of policy instantiations that should never be explored, so they also serve as a mechanism to bound the size of the policy search space. The outputs consist of the policy representations for the policies that have been found to be optimal given the conditions of the AMS operation, and the policy violations that have been found during the analysis and learning of policy decisions.

## 5.2 GPM Components

Beyond the traditional components of a PBMS, which include a PDP, a PEP, and a policy repository, the GPM follows the general architecture of the evolved PBMS described in Sect. 3.2. The GPM includes three new components, a Policy Adaptation Point (PAP) at the AMS, and a Policy Refinement Point (PRP) at the management tool and at the AMS. Also, two additional repositories are defined for the AMS, the context information repository and the data structures repository, which are described below along with the new components.

**Global Policy Refinement:** Policy refinement refers to the process of interpreting the policy grammar, making modifications accordingly, e.g., to correct possible violations or inconsistencies, and generate policies according to the revised (modified) grammar. Policy refinement is done at both the global level (i.e., in the management system), and at the local level (i.e., inside the autonomous managed system) in a Policy Refinement Point (PRP) as shown in Fig. 2. Global policy refinement allows the policy management system to consider policies that are within the prescribed bounds, and to obtain the right representation for the policies (i.e., grammar or template). In the case that the system is collaborative—i.e., multiple managed systems agree to collaborate to perform tasks together, then global refinement is in charge of defining the Interaction Graph (IG) and the Computation Graph (CG) described below.

*Interaction Graph (IG):* The interaction graph is a graph where entities (AMSs) in the global system are the vertices, and the interactions between them are the edges. The IG is a representation of the relationships between entities in different roles in the system and its environment. From the IG the PRP can figure out the type of services a given entity may expect to see in the system's environment.

*Computation Graph (CG):* A computation graph describes how different entities are allowed to interact to fulfill a common task. This graph is composed based upon the IG and the services needed to accomplish the system objectives. In a distributed environment, the CG captures the configurations needed and the sequenced rules (e.g., state transition, transport) for control of the execution of the distributed multi-agent system.

**Data Structures Repository:** The data structures repository stores the policy representations (e.g., grammar), policy constraints, and interaction graphs, along with their versions (i.e., initial version specified by the admin user, and the subsequent versions generated by the AMS during its operation).

**Context Information Repository:** For each AMS, the context information repository holds information about the status of the elements of the overall system that affect its operation. The monitoring of decisions in the associated PDPs, and the status of resources in their associated PEPs are also stored in this repository. The information in the context repository is key to the refinement and adaptation of policies, as it characterizes the current system state and environment as seen by the local ASM.

**Policy Adaptation Point (PAP):** The PAP component is in charge of analyzing the history of policies' decisions, and adapting the generative policy model so that it is representative of the types of policies used in the managed system. The PAP updates the policy representation (e.g., policy grammar or template) to include aspects of new policies that are considered to be useful to the managed system based on the analysis of policy decisions and context. Contextual information is obtained either from the monitoring of PDPs and PEPs, or from the context information repository. There are two key sub-components of the PAP and below we briefly describe them.

*Policy Representation Analyzer:* This sub-component of the PAP performs analytics over the policy decisions and managed resource status to inform the policy learner about conditions and actions that need to be considered to adapt the current policy representation (see [3] for initial analysis approaches for access control policies). This component ensures that the policies being generated satisfy policy metrics, such as response time, confidence, consistency, and completeness.

*Policy Representation Learner:* By using the information from the policy analyzer, the policy learner in the PAP modifies the current policy representation to incorporate information that instantiates policies that comply with the business objectives of the managed system as well as new policies that allow the managed system to behave autonomously.

**Policy Refinement Point (PRP):** At the local level, the refinement of policies inside the PRP uses the information from the global refinement, the context information repository, the policy repository, and the PAP to create a generative policy model (e.g., policy template, or policy grammar) that supports the instantiation of policies that can be used by the managed system. There are two key sub-components of the PRP and below we briefly describe them.

*Policy Model Analyzer:* This sub-component of the PRP performs analytics over the policy representation, obtained from the data structures repository, and the context repository to identify the set of policies that will be used by the learner to find and update the generative policy model.

*Policy Model Learner:* With the results from the policy analyzer, the policy model learner creates or modifies the current policy model to incorporate information that enables the instantiation of generative policies. The policy model learner provides the policy model analyzer with the latest policy representation derived for the generative policy model.

Once a generative policy model has been created, either in the form of a grammar or policy template, policies are instantiated and stored in the Policy Repository from where the PDP can access them.

# 6    AGENP: ASGrammar-based GENerative Policy Framework

Based on the architecture of the GPM, we designed AGENP, an instantiation of the GPM that uses ILASP as the mechanism to learn the policy representa-

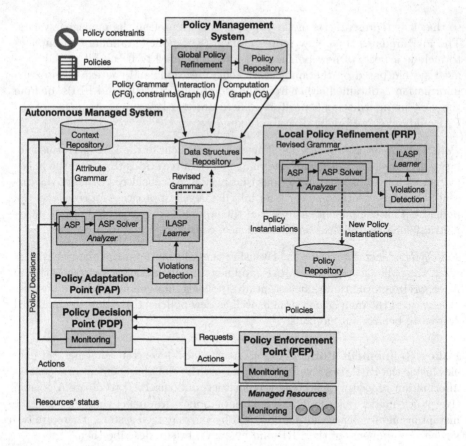

**Fig. 3.** Overview of the ASGrammar-based GENerative Policy Framework (AGENP)

tions and to enable the self-generation of policies on AMSs. Following the same structure of the GPM, in Fig. 3, we show an overview of the AGENP framework components using inductive learning mechanisms inside the PAP and PRP components, which are described in detail below.

### 6.1   Inputs and Outputs

AGENP accepts as inputs policies represented by a CFG, the policy constraints, the IG, and the CG. AGENP outputs include an attribute grammar with ASP constructs that represent the policies for the AMS. The next section explains how these constructs are created inside the AGENP framework.

### 6.2   Overview of AGENP

Below we describe the details of the GPM components that are instantiated in a specific way in the AGENP framework. Components that are not detailed here follow the same structure as previously defined in Sect. 5.

**Data Structures Repository:** In the AGENP framework, this repository keeps track of the interaction graph, the policy grammars (CFG, and attribute grammars), and the policy constraints.

**Policy Refinement Point (PRP):** The analyzer in the PRP uses the information contained in the data structures repository to get the policy grammar needed by the ASP component. If there does not exist an attribute grammar in the data structures repository, then the PRP first transforms the CFG to an attribute grammar. Then, the attribute grammar is translated to an ASG in the ASP subcomponent, using information from examples of policy instantiations, obtained from the context and policy repositories. Policy examples could also be acquired from distributed repositories which contain policies from various related domains as per the system presented by Bertino *et al.* [2].

The ASP solver takes the ASG information and using a search algorithm finds the set of policy solutions and policy violations. Policy solutions are passed to an inductive learner for ASP, such as the ILASP system [11], which both learns the ASP rules in the ASG, and finds a representative model of the generative policies—i.e., the *revised* ASG, that can be used to instantiate policies. The generated *revised* ASG is shared back to the ASP subcomponent. Once there are no changes between consecutive versions of the grammar being generated, the *revised* ASG is stored in the data structures repository. Policy instantiations, created from the ASG are saved in the policy repository so that the AMS can use them for its operations. For a formalisation of how ASP can be learned, the reader is referred to [11].

**Policy Adaptation Point (PAP):** The policy adaptation process uses the latest policy representation, i.e., grammar, from the policy data repository. The history of policy decisions and contextual information, such as resource status and availability, and background knowledge are used as examples by the analyzer, where positive examples can be policies with high quality (i.e., policies that are consistent, complete, minimal, relevant, and correct [9]). The grammar is converted into an ASG in the ASP component and then it is passed to the ASP Solver to find the optimal set of policy solutions along with policy violations. Policy solutions are then passed to a learner for ASP, such as the ILASP learner [12], that is able to learn the constraints, in the form of ASP, for the generative policy model. Also, the learner returns a preference ordering for instances of the generative policy model. Both the preference ordering and the revised ASG are stored in the data structures repository.

## 7  Applying AGENP for Connected and Autonomous Vehicle (CAV) Domain

In this section we present the description and preliminary results of an AGENP instantiation for CAV policies. As discussed in Sect. 2.2, CAVs are systems where

| SAE level | SAE name | SAE narrative definition | Execution of steering and acceleration/deceleration | Monitoring of driving environment | Fallback performance of dynamic driving task | System capability (driving modes) |
|---|---|---|---|---|---|---|
| *Human driver* monitors the driving environment | | | | | | |
| 0 | No Automation | the full-time performance by the *human driver* of all aspects of the *dynamic driving task*, even when enhanced by warning or intervention systems | Human driver | Human driver | Human driver | n/a |
| 1 | Driver Assistance | the *driving mode*-specific execution by a driver assistance system of either steering or acceleration/deceleration using information about the driving environment and with the expectation that the *human driver* perform all remaining aspects of the *dynamic driving task* | Human driver and system | Human driver | Human driver | Some driving modes |
| 2 | Partial Automation | the *driving mode*-specific execution by one or more driver assistance systems of both steering and acceleration/deceleration using information about the driving environment and with the expectation that the *human driver* perform all remaining aspects of the *dynamic driving task* | **System** | Human driver | Human driver | Some driving modes |
| *Automated driving system* ("system") monitors the driving environment | | | | | | |
| 3 | Conditional Automation | the *driving mode*-specific performance by an *automated driving system* of all aspects of the *dynamic driving task* with the expectation that the *human driver* will respond appropriately to a *request to intervene* | System | **System** | Human driver | Some driving modes |
| 4 | High Automation | the *driving mode*-specific performance by an *automated driving system* of all aspects of the *dynamic driving task*, even if a *human driver* does not respond appropriately to a *request to intervene* | System | System | **System** | Some driving modes |
| 5 | Full Automation | the full-time performance by an *automated driving system* of all aspects of the *dynamic driving task* under all roadway and environmental conditions that can be managed by a *human driver* | System | System | System | **All driving modes** |

**Fig. 4.** SAE: levels of autonomy obtained from [8]

generative policies can assist in managing the behavior of vehicles according to contextual changes or user (driver or passenger) preferences. In this section we demonstrate how the ASG can be used to represent policies, and how the ILASP-based learner can find the proper constraints in the general policy representation (i.e., grammar) to create a generative policy model that contains the proper constraints for CAV policies.

## 7.1 Policies for CAVs

Figure 4 depicts the five levels of autonomy, excluding the zero-th level, that have been defined for CAVs by the Society of Automotive Engineers (SAE) international [8]. According to the SAE levels, the Advanced Driver Assistance System (ADAS) or the Automated Driving Systems (ADS), can help drivers, allowing them to disengage from some of their driving tasks (e.g., steering or acceleration), starting from level 2 autonomy—i.e., the partial automation level. However, except for level five, where full automation is in place, the driver must always be ready to take control of the vehicle, and it is the driver who is responsible for safety-critical functions. Policies for CAVs can be designed to assist during the vehicle operation while capturing preferences from the driver or passengers in specific contexts and scenarios. Here we present CAV policies that dictate whether a task can be performed or not based on the level of autonomy of the vehicle for which the task was requested, the road where the vehicle is located, and the level of autonomy of the requested driving task, considering the SAE levels of autonomy. We leveraged the system proposed in [15] using ITA Controlled English[2] (CE) [4]—a formal language to model domains semantically—to model and generate policy instances for CAVs.

The authors of [15] define applicable CAV policy instances as follows: given a set of levels of autonomy $\mathcal{L} = \{x \in \mathcal{Z} \mid 0 \leq x \leq 5\}$, a set of regions (i.e., $\mathcal{R}$) are identified, where each region $\mathcal{R}_i$ permits a level of autonomy $loa_r \in \mathcal{L}$. They then create a set of vehicles $\mathcal{V}$, where each vehicle $\mathcal{V}_j$ represents a vehicle located within region $\mathcal{R}_i \in \mathcal{R}$, and is capable of operating at the level of autonomy $loa_v \in \mathcal{L}$. Finally, a set of driving tasks $\mathcal{T}$ is created, where each driving task $\mathcal{T}_k$ requires a vehicle with level of autonomy $loa_t \in \mathcal{L}$ in order to be executed. A policy instance can therefore be defined as $\mathcal{P}_{vrt}$ to denote a vehicle $v$ located in a region $r$ attempting to execute task $t$, thus the set of all possible policy instances $\mathcal{P}$ is defined as $\mathcal{P} = \{P_{vrt} \mid v \in \mathcal{V}, r \in \mathcal{R}, t \in \mathcal{T}\}$ over the domain of vehicles, regions and tasks.

After policy instances have been generated, each policy instance is annotated as either *accepted* or *rejected*. A policy instance $P_{vrt}$ should be *accepted* iff $loa_t \leq loa_v$ and $loa_t \leq loa_r$ otherwise the policy instance should be *rejected*—e.g., a vehicle with level of autonomy 3 in a region which permits level of autonomy 4 attempting to execute a driving task which requires level of autonomy 3 should be *accepted*, whereas the same vehicle attempting to execute the same driving task in a region which permits level of autonomy 2 should be *rejected*.

## 7.2   Instantiating AGENP for CAVs

According to the AGENP architecture shown in Fig. 3, we describe the inputs to the PRP and PAP that we used to take the first step in evaluating the effectiveness of using the ASG along with an ILASP learner to find the generative policy model that represents the set of CAV policies described above.

**Initial Grammar:** We define the input ASG grammar for the CAV policies in terms of the vehicle initiating the driving task, the location of the task, and the task being executed. Each production rule for these attributes is *annotated* with a single fact describing the corresponding level of autonomy, as shown in Listing 1.1. The production rule (i.e., **start**) does not contain any annotations in the initial grammar. As the annotations of the grammar contain only facts and no ASP constructs (such as constraints) that could eliminate a string from the language, the language of the initial grammar is equal to the language of

---

[2] https://github.com/ce-store/ce-store.

the context free grammar (with the ASP conditions ignored). The task in these experiments is to learn a set of constraints to annotate the first production rule that eliminate exactly those strings which represent policies that should be rejected.

**Listing 1.1.** Part of the input grammar for the CAV policy experiment. Note that the full grammar contains 12 vehicles, 12 regions and 12 driving tasks.

```
start -> vehicle ';' region ';' driving_task {}
vehicle -> 'Kia Seed' { vehicle_loa(3). }
region -> 'Christchurch' { region_loa(4). }
driving_task -> 'Parking' { driving_task_loa(2). }
...
```

**Positive and Negative Examples:** In this experiment, positive examples are strings corresponding to policy instances that should be *accepted* by the generative policy model. For instance, the string `Kia Seed; Christchurch; Parking` is a positive example, whereas the string `Vauxhall Astra; Christchurch; Parking` is a negative example as according to the vehicle definition the Vauxhall Astra has level of autonomy 1 which does not support assisted parking. For our evaluation, we generated 1728 policy instances, of which 728 instances were positive.

**Language Bias:** The language bias is a key part of the input of any ILP task, as it defines the language in which learned hypotheses can be constructed. In this experiment, we defined a language bias which meant that the first production rule of the input grammar (i.e., `start`) can be annotated with constraints defined using the predicates `driving_task_loa`, `region_loa` and `vehicle_loa` and the less than operator.

## 7.3   Constraint Generation with AGENP

Using the inputs described above, and the ILP learner described in Sect. 6, the AGENP framework outputs the generative policy model represented as an ASG, when given sufficient examples. Listing 1.2 shows the learned ASG that specifies the ASP constraints for the production rules in the ASG, which represent the policy model. The learned constraints state that the level of autonomy for the driving task may not be lower than either the level of autonomy of the region where the vehicle is trying to execute the driving task, or the level of autonomy of the vehicle trying to execute the task. Note that the atoms representing the levels of autonomy end with @n for some integer n. This indicates that the atom is defined in the $n$th node of the right hand side of the production rule; for instance, the `driving_task_loa` is defined in the 5th node (`driving_task`) on the right hand side of the production rule.

**Listing 1.2.** Part of the learned grammar for the CAV policy experiment, which represents the generative policy model.

```
start -> vehicle ';' region ';' driving_task {
:- driving_task_loa(X)@5, region_loa(Y)@3, X < Y.
:- driving_task_loa(X)@5, vehicle_loa(Y)@1, X < Y.
}
vehicle -> 'Kia Seed' { vehicle_loa(3). }
...
region -> 'Christchurch' { region_loa(4). }
...
driving_task -> 'Parking' { driving_task_loa(2). }
...
```

### 7.4 Preliminary Evaluation

The aim of this evaluation was to investigate how many examples are necessary to learn the CAV policy as described above. For $n = 0, 5, 10, \ldots, 50$, in each experiment, we randomly drew $n$ examples from the full set of 1728 policy instances. The ILP learner was used to learn (the annotations of) an ASG, which was then tested on the remaining $(1728 - n)$ policy instances checking that those policy instances which should be *accepted* (resp. *rejected*) were (resp. were not) in the language of the learned ASG. The graph in Fig. 5 show the average accuracy of the learned ASG over 50 repetitions of this experiment. The learner achieves over 95% accuracy on average when given 15 examples or more. For every experiment with 35 or more examples, the learner achieved 100% accuracy.

## 8   Discussion

Autonomic management is an area where the policies used to manage a system are automatically generated. In this area tools like Madison [14], a library for automatic policy generation for SELinux policies, have been developed to provide modules that guide the policy definition process, and modules that extract information from reference policy interface files to allow the creation of policy templates from knowledge of accesses to a system. However, to the best of our knowledge, none of the current autonomic management approaches consider the evolution of policies according to the common decisions made by the managed system.

The closest work related to ours is by Quiroz et al., that presents a framework for autonomic policy adaptation based on online analysis and characterization of system operation based on decentralized clustering techniques [16]. Our approach is different to theirs in that we use symbolic learning to capture common and optimal policies based on the system operation without relying on large amounts of data but on a small set of examples and background knowledge about the managed system policies, its components, and operation. Jabal *et al.*, presents a review of policy analysis approaches and tools in [9], including policy examples

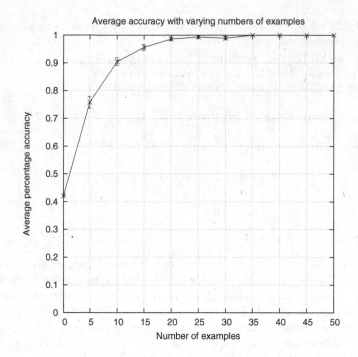

**Fig. 5.** The average accuracy of the learner when evaluated on the CAV policy model.

for access control (e.g., role-based access control policies), and network (e.g., firewall policies, SDN policies), as well as the policy analysis process, and the available analysis frameworks and tools. As we have discussed in this paper, different policy types and analysis tools can be leveraged by other instantiations of the GPM, and in the AGENP framework to analyze and select optimal polices for different AMSs and scenarios.

## 9   Conclusions

We have presented the design of AGENP, a generative policy framework for AMS based on ILP and ASP. AGENP enables the reasoning, refinement, and learning of policies autonomously using ILP as the mechanism to learn a generative policy model from a set of examples and background knowledge from the managed system. In AGENP, policies are represented as ASGs to express generated policies in a human understandable form and to facilitate the learning of policy attributes and constraints via ILP. We described how existing algorithms and tools for learning ASG solutions can be leveraged in the AGENP's implementation to learn generative policies for autonomous managed systems. We presented two representative scenarios, including federated learning and CAVs, where generative policies and the AGENP instantiation can be useful, and included preliminary results that show the potential of using ASG and the AGENP framework to find and adapt the generative policy model for CAV policies. Future work includes an empirical evaluation of AGENP instantiations for different scenarios and a comparison of AGENP's approach for generative policy learning with other learning approaches. For the former, we plan to consider scenarios where the system context is taken as input, e.g, via policy attributes that represent contextual information such as weather conditions and driver preferences for CAV policies, and evaluate how generative policies can help the system to decide more autonomously about optimal policies.

As a general framework for generative policies, the symbolic logic approach used in AGENP can be applied to the policy domains that are described in the other chapters of this volume, notably safety and autonomy in collaborative, federated systems.

**Acknowledgement.** This research was sponsored by the U.S. Army Research Laboratory and the U.K. Ministry of Defence under Agreement Number W911NF-16-3-0001. The views and conclusions contained in this document are those of the authors and should not be interpreted as representing the official policies, either expressed or implied, of the U.S. Army Research Laboratory, the U.S. Government, the U.K. Ministry of Defence or the U.K. Government. The U.S. and U.K. Governments are authorized to reproduce and distribute reprints for Government purposes notwithstanding any copyright notation hereon.

# References

1. Bertino, E., Calo, S., Toma, M., Verma, D., Williams, C., Rivera, B.: A cognitive policy framework for next-generation distributed federated systems: concepts and research directions. In: IEEE 37th International Conference on Distributed Computing Systems (ICDCS), pp. 1876–1886 (2017)
2. Bertino, E., de Mel, G., Russo, A., Calo, S., Verma, D.: Community-based self generation of policies and processes for assets: concepts and research directions. In: IEEE International Conference on Big Data, pp. 2961–2969 (2017)
3. Bertino, E., et al.: Provenance-based analytics services for access control policies. In: Proceedings of the 2017 IEEE World Congress on Services (SERVICES). IEEE (2017)
4. Braines, D., Mott, D., Laws, S., de Mel, G., Pham, T.: Controlled English to facilitate human/machine analytical processing. In: Next-Generation Analyst, vol. 8758, p. 875808. International Society for Optics and Photonics (2013)
5. Coppola, R., Morisio, M.: Connected car: technologies, issues, future trends. ACM Comput. Surv. **49**(3), 46:1–46:36 (2016)
6. Fok, C.L., et al.: A platform for evaluating autonomous intersection management policies. In: 3rd International Conference on Cyber-Physical Systems, pp. 87–96 (2012)
7. Gulwani, S., Hernández-Orallo, J., Kitzelmann, E., Muggleton, S.H., Schmid, U., Zorn, B.: Inductive programming meets the real world. Commun. ACM **58**(11), 90–99 (2015)
8. Taxonomy and Definitions for Terms Related to Driving Automation Systems for On-Road Motor Vehicles. Standard, SAE International, June 2018

9. Jabal, A.A., et al.: Methods and tools for policy analysis. ACM Comput. Surv. (2018)
10. Kazakov, D., Kudenko*, D.: Machine learning and inductive logic programming for multi-agent systems. In: Luck, M., Mařík, V., Štěpánková, O., Trappl, R. (eds.) ACAI 2001. LNCS (LNAI), vol. 2086, pp. 246–270. Springer, Heidelberg (2001). https://doi.org/10.1007/3-540-47745-4_11
11. Law, M., Russo, A., Broda, K.: Inductive learning of answer set programs. In: Fermé, E., Leite, J. (eds.) JELIA 2014. LNCS (LNAI), vol. 8761, pp. 311–325. Springer, Cham (2014). https://doi.org/10.1007/978-3-319-11558-0_22
12. Law, M., Russo, A., Broda, K.: Learning weak constraints in answer set programming. Theory Pract. Log. Program. **15**(4–5), 511–525 (2015)
13. Law, M., Russo, A., Broda, K.: The complexity and generality of learning answer set programs. Artif. Intell. **259**, 110–146 (2018)
14. MacMillan, K., Hat, R.: Madison: a new approach to policy generation. In: SELinux Symposium, vol. 7. Citeseer (2007)
15. de Mel, G., Cunnington, D., Manotas, I., Calo, S., Bertino, E., Verma, D.: A generative policy model for connected and autonomous vehicles based on local knowledge. In: The 5th International Workshop on Middleware and Applications for the Internet of Things. ACM (2018)
16. Quiroz, A., Parashar, M., Gnanasambandam, N., Sharma, N.: Autonomic policy adaptation using decentralized online clustering. In: Proceedings of the 7th International Conference on Autonomic Computing, ICAC, pp. 151–160. ACM (2010)
17. Verma, D., et al.: Generative policy model for autonomic management. In: IEEE SmartWorld, Ubiquitous Intelligence Computing, Advanced Trusted Computed, Scalable Computing Communications, Cloud Big Data Computing, Internet of People and Smart City Innovation, pp. 1–6 (2017)
18. Verma, D., Bent, G., Taylor, I.: Learning neural network policies with guided policy search under unknown dynamics. In: Proceedings of the 9th International Conference on Advanced Cognitive Technologies and Applications. COGNITIVE (2017)
19. Verma, D., Calo, S., Cirincione, G.: Distributed AI and security issues in federated environments. In: Proceedings of the Workshop Program of the 19th International Conference on Distributed Computing and Networking, Workshops ICDCN. ACM (2018)
20. Yu, L., Zhang, T., Luo, X., Xue, L.: AutoPPG: towards automatic generation of privacy policy for android applications. In: Proceedings of the 5th Annual ACM CCS Workshop on Security and Privacy in Smartphones and Mobile Devices, SPSM, pp. 39–50. ACM (2015)

# Value of Information: Quantification and Application to Coalition Machine Learning

Gavin Pearson[1], Dinesh Verma[2(✉)], and Geeth de Mel[3]

[1] Defence Science and Technology Laboratory, Ministry of Defence,
Porton Down, Salisbury SP4 0JQ, UK
agpearson@mail.dstl.gov.uk
[2] Distributed AI Department, IBM TJ Watson Research Center,
Yorktown Heights, NY 10549, USA
dverma@us.ibm.com
[3] IBM Research UK, Harytree Center, Warrington, UK
geeth.demel@uk.ibm.com

**Abstract.** The creation of good machine learning models relies on the availability of good training data. In coalition settings, this training data may be obtained from many different coalition partners. However, due to the difference in the trust level of the coalition partners, the value of the information provided by the coalition partners could be questionable. In this paper, we examine the concept of Value of Information, provide a quantitative measure for it, and show how this can be used to determine the policies for information fusion in the training of machine learning models.

## 1 Introduction

The most important use of information is to enable "understanding and decision making" [1]. Furthermore, given the major trends within socio-technical information systems, the most critical resources in exploiting data and information for understanding and decision-making are (firstly) human attention units and (secondly) communications bandwidth [2]. Hence it is important to be able to measure the value of different pieces of information due to its impact on understanding and decision making, as opposed to other metrics such as the cost of collecting or replacing the information. This resulting measure of value can be used to make decisions about how to prioritize the use of information system resources. Thus, a quantitative method of assigning value to information is needed to enable fusion resource management [3] to operate effectively, especially in a resource constrained setting.

This paper begins with a discussion on specific scenarios for coalition operations that motivate the need for quantifying the Value of Information (VoI). We then review the meanings of different terms related to measuring the value and quality of information (QoI) in existing literature, and map them to a framework

© Springer Nature Switzerland AG 2019
S. Calo et al. (Eds.): PADG 2018, LNCS 11550, pp. 21–41, 2019.
https://doi.org/10.1007/978-3-030-17277-0_2

defined by NATO. Subsequently, we propose a definition of VoI and QoI derived from our scenario requirements. We apply these definitions to machine learning in the context of coalition operations. We then show how the definition of VoI can be used for different goals, such as defining policies in coalition machine learning, and determining how much data to be acquired for a machine learning process.

Machine Learning is a key technology that can be used to enable autonomy in many different contexts. In order to obtain distributed autonomy, machine learning processes need to be able to understand the attributes of information assets obtained from other peer processes. The characterization of VoI and QoI provides a means to obtain distributed autonomy. This chapter makes contributions to the area of distributed autonomy, and by helping generate policies required for assessing models and information obtained from partners, partially helps in the goal of supporting autonomy using generative policies.

## 2    Coalition Machine Learning Scenario

In a coalition, be it military or humanitarian, many nations work together to achieve a set of shared goals. These goals may in turn result in a series of missions and tasks including, for example, peace-keeping, surveillance and humanitarian operations in a given region. In such operations, there will often be a need for coalition members to share information, subject to a range of constraints. The shared information can be valuable in creating the models used within Artificial Intelligence (AI) systems, which are then in turn used to improve situational understanding and the effectiveness of decision making.

### 2.1    Exemplar Coalition Environment

As an example, let us consider the case where multiple coalition partners are conducting surveillance operations in a region containing two adversarial nations and the goal of the coalition is to stabilize the region. After a period of active aggression, the two adversaries have reluctantly agreed to a cease-fire line.

The coalition consists of the U.S., the UK and the imaginary country of Kish. Kish is an imaginary nation created to demonstrate coalition scenarios in the context of the DAIS research alliance activities [4], and is similar to other hypothetical countries such as Holistan [5] used in related works. The U.S. and the UK trust each other more than Kish, but Kish has more influence with the two adversarial nations. The coalition forces are positioned as observers to maintain peace along the cease-fire line. Surveillance equipment along the border monitors the forces of both adversaries and would notify the coalition members in case they need to mobilize additional forces and attempt to diffuse the situation. Figure 1 illustrates the scenario.

The adversaries, or insurgent sub-groups within the adversarial nations, are continuously seeking opportunities to conduct clandestine infiltration operations and attack the other side. Advance warning of such infiltrations and attacks is

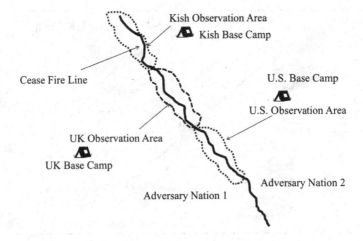

**Fig. 1.** Coalition surveillance scenario

one of the goals of the coalition surveillance operation. On the identification of any such infiltration, the coalition members inform the two adversarial nations to deter the insurgents. Base camps of coalition members are used by analysts of each nation to examine the surveillance data and identify any incursions or infiltrations that could disturb the peace.

Insurgents trying to cross the border are aware that the coalition has surveillance equipment in the theater and adopt various camouflage and deception techniques to hide their movement. The coalition forces need to continuously learn and upgrade their models for identifying the insurgents from the general population. Due to differences in the terrain, the UK is likely to get much more data and video footage of insurgents operating from one adversary nation, while the U.S. is likely to get more data and footage of those operating from the other adversary nation. Additionally, Kish may be able to collect some video footage from the two adversaries. In order to make the joint surveillance more effective, all coalition members want to share their knowledge and data with each other. The constraints on sharing lead to two possible scenarios.

## 2.2  Data Sharing Scenario

In this scenario, the coalition partners are able to share the raw data and video footage of the insurgents with each other. As an example, let us consider the situation where the U.S. is using machine learning techniques to learn the properties of the insurgents, and obtains information from all of the other coalition partners. The situation is as shown in Fig. 2.

The U.S. machine learning system will get part of its training data from the U.S., part of it from the UK, and part of the learning data from Kish. The base camps of the different nations are interconnected via a network protected by their firewalls, but with security policies established to enable data to be

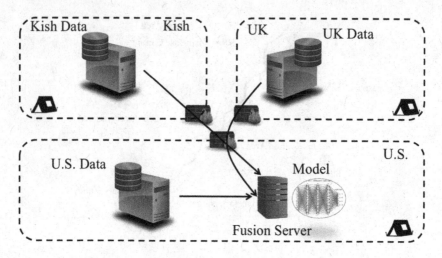

**Fig. 2.** Machine learning with data from partners

retrieved from different coalition partners by the U.S. machine learning server. As the U.S. machine learning algorithm builds its model (e.g., a neural network), it needs to determine the value it is getting from the training data provided by each of the partners. Depending on the value being provided, the U.S. may decide to accept all, some or none of the data being offered by the UK or Kish.

### 2.3   Model Sharing Scenario

In this scenario, depicted by Fig. 3, the three nations, the U.S., the UK and Kish are each creating their own machine learning models. National policies prevent the sharing of raw data and video footage of the insurgents, some of which has been provided to each country under special arrangements, and each country is concerned about possible leakage or misuse of the raw video by the other country. The analysts at the base camps of coalition members have verified that their national policies allow them to share their models. Each country may combine the models with those of other countries to get a better model.

In this situation, the U.S. needs to decide how much value it is receiving by using the model provided by Kish and the the UK respectively. If the fused model becomes more accurate by including the models provided by the UK or Kish, they have a high value. On the other hand, if the model barely changes, not much value is being provided. In both of the scenarios described above, a quantitative estimate for VoI can prove useful to determine whether or not to accept the data or model offered by a partner.

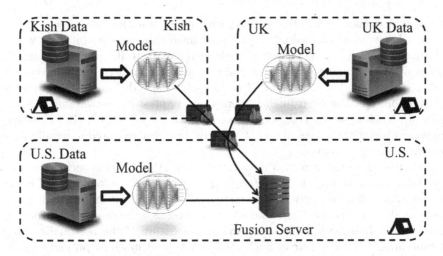

**Fig. 3.** Machine learning with models from partners

## 3   Terms: Value, Relevance and Quality

It will be useful to review the various terms associated with value and quality of information that are found in the existing literature. There are a range of terms which can be used to describe information and which affect its impact on understanding and decision making.

Some definitions are provided by documents such as the NATO Code of Best Practice for Command and Control (C2) Assessment [6], which is intended to provide a framework for discussing measures of merit associated with the impact of information on understanding and decision making.

Specifically, the framework identifies the following types of measures of metrics:

- **Measures of Policy Effectiveness (MoPE)**, which focus on policy and societal outcomes;
- **Measures of Force Effectiveness (MoFE)**, which focus on how a force performs its mission or the degree to which it meets its objectives;
- **Measures of C2 Effectiveness (MoCE)**, which focus on the impact of C2 systems within the operational context;
- **Measures of Performance (MoP)**, which focus on internal system structure, characteristics and behavior; and
- **Dimensional Parameters (DP)**, which focus on the properties or characteristics inherent in the physical C2 systems.

While the NATO document [6] defines an overall framework for information measures/metrics, it does not have definitions that we can apply directly to the scenarios described in Sect. 2.

A concrete definition of Quality of Information (QoI) and Value of Information (VoI) was articulated in [7] with a focus on sensor information fusion. Both terms were defined qualitatively along with an information model to describe the attributes required for both. QoI was defined as a measure intrinsic to the information which can be measured without reference to its usage, i.e., the situational understanding or decision making task that utilized the information. VoI was articulated as a measure of merit which depended on the usage of the information. QoI has been further refined and applied for networking applications [8], wireless sensor networks [9], and mobile crowd sensing [10]. However, equivalent quantitative definitions of VoI have not been explored in detail in the current research literature.

In statistics and information theory, measures of information such as the Fischer Information Index [11] and information entropy [12] are found. The Fischer Information Index measures the amount of information that an observable random variable carries about an unknown parameter in a distribution that models the variable. Information entropy provides a measure of the information that is contained in a data source. Such measures are an inherent property of the information being collected, and they can be viewed as a dimensional parameter in the NATO measures of merit framework.

The Quality of Information metrics, on the other hand, measure the effectiveness of the system structure used to collect the information, including errors that may have been introduced within the information collection system, therefore they can be viewed as belonging to the Measure of Performance family of metrics as defined in the NATO framework.

In order to assess the value of information, it is necessary to know the analysis task, or at least the type of analysis task, that is using the information. Value measures are not intrinsic to the information, and as such they cannot be measured or assessed without knowledge of the analysis task. The weakest such measure, in terms of its usefulness as a measure of merit for system design and operation, is relevance; this is simply an assessment that the information is pertinent to a task. As such relevance provides only a weak measure of performance within the NATO measure of merit framework.

We assert that an item of information has value to a task if:

- (a) it is relevant to the task; and
- (b) it changes the information state of an entity to such a degree that the entity conducting the task will come to a different understanding or decision than it would without the information.

Thus, the VoI measure of information applied in the context of the decision making within a C2 system provides a Measure of C2 Effectiveness (MoCE) within the measure of merit hierarchy. Summarizing, metrics such as Fischer Information Index and information entropy can be equated to dimensional parameters (DP), measures of QoI can be equated to a Measure of Performance (MoP), and VoI measures can be equated to a Measure of C2 Effectiveness (MoCE) within the NATO measures of merit hierarchy [6].

## 4  Definition of VoI and QoI

In order to define QoI and VoI in a quantitative manner, we consider an abstract model for decision making which is shown in Fig. 4. This model is applicable to many common information processing scenarios. Three types of data are present in any scenario, which we are referring to as ground truth, information, and decision. The ground truth is the actual data that is of interest, and can be any digital asset, e.g., a file, a model, a bundle of information, etc. The ground truth may also be non-digital, e.g. the physical attributes of an environment. A collection task is used to convert the ground truth into information. The information is a digital asset, which can be stored and manipulated on a computing system. The information is passed through an analysis task, after which it is converted to a decision. The decision could be digital (e.g., a file, a machine learning model, another measurement, etc.) or a digital representation of a physical outcome (e.g., a decision to turn on/off a switch on a device, move some assets, or any other action that needs to be taken). Let us examine the terms of Fig. 4 in the context of the scenarios described in Sect. 2. For the data sharing scenario, the ground truth would be the non-digital behavior of insurgents, while the collected information would be the footage present at U.S., UK, and Kish repositories respectively, resulting from the collection process used by each country. The decision is the machine learning model built by the U.S., where the analysis is the process of training that model. For the model sharing scenario, the ground truth is the "true" model that characterizes the insurgents' behavior in the environment of each country, while the information is the model trained by each individual country. The decision is the fused model that results by combining all the models together.

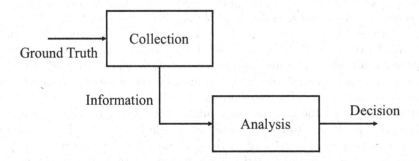

**Fig. 4.** Model assumed for definitions of QoI and VoI

We can now define QoI as the fidelity with which the information follows the ground truth. The VoI would be the degree to which the information impacts the decision that is the output of the analysis. For the data sharing scenario, QoI measures how closely the collected footage is to that of the actual behavior of insurgents, while VoI would be the impact of the collected data on the model trained by the U.S. For the model sharing scenario, the QoI of the model provided by the UK or Kish would be an accuracy metric of the individual country model to predict insurgent behavior. The VoI of an individual country model would be its impact on the fused model. Let us consider the situation where the ground truth $g$ is a metric like the temperature in an environment, and the information $f$ is the value reported by a sensor. The decision $d$ is a binary value that determines whether an air-conditioner has to be turned on or off. Each of these can be measured as a function of time $t$ as shown in Fig. 5.

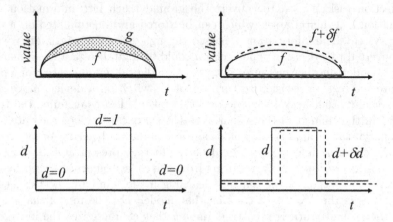

**Fig. 5.** Illustration of QoI and VoI for functions

The left-hand side of Fig. 5 shows the ground truth and the information collected on the top, and the corresponding decision in time on the bottom. The difference between $f$ and $g$, as shown by the shaded area in the figure reflects the QoI (rather the inverse of the QoI). The (inverse of) QoI of information $f$ can be measured by the ratio of the shaded area in the figure to that of the overall area between the horizontal axis and the ground truth $g$. While $f$ and $g$ are measured in the same units, the decision $d$ is measured in different units, a binary unit in this case and is shown at the bottom. The right-hand side of Fig. 5 shows what happens when the information changes, from the figure shown in a solid line on the top left as $f$ to the figure shown in a dashed line on the top right as $f + \delta f$. This change causes a shift in the decision from the solid line shown on the bottom left as $d$ to the dotted line on the bottom right as $d + delta d$. The relative change in the decision due to a change in the information is the VoI.

These concepts are not limited to that of functions of time but can be applied to any relationship between the ground truth, measured information and decision making. Let us consider the task where we need to make a decision about the location and strength of a transmission system that is to be installed to provide communication coverage to an area. The ground truth may be the need to have good coverage over some strategic locations in the area, identified by the points on a two-dimensional plane representing the map of the area. In this case, the ground truth consists of the locations of the points needing coverage, and information about the power at any location may come from collections of data, or using some models to predict the power at different locations. From the collected information, the decision is to select the location of the transmission system, which is characterized by a center (the location of the system to be installed) and radius (determined by the power of the transmission system) indicating the area covered by the transmission system.

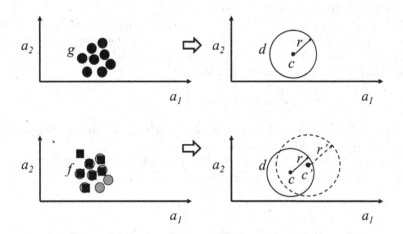

**Fig. 6.** Illustration of QoI and VoI for relational information

In such a system, the ground truth and the information consist of several information items, each item represented with a pair of attributes (e.g., $a_1$ and $a_2$ in Fig. 6), which are the coordinates in the plane. The top part of Fig. 6 shows the information collected at one instance, which is represented by the dark circular dots, each circle representing a specific information item. If the information at top were analyzed, the analysis task would have determined that it represented a circular area defined by its center $c$ and a radius $r$. The bottom part of Fig. 6 shows a change in the information collected, where the new information coming in is shown as square shapes overlaid on the original ones. As a result of the new information, the decision regarding the center and radius changes. The shift in the decision of the center and the change in radius compared to the original location provide a measure of the value of the new information.

In general, information such as the once described previously can be viewed as structured information that can be stored in a relational database. This forms the most common type of information used in machine learning activities – where each attribute reflects a feature in the training or test data, and for the classification problems, another attribute is the label assigned to the set of features. The analysis could map the information into decisions with completely different attributes (the center and radius in Fig. 6).

More generally, we can view the ground truth and information as representing functions in an information space ($\textbf{\textit{IS}}$), which is distinct from that of the decision space ($\textbf{\textit{DS}}$). The information space is defined by the attributes that define the specific attributes of the information being collected, or the ground truth, and may include time as one of the attributes. The ground truth and information are elements of the information space. We assume that a distance metric $\Delta$ is defined over the information space, so that $\Delta(f,g)$ measures the distance between any two elements. Similarly, a distance metric $\delta$ is defined in the decision space to measure the distance between two decisions.

The analysis task is a mapping from the information space to the decision space. Denoting the decision corresponding to an existing information $I$ as $a(I)$, the VoI for a new information $J$ for an analysis task denoted as $A$ which is already using a given information I, would be given by

$$VoI(J|I,A) = \delta(a(J+I),a(I))$$

Note that VoI depends both upon the analysis task, as well as the available information that is used for analysis.

Given any piece of information $I$ ($I \in \textbf{\textit{IS}}$), which is supposed to be representing a ground truth $G$ ($G \in \textbf{\textit{IS}}$), the QoI of $I$ is given by

$$QoI(I) = \Delta(I,G)$$

where $\Delta$ measures the distance between two points in the information space.

In contrast to VoI, measures of QoI are dependent only on the attributes of the collected data and the properties of the collection process, and independent of the analysis task or the amount of current information available to the system.

## 5   VoI for Coalition Machine Learning

In this section we apply the concepts of the previous Sect. 4 to the coalition machine learning scenarios described in Sect. 2. Two scenarios that we examined were those of data sharing and model sharing.

### 5.1   Data Sharing Scenario

In the data sharing scenario, training data from coalition partners is used to create machine learning models for the U.S. Let us consider the situation where a set of existing training data ($T_0$) is available in the U.S. environment to train a model. An incremental set of training data ($T_i$) is available from a coalition partner, and we would like to know $VoI(T_i|T_0)$.

For supervised learning problems, each instance of training data consists of a tuple $[x_1, x_2, \ldots x_n, y]$ where $x_1, x_2, \ldots x_n$ are the features and $y$ is the label assigned to an item with those features. The information space ($\textbf{\textit{IS}}$) consists of all possible such tuples, with $T_0$ and $T_i$ being elements of this space. The trained model is a function that maps a tuple $[x_1, x_2, \ldots x_n]$ into a label $y$, and the decision space becomes the set of all such functions. Let $m(T)$ be the model built from training data $T$. Given two functions $m_1$ and $m_2$ representing two models, we define the distance between these two functions as

$$(m_1, m_2) = \Sigma \delta(m_1(x), m_2(x)),$$

where $\delta$ is a distance function between two labels, and the summation is over all possible tuples. The distance function would be selected based on the nature of the labels used in the machine learning process. For classification problems, the distance could be the equality indicator taking the value of 0 when the output labels are the same and the value of 1 when they are not. On the other hand, if the output is not a label but an estimate/prediction (e.g., the predicted temperature 5 min into the future), the distance metric could be a measure of difference in the estimate. If the output is a probability distribution among different possible output labels, it could be a histogram based difference metric, e,g., like one described in [13].

With these definitions,

$$VoI(T_i|T_0) = \delta(m(T_i|T_0), m(T_0))$$

In other words, the VoI is measured by the change in the prediction of the model that is caused by the addition of new training data.

## 5.2   Model Sharing Scenario

In the model sharing scenario, the information being provided is a machine learning model itself, and the analysis task is the task of combining or fusing models together. The decision is the model that results from the fusion of the different models that are provided to the environment.

We can represent the VoI of a new model that is coming from a coalition partner relative to the current model. Let us consider the fusion process as $\phi$, so that the result of the fusion of two models $m_1$ and $m_2$ is $\phi(m_1, m_2)$. When a new model $m_n$ is received, the VoI of the new model resulting from the fusion of that with the current model $m$ is given by:

$$VoI(m_n|m) = \delta(\phi(m_n, m), m)$$

## 5.3   Practical Considerations

In order to estimate the VoI in a practical setting, we need to have a way to measure the distance between two different models. While the definition of distance among two models is easy to provide, in practice machine learning models such as neural networks are representations of complex non-linear functions, and the information space is very large. Thus distance measures like $\Sigma \delta(m_1(x), m_2(x))$ over all tuples of x cannot be computed in practice.

A similar challenge exists in the estimation of the QoI of information in many contexts. The QoI is the distance between the collected information and the ground truth. In most cases, the ground truth is not known and the information is the only data that is available. In those cases, estimating QoI may not be viable. If we consider the two scenarios of Sect. 2, the QoI of a training data set offered by a partner would be the fidelity with which the partner collected its information. Without any detail of how it was done, the QoI of partner supplied training data cannot be ascertained. Similarly, when a partner provides a trained model in the model training scenario, the QoI of the provided model cannot be determined since there is no ground truth available. Any supporting information is only available to the partner making the measurement, and not the one fusing the various models together.

In order to make the calculation of VoI practical for machine learning scenarios, we can assume that some amount of validation data is available to the model building partner. This validation data can be used to compute the distance function among two models. Using this methodology, the distance between two models is the difference in the prediction they make over the validation data. In the case where the two models are classifiers, the distance would be the fraction of the validation data set on which the two models differed. The validation data can also be used to determine the QoI, by comparing the provided training data or trained model against the properties of the validation data.

In the specific scenarios described in Sect. 2, if the U.S. has a set of validation data available to it, then it can use that validation set to determine whether or not it is getting enough value out of acquiring training data from its partners (in the data sharing scenario), or from using the models from the partners. The quality of training data in the data sharing scenario can be compared by checking it against the properties of the validation data, and the quality of a model provided in the model sharing scenario can be compared by checking its accuracy on the validation data.

## 6    Applications of VoI

In this section, we look at some of the use-case scenarios where VoI and its quantification can be valuable in machine learning scenarios. We begin with the examination of VoI for deciding whether or not to accept data from partners in coalition environments, as well as non-coalition environment applications of VoI.

### 6.1    Defining Policies for Coalition Environments

The quantification of VoI is useful for determining whether or not to accept the information offered by a coalition partner. The decision would depend on the mixture of QoI and VoI of the information. These can result in the automatic generation of policies for acceptance or rejection of data provided by partners, a special case of the general approach for systems to automatically generate access control policies [14]. In order to accept information, a decision matrix like that shown in Fig. 7 can be used.

If the VoI and QoI are both high (i.e., they are larger than some threshold) the data should be accepted. However, if they are both low, it makes sense to reject the data. If one is low and the other is high, the decision whether to accept or reject the data depends on the context. Information with low QoI but high VoI may be dangerous and requires additional input regarding whether it ought to be used. Information with high quality but low value may not be suitable for the current analysis task, and should be rejected for the current task, but one may want to keep the information around and use it for future analysis tasks, given that it is of high quality.

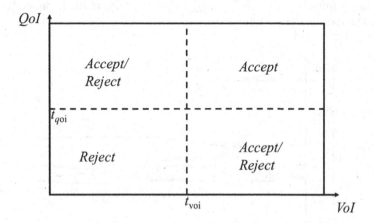

**Fig. 7.** Acceptance of coalition data

Since the VoI is highly dependent on the analysis task as well as the current information that is available, defining the threshold for VoI manually is difficult. However, a system can generate the policies with the right threshold to determine the acceptance by analyzing the data that is available. A human being provides the template for the policies, and an analysis of the data determines the threshold for accepting or rejecting the data.

In order to define the policies, we need to have an approach to determine both the VoI and QoI of data in different scenarios. Below we discuss the assessment of these two metrics in the context of the two scenarios described in Sect. 2.

For the assessment, we have used the MNIST data set [15] to estimate the VoI and QoI of the data. It is a data set that is publicly available, and used widely in the machine learning literature. There are 70,000 images in the MNIST database, divided into 60,000 images for training and 10,000 for testing.

In order to use this data in the coalition setting, we assumed that this training data, instead of being available in a central location, was collected in three different portions by the U.S., the UK and Kish. To achieve this, the training data was randomly split into a portion owned by the U.S., one owned by the UK and one owned by Kish. The VoI of partner data would depend on the share of data that is owned by each country. We assume that all of the test data remains with the U.S., which is the only nation creating a machine learning model in the data sharing scenario, and the only nation fusing different models together in the model sharing scenario. The test data was used by the U.S. for determining the QoI of the provided data.

## 6.2   Data Sharing Scenario

In the data sharing scenario, the UK and Kish provide data to the U.S. so that the U.S. can build a training model. The VoI of the data provided is measured by how much impact it has on the model that the U.S. built. It depends on the share of the data set that different clients own.

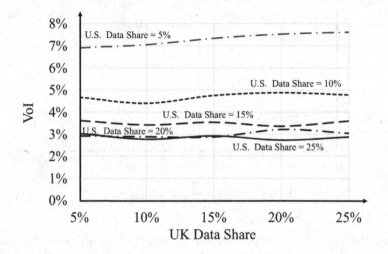

**Fig. 8.** Data sharing scenario: VoI of UK data

Figure 8 shows a quantitative evaluation of the VoI of UK data, which is measured by the fraction of the validation data that were labeled differently when data from the UK was combined to train the model, as compared to when the data from the UK was not used. The VoI for various configurations (different combinations of splits between the three nations) were simulated for 20 iterations, and averaged. The standard deviation from the plotted results was in the range of 10–15% of the mean value.

The VoI is dependent primarily on the amount of data share that the U.S. started with originally, and it remains relatively unchanged as the amount of data provided by the UK increases. When the U.S. had more than 20% of the data of the original set, the VoI provided by the addition of UK data was a modest 3% regardless of its size.

The addition of Kish data provides an incremental value when added to the UK data, but the VoI added is significantly less. This result is reasonable since the value of adding incremental training data is reduced and more value is needed. Figure 9 shows the incremental value of adding the data from Kish for two configurations, the first one when the U.S. has 5% share of the complete data, and the other one when the U.S. has 25% if the complete data.

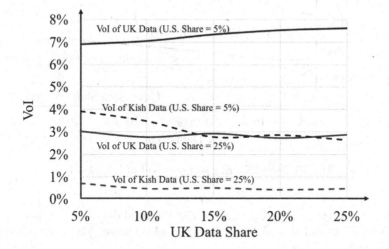

**Fig. 9.** Data sharing scenario: VoI of Kish data

The QoI of additional data provided by each of the partners is significant. Looking at the value provided by each of the partners, the U.S. may want to determine a threshold of 3% or more for accepting the data from any partner for the data provided in this particular context.

## 6.3   Model Sharing Scenario

In the model sharing scenario, the VoI is determined by comparing the difference in the classification that results from incorporating the model provided by the partner into the original model developed by the U.S. We assume that an ensemble approach is used for integrating the models, as described in [16]. In this case, the VoI is measured by examining how the VoI changes when the models are incorporated.

Figure 10 shows the VoI for integrating the models provided by the UK to create an integrated model. The VoI is calculated by modeling the changes to the values predicted on the validation data set. As in the case with data sharing, the VoI is impacted more by the amount of data that the U.S. originally had in its partition, than by the amount of UK data.

As in the case of data sharing, the incremental value of incorporating the model from Kish, when the model from U.S. is already incorporated, is relatively modest. The changes in VoI is shown in Fig. 11. Two sets of curves are shown, one corresponding to the case where the U.S. had 5% of the total data and the

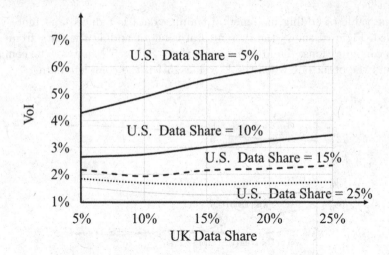

**Fig. 10.** Model sharing scenario: VoI of UK model

other to the case where the U.S. had 25% of the total data. For comparison, the VoI of the UK model as well as the Kish model is shown. The cases are similar to those shown in Fig. 8.

As in the case of data sharing, the additional VoI provided by the incorporation of Kish data is much less than that due to that provided by the U.S. data. The VoI of getting additional data seems to follow a trend of diminishing marginal utility.

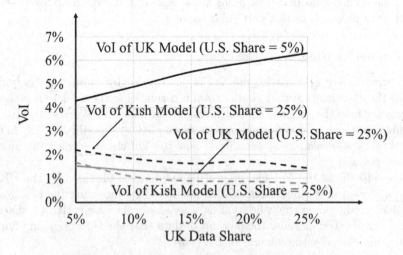

**Fig. 11.** Model sharing scenario: VoI of Kish data

## 6.4    VOI and Size of Training Data

In machine learning based applications, VoI as formulated above can be used to determine whether including additional data sets is likely to provide an improvement in the function that is being learned. The effectiveness of training process depends significantly on the amount of training data that is available. However, acquisition of training data remains the most time-consuming process in creating machine learning based solutions for specialized domains, and is a major impediment in creating AI enabled solutions for special industrial or military domains.

In general, having a large but varying and domain-specific training data set is more beneficial for machine learning applications. The improvement in accuracy of the training data can be captured as learning curves, and theoretical estimations of the learning curves are available when statistical assumptions about the type of data being seen can be made. However, in real-life, data rarely conforms to any stable statistical properties. Thus, it is still something of an art to determine whether one has obtained sufficient training data.

A quantitative formulation of the VoI provides a way to determine whether one has obtained sufficient data in order to train the model, making data acquisition more of a science than an art. For each set of training data that is obtained, one can determine what the VoI of the additional training data obtained would be. This would allow the determination of the point where the increase in VoI offered by the collection of additional data falls below the threshold where the effort to collect additional data is warranted.

As a concrete example, let us consider the scenario shown in Fig. 12, where a camera is used to read the gauge dials associated with an underwater gas pipeline. When the camera notices a reading which exceeds some threshold, it would send an alert and/or take corrective actions like shutting off the gas supply. In order for the camera to perform this action, it needs to be trained to recognize the characters displayed on the dial. This requires training the camera with machine learning software with training samples showing different values of the digits in the dial. The MNIST data set [15] is used as a proxy for this scenario to train the machine learning model.

The training algorithm used was that of a convolutional neural network [17] implemented using the TensorFlow package using the Keras API [18]. The neural network consisted of an input layer accepting the $28 \times 28$ pixel images, followed by 2 convolution layers with a kernel area of $5 \times 5$ pixels, followed by a flattening layer to take their output and feed to a dense layer of 128 neurons. The final layer was a 10 node layer using the softmax activation function to identify one of the 10 possible digits as the likely one represented in the input image.

The collection of training data for some specialized applications is often the most expensive and time-consuming part of creating an AI solution. While different amounts of training data can be collected, one needs to assess the value of the additional information that is collected. Suppose training information is collected in bundles of 5000 images each. We would like to understand how many such bundles are required and what is the value of each new bundle of informa-

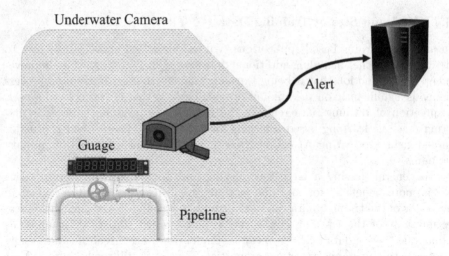

**Fig. 12.** Underwater surveillance scenario

tion that is collected in this manner. Traditional machine learning wisdom would indicate that one should collect as much information as possible, but that comes with additional costs of collection. Measures of accuracy of learning algorithms are calculated on portions of the training data and by themselves are not useful for predicting when sufficient data has been collected.

Usually, training data is collected in batches incrementally. In many use-cases, the collection effort is about the same for each batch of training data. The additional VoI provided by each new training data set, however, will keep on decreasing as a general trend. When the VoI falls below a predefined threshold, collection of additional training data could be stopped.

If we follow the paradigm of collecting data in information bundles of 5000 images each, it would be useful to know the value of information delivered by each of the information bundles. When the VoI delivered by an additional increment is not high enough, we can determine that enough samples have been collected.

Figure 13 shows the VoI that is delivered by each incremental information bundle that is collected.

The VoI provided by each of the information bundles is shown. Twelve bundles of images in the MNIST database are used for training. The first bundle of 5K images is the base reference and is marked as no change in the function. The VoI graph can now be used to determine how much training data is adequate.

If for our applications, we decide that a change of less than 5% in the classification function is sufficient for the task, 4 bundles of information, or 20,000 images will be adequate. On the other hand, if we decide that the system requires a change of less than 3% in the realized classification, we need to have more than 7 bundles or 35,000 images from the training set. A requirement of less than 2% change in VoI would require that we have more than 60,000 images, which exceeds the amount available in the MNIST database. An analysis of the

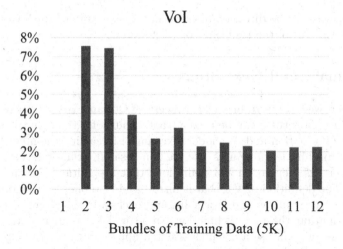

**Fig. 13.** VoI as measured for MNIST data

MNIST dataset, coupled with the problem requirements, provides a good way to determine the amount of data required for training digital number recognition for the undersea gauge problem.

Note that this VoI is not the same as accuracy metric, but simply a measurement of how much the estimated function is changing. Since the MNIST data set is a well-studied one in machine learning applications, the basic algorithms can provide high accuracy. The accuracy of the model being discussed was 89% using only one bundle of information, which grew to 94% with four bundles, and 96% with 7 bundles. The neural network using all of the data could reach an accuracy of 98% eventually. While the fluctuation of VoI has an impact on the accuracy, the stabilization of the function being learned may happen at any accuracy level depending on the characteristics of the model. The VoI measure provides a way to assess the effort required to collect the new bundles of information, as compared to the additional accuracy that will be gained.

## 6.5   Other Usage of VoI

VoI is useful in empirical situations beyond just machine learning applications. It has been shown that it is possible to run games [19–21] in which human players (both experts and non-experts) need to make decisions (single or sequential) and are presented with a stream of items of information on cards (with information divided into a number of categories), and produce a probabilistic model of the value of different categories of information to the decisions made (aka operational task).

It has yet to be shown how to take such models of value and build a VoI enabled fusion graph. However, it has been shown how to bundle information system assets to meet the needs of operational tasks [22]. Those can be viewed as an initial step in the direction of creating a fusion graph, which can be used to estimate the VoI of the resulting complex system.

## 7   Summary and Next Steps

In this paper, we have introduced the concept of QoI and VoI for machine learning, and shown how these can be used advantageously for the policy based coordination of information and AI models exchanged in coalition contexts.

Because machine learning uses discrete bundles of information, the discussion in this paper has focused on VoI definitions that are suitable for that type of operation. The definition of VoI that is introduced is applicable to more general class of information fusion and processing approaches. In signal processing based uses of information, the analysis function can be modeled as an analytic function. In those cases, we can use a calculus-oriented approach to define QoI and VoI, and obtain analytical definitions for them. For complex information fusion tasks, which often include a network of cascading analysis functions, the analytical definition must be composed in other ways.

The concept of VoI can be applied in many other scenarios and can be used to improve analysis operations in many contexts.

**Acknowledgments.** This research was sponsored by the U.S. Army Research Laboratory and the U.K. Ministry of Defence under Agreement Number W911NF-16-3-0001. The views and conclusions contained in this document are those of the authors and should not be interpreted as representing the official policies, either expressed or implied, of the U.S. Army Research Laboratory, the U.S. Government, the U.K. Ministry of Defence or the U.K. Government. The U.S. and U.K. Governments are authorized to reproduce and distribute reprints for Government purposes notwithstanding any copyright notation hereon.

Dstl/CP107670. Content includes material subject to © Crown copyright (2018), Dstl. This information is licensed under the terms of the Open Government Licence except where otherwise stated. To view this licence, visit http://www.nationalarchives.gov.uk/doc/open-government-licence/version/3 or write to the Information Policy Team, The National Archives, Kew, London TW9 4DU, or email: psi@nationalarchives.gsi.gov.uk.

## References

1. Ministry of Defence, United Kingdom: UK defence doctrine, 5th edn. MoD Concepts and Doctrine Centre Joint Doctrine Publication, U.K. (2014)
2. Pearson, G., Lemon, J.: Vision and critical challenges in exploiting distributed data for distributed decision making. In: Proceedings of the International Society for Optics and Photonics Conference on Defense Transformation and Net-Centric Systems 2011, Orlando, FL, USA (2011)
3. Steinberg, A., Bowman, C.: Rethinking the JDL data fusion levels. In: National Symposium on Sensor and Data Fusion (NSSDF) (2004)

4. Pham, T., Cirincione, G., Swami, A., Pearson, G., Williams, C.: Distributed analytics and information science. In: IEEE 8th International Conference on Information Fusion (2015)

5. Roberts, D., Lock, G., Verma, D.: Holistan: a futuristic scenario for international coalition operations. In: IEEE International Conference on Integration of Knowledge Intensive Multi-Agent Systems (2007)

6. Stenbit, J., Wells, L., Alberts, D.: NATO code of best practice for C2 assessment. Office of the Assistant Secretary of Defense (OASD), Command and Control Research Program (CCRP), Washington, DC 20301 (2002)

7. Bisdikian, C., Kaplan, L., Srivastava, M., Thornley, M., Verma, D., Young, R.: Building principles for a quality of information specification for sensor information. In: IEEE International Conference on Information Fusion, pp. 1370–1377 (2009)

8. Bar-Noy, A., et al.: Quality of information aware networking for tactical military networks. In: IEEE International Conference on Pervasive Computing and Communications (2011)

9. Sachidananda, V., Khelil, A., Suri, N.: Quality of information in wireless sensor networks: a survey. In: Proceeding of the International Conference on Information Quality (2010)

10. Jin, H., Su, L., Nahrstedt, D.C.K., Xu, J.: Quality of information aware incentive mechanisms for mobile crowd sensing systems. In: Proceedings of the ACM International Symposium on Mobile Ad-Hoc Networking and Computing, pp. 167–176 (2015)

11. Rissanen, J.: Fisher information and stochastic complexity. IEEE Trans. Inf. Theory $42(1)$, 40–47 (1996)

12. DeDeo, S.: Information theory for intelligent people. May simon/it.pdf (2018). http://tuvalu.santafe.edu/

13. Olivier, C., Courtellemont, P., Colot, O., de Brucq, D., Matouat, A.E.: Comparison of histograms: a tool for detection. Eur. J. Diagn. Saf. Autom. $4(3)$, 335–355 (1994)

14. Calo, S., Chakraborty, S., Verma, D., Bertino, E., Lupu, E., Cirincione, G.: Self generation of access control policies. In: Proceedings of ACM SACMAT (2018)

15. Yann, L., Corinna, C., Christopher, J.: The MNIST database of handwritten digits (1998). http://yann.lecun.com/exdb/mnist/

16. Verma, D., Chakraborty, S., Calo, S., Julier, S., Pasteris, S.: An algorithm for model fusion for distributed learning. In: SPIE Defense and Commerical Sensing Symposium, Ground/Air Multisensor Interoperability, Integration, and Networking for Persistent ISR (2018)

17. LeCun, Y., Bengio, Y.: Convolutional networks for images, speech, and time series. Handb. Brain Theory Neural Netw. $3361$, 10 (1995)

18. Abadi, M., et al.: Tensorflow: a system for large-scale machine learning. In: Proceedings of OSDI, vol. 16, pp. 265–283 (2016)

19. Moffat, J., Medhurst, J.: Modelling of human decision making in simulation models of conflict using experimental gaming. Eur. J. Oper. Res. $196$, 1147–1156 (2009)

20. Medhurst, J., Stanton, I., Bird, H., Berry, M.: The value of infomration to decision makers: an experimental approach using card based decision gaming. J. Oper. Res. Soc. $60$, 747–757 (2009)

21. Medhurst, J., Stanton, I., Bird, H., Berry, M.: Risk taking by decision makers - using card-based decision gaming to develop models of behavior. J. Oper. Res. Soc. $61$, 1561–1571 (2010)

22. Braines, D., Preece, A., de Mel, G., Pham, T.: Enabling CoIST users: D2D at the network edge. In: IEEE International Conference on Information Fusion (FUSION) (2014)

# Self-Generating Policies for Machine Learning in Coalition Environments

Dinesh Verma[1], Seraphin Calo[1(✉)], Shonda Witherspoon[1], Irene Manotas[1], Elisa Bertino[2], Amani M. Abu Jabal[2], Greg Cirincione[3], Ananthram Swami[3], Gavin Pearson[4], and Geeth de Mel[5]

[1] Distributed AI Department, IBM TJ Watson Research Center, Yorktown Heights, NY 10549, USA
{dverma,scalo,Shonda.Adena.Witherspoon,Irene.Manotas}@us.ibm.com
[2] Computer Science Department, Purdue University, West Lafayette, IN 47907, USA
{bertino,aabujaba}@purdue.edu
[3] Army Research Labs, 2800 Powder Mill Road, Adelphi, MD 20783, USA
{gregory.h.cirincione.civ,ananthram.swami.civ}@mail.mil
[4] Defence Science and Technology Laboratory, Ministry of Defence, Porton Down, Salisbury SP4 0JQ, UK
agpearson@mail.dstl.gov.uk
[5] IBM Research UK, Hartree Center, Warrington, UK
geeth.demel@uk.ibm.com

**Abstract.** In any machine learning problem, obtaining and acquiring good training data is the main challenge that needs to be overcome to build a good model. When applying machine learning approaches in the context of coalition operations, one may only be able to get data for training machine learning models from coalition partners. However, all coalition partners may not be equally trusted, thus the task of deciding when, and when not, to accept training data for coalition operations remain complex. Policies can provide a mechanism for making these decisions but determining the right policies may be difficult given the variability of the environment. Motivated by this observation, in this paper, we propose an architecture that can generate policies required for building a machine learning model in a coalition environment without a significant amount of human input.

## 1 Introduction

Machine learning and the broader area of Artificial Intelligence have many applications across a wide range of domains, including battlefield operations [1]. In general, machine learning based solutions create a model that characterizes patterns present in a corpus of training data, and subsequently use the model for decision making.

As an example, a machine learning model can be trained to recognize patterns in sounds, video or images to characterize the actions a group of insurgents may be employing to disturb peace in an area under the oversight of a coalition peacekeeping force. These may include recognizing the type of vehicle that insurgents

S. Calo et al. (Eds.): PADG 2018, LNCS 11550, pp. 42–65, 2019.
https://doi.org/10.1007/978-3-030-17277-0_3

use, how a vehicle is loaded for different activities, recognizing the type of gear they wear when involved in a disturbing activity versus the type of clothes they wear when participating in a social activity and so forth. However, these patterns vary from context to context, which implies that the training data for the models has to be acquired in the field.

In general, more training data leads to better machine learning models [2,3]. However, obtaining a sufficient amount of training data to build a model is an onerous and time-consuming process even in the best of circumstances, and the difficulties are exacerbated when the operations are conducted in the field. The collection of data is relatively simple since sensing equipment and data collection technologies are inexpensive and widely available. However, the quality of the collected data will remain an issue. As a result, the task of accessing the data, and deciding whether or not a piece of data is suitable for the training process is a challenge.

In a coalition environment, we envision a data curation system that examines the data available from different partners, evaluates their properties, and selectively determines the right data to use which is best suited for building a desired machine learning model. The data curation agent can use policies defined by an administrator to automate its task of selecting data sets. However, since data and machine learning models vary tremendously, specifying the policies for curation manually could be difficult. We suggest the use of self-generating policies [4] to drive the operations of the data curator. This contributes to advancing the state of autonomy in distributed coalition environments using generative policies.

This paper begins with a specific scenario of coalition operation in which it would be appropriate to share training data. It then discusses how a policy-based approach can help create a general data curator that can safely collect data from the coalition partners. We look at the set of policies that are needed for data curation. We discuss the limitations that will arise if those policies are specified manually. We then define an approach for the data curator to generate the policies automatically. Finally, we present some simulations to show that a data curator based on self-generating policies can be realized in practice.

While the design and operation of data curation are motivated by the coalition operation scenario, we believe the curation technologies can be applicable in many other scenarios where data needs to be collected from diverse sources. Specifically, when training data is collected from public sources like the Internet, or from crowd-sourced data, similar concerns about the reliability and trustworthiness of training data being acquired will arise. The data curation approach specified in this paper should be applicable to those environments as well.

## 2  Coalition Data Sharing Scenario

We consider a scenario where multiple partners have training data that can be combined together for the purpose of training a machine learning model, and exactly one of the partners in the coalition is creating that model. The different partners have collected the training data independently and have agreed to share their data with the partner that is building the machine learning model.

In the case of military coalition operations, such a scenario may arise when the coalition is trying to maintain peace in a disturbed area. Coalition members may have surveillance that could monitor the movement of people and personnel, and the video and audio footage acquired in the process provides the training data to look for possible insurgents and to distinguish them from the civilians who may be moving around.

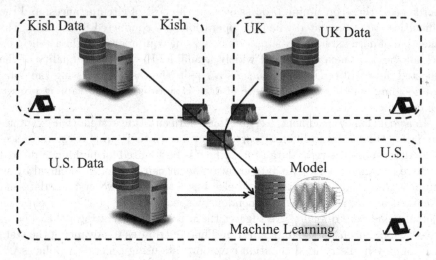

**Fig. 1.** Machine learning with data from partners

Figure 1 illustrates one such scenario, which has been borrowed from [5]. Three partners, the U.S., the UK and Kish, are shown. Kish is an imaginary nation created to demonstrate coalition scenarios in the context of the DAIS research alliance activities [6], and is similar to other hypothetical countries such as Holistan [7] used in related works. Each of the partners has access to a set of training data. One of the partners, namely the U.S., is running a machine learning training process to create a model out of the data, which is distributed to each of the partners in the system. The partner running the machine learning algorithm (U.S.) can choose to use only the training data that it has. However, a better model can be built by using the training data available from the other partners. The concern would be that the data obtained from the partners may not be as reliable as the data generated and curated in-house.

The U.S. machine learning system may get part of its training data from the U.S., part of it from the UK, and part of the learning data from Kish. The base camps from different nations are interconnected into a communication network protected by their firewalls. Due to the arrangements between the coalition partners, the firewalls between the camps would allow network level access for the server training from the U.S. to data servers in Kish and the UK. As the U.S. machine learning algorithm builds its model, such as a neural network, it needs to determine the value of information [8] it is getting from the training data provided by each of the partners, and whether the additional data would be useful to have.

While having access to a partner's data is likely to improve the model if the data has good quality and value, there may be concerns about the quality of partner data. The partner training data may be inaccurate or may even have been maliciously manipulated to lead to inaccurate results, e.g. as a form of data poisoning attack. Thus, accepting all partner data for training purposes may result in a poorer model. Therefore, an approach for judiciously selecting which data from which partners needs to be developed.

In addition to coalition environments, the situation for obtaining training data from partners or sources with limited amounts of trust may arise in many situations, e.g., data sources such as medical records or information about the spread of infectious diseases have varying degrees of trust/confidence associated with them across many different countries. Building a machine learning model that works across data obtained from many different sources has similar issues, since not all sources may follow the same standards for maintaining and checking the quality of data.

## 3   Data Curator for Machine Learning

In order to accept only valid data for training its machine learning model, the partner running the training operation can choose to implement a data curator. The logical role of the curator is shown in Fig. 2, where the data curator acts like a filter and a funnel; the funnel to collect data from partners and the filter to clean and process the data provided by them. The resulting data is clean and suitable for model training. The data curator has the task of checking the data provided by each partner, and deciding whether or not the data should be accepted for training the model. The acceptance may be done at the granularity

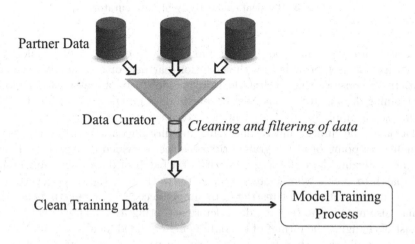

**Fig. 2.** Logical concept of data curator

of the entire data set provided by a partner, at the granularity of a subset of the data set, or on each individual data sample that is provided.

In order to perform its task, the physical layout of the interconnections that the data curator needs is shown in Fig. 3. The data curator would need to interface with the data servers in the other domains, be able to communicate with them using the data transfer protocol supported by the partner, be able to understand the format in which the data is stored, be able to analyze, process, combine and store the data, and formulate a coherent set of training data that is in a format suitable for training. Some of the data may be acquired previously and stored in a data server accessible to the partner that is running the data curator. In other cases, the data curator may be able to interface directly with the data sources in the partner environments.

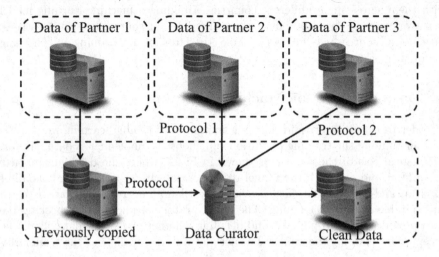

**Fig. 3.** Physical connectivity of data curator

The data curator may be filtering and analyzing data at the granularity of the entire data set provided by the coalition partner, or at a smaller segment of it. If we consider the machine learning model to be a classification model, the training data is likely to consist of several data points, with each data point having some input features (e.g., image, voice samples, FFT coefficients, etc.) and a class. The curator may be analyzing and filtering data at the granularity of a single data point, or at the granularity of a class provided by a partner. It may also be analyzing data at the granularity of a batch of data points, examining each batch to decide whether to accept or reject them at the batch-level.

The data curator is not restricted to simply accepting or rejecting the data. It may also modify the training data before accepting it. This modification may consist of changing the format of the data being provided, relabeling a data point with a class different than the one the original partner has provided, changing all the class names to some other local convention, or performing other types of transformations on the data.

It would be desirable to have the data curator be independent of the specifics of the machine learning algorithm being used, or the exact number of partners, or the specific schema they may be using. In order to create a flexible data curation system, the operation of the data curation system could be based on policies. These policies would need to satisfy several requirements, as described in [9]. The requirements may be applicable to both the providers of the data as well as the recipients of the data. From the perspective of the data receiver, which is the organization driving the operation of the data curator, the following requirements may need to be imposed on any data set that is received:

- conditions on data content specify whether that content should be received;
- data content should be in a specific format or contain a specific number of fields;
- data content may only be received from selected partners with a pre-existing agreement in place;
- data may require special transformations after it is received in order to pre- serve privacy, or transform its format, depending on the partner and the content of the data being provided;
- data should be received if it improves the quality of the machine learning model; and
- data should be examined to check for biases or attempts at data poisoning attacks on the machine learning system.

In order to satisfy these requirements, the data curator may need to use several helper functions that help it analyze the content or transform the content.

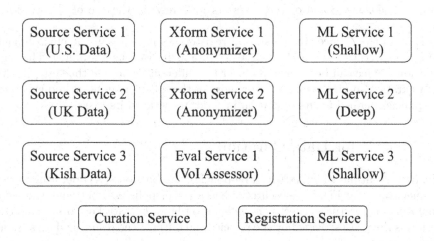

**Fig. 4.** Helper services for curation

From an operational perspective, we can view the curator as well as the helper functions available in the U.S. environment as a set of micro-services.

Each micro-service registers itself to a registration service, which allows the micro-services to discover each other. Other micro-services would include one or more machine learning services, data transformation services, data evaluation services and the data source services. Data source services provide access to the repositories holding the actual data before the curator accesses them. A typical setup for the coalition scenario is shown in Fig. 4.

In this approach, the raw data available from each of the partners is available from data source services, one or more for each partner. A data source service may be a front-end to an actual data set (e.g. for the U.S. data) or may be a proxy for a data set that is available remotely. The proxy service provides access to the partner data and may require special protocols to access the data. Such proxy services may either query the data available in the partner network, or they may have pre-copied the data from the partner and are providing access to that data to the group in the U.S. trying to access them.

The data transform services provide different transformations on the data that is received. The transformations may include changing the format of data, changing the labels assigned to data, or any other required modification. The data evaluation services can compute attributes such as the Value of Information (VoI) or Quality of Information (QoI) [8] of the data or a subset thereof.

The system may use one or more machine learning processes in its task. Depending on the type of algorithm used in the machine learning process, the learning service is characterized as shallow or deep. The shallow learning processes can build models more quickly, and may be using algorithms such as decision trees, kNN-clusters or neural networks with a small number of layers. The deep learning models may be using algorithms that require significantly more computation time to build, e.g., variations of neural networks with many layers of neurons. Some of the assessors may rely on the use of the machine learning processes.

Each of the services in the system registers its presence in the environment using a registration service, which also contains its various attributes. The registration service can be used to discover the different devices in the system. The data curation service invokes one or more of these helper services, and executes the policies defined for its operation in order to perform its tasks.

## 4   Policies for Data Curation

The data curation, which is driven by policies, can be viewed as operating in the manner shown in Fig. 5. The curator has a set of policies. It obtains the data from different partners, checks the policies on how the data has to be handled, performs the tasks specified by the policies and outputs the resulting data stream as its output.

In order to perform its tasks, the data curation system needs to have many different types of policies. These include policies for data format transformation, policies for deciding the order for obtaining information from partners, and policies for accepting or rejecting datasets.

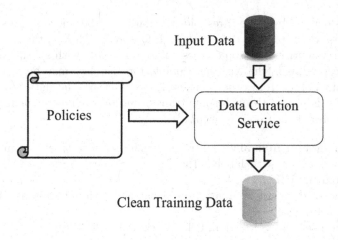

**Fig. 5.** Policy based data curator

Data format transformation policies are required to deal with differences in the formats of data among different partners. In order to produce a clean training data set, all data from all partners needs to be transformed and stored in the same format. Once the format for the machine learning data is determined, all remaining data has to be transformed to that format. The transformation would require passing the data through a transformer. In case a transformer is not available that does a direct transformation from the format of the partner to the format desired, a sequence of transformations that can achieve the same goal would need to be undertaken. A typical transformation policy may look like the following:

- If data is from the UK, call DataXformService1.
- If data is from Kish, call DataXformService1 then DataXformService2 and DataXformService3.

The transformation may deal with changes such as renaming data entries, converting image or audio formats, supplying missing entries, etc. The exact transformation would be specific to the transformation service, and may be opaque to the curator process, which only needs to worry about the policy to invoke.

Policies for determining the order in which partner data is acquired are needed because the value of information provided by a partner depends on the amount of data that is already available in the system. Such policies may look like the following:

- Process U.S. data before processing Kish data.

Policies for accepting or rejecting data would depend on the QoI and VoI of the data from each partner. For partners which provide data with low QoI and low VoI, as defined by some threshold, the data may be rejected in its entirety. For partners which provide data with high QoI and high VoI, the data may be accepted in its entirety. In some cases only data points with specific attributes may be accepted, e.g., the Kish data points for one class may be accepted but not the data points from other classes. In some cases, the data may only be accepted if it is passed through some transformation such as relabeling of data. Some examples of such policies would be

- Reject a data set from any country in which attribute labels are missing.
- Reject a data set with labels "Tank" and "Sniper" from Kish, but accept them from the UK.
- If a data set does not originate from a partner with a certain attribute, call DataXformService2.
- If the data set QoI is less than 0.4, call the relabeling service.

These policies can be viewed as more precise specifications of the requirements that were described in Sect. 3. The English sentence representations above can be implemented in any policy language that supports an event-condition-action model such as EPAL, XACML [10], CIM-SPL [11] or any other similar language [12].

Once the policies are specified and the data curation service has access to all of the available services (through the registration service or equivalent), the curation service can simply execute all of the policies on each partner dataset. This will allow the curation service to automate the task of accepting data from the partners, processing the data and making them ready to be stored in a format that the machine learning process can use to build a model.

## 5   Self Generation of Policies

Although the policy-based approach for data curation is simple and can be implemented readily within our environment, the number of policies can grow rapidly. If there are N data sources with N1 attributes, P partners each with P1 attributes, and Q data assessment services with Q1 measures and thresholds each, the number of possible policies would be N*N1*P*P1*Q*Q1. If each of these attributes is constrained to take 5 values, the set of possible policies we can have is 15,625. The set of policies can grow unwieldy and would be very difficult to specify manually.

Another challenge is that the policies and their parameters depend on the type of data and content that is being provided by the partners. The specification of the right policies would depend on the properties of the data, and how much value they provide to the learning task. This analysis can be hard to do manually.

New data quality and value measure assessments can be introduced in the environment over time and may require addition of new policies. For all of these reasons, it would be hard to specify policies manually, and the only practical way is for the data curation policies to be generated by the system itself.

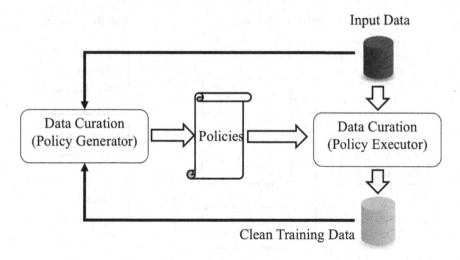

**Fig. 6.** Self-generation of policies for data curation

The data curator in this case consists of two components, a policy generator and a policy executor. The policy executor is a component of the data curator shown in Fig. 5. The policy generator is an additional component that analyzes the partner data content, uses the helper services, and creates the policies. This operation of the data curator is shown in Fig. 6.

The data curator in Fig. 6 can be viewed as operating in two stages. In the first stage, the policy generator component examines the data from the partners, and the currently available set of accepted training data in order to generate the policies for data curation. In the second phase, the policy executor runs the data curation policies to generate the clean training data. The process could be done in a staged manner, with one batch of data examined and policies for the next batch to be generated.

The policy generator requires some information from a human in order to generate the set of policies for a given coalition scenario. This information can be provided via a management system. The information obtained from the management system is shown in Fig. 7.

The manager provides an interaction graph, which defines the type of other services the curator may expect to see in the environment. These would include the data source services, the data transform services and the machine learning services that can be viewed in the system. The manager also provides generation information to the curator, which consists of a context, a set of policy templates and a set of restrictions on the templates. The approach follows the concepts mentioned in [13].

The interaction graph helps the curator in finding other helper services in the environment. It queries the registration service for services that have a role defined in the interaction graph. For the data curation part, this would indicate the set of services that have the role of data transformation, data assessment,

Information from Manager                    Curator Action

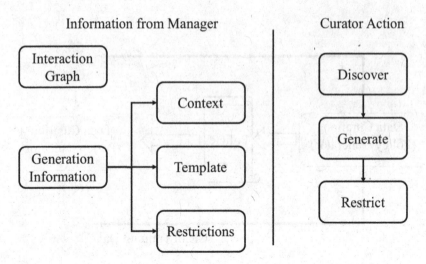

**Fig. 7.** Information for policy generation

data relabeling or creating a machine learning model. The curator would be able to discover the properties of those services and use them to create policies using the generation information.

**Start → TrustedSourcePolicy | UnTrustedSourcePolicy | Default**

**TrustedSourcePolicy → if** (dataSource.origin == **TrustedNation) then accept**

**UnTrustedSourcePolicy → if** (dataSource.origin ==   **UnTrustedNation) and**

[{*isMissingTrustedClass*(dataSource.class)}] **then accept**

**UnTrustedSourcePolicy → if** (dataSource.origin == **UnTrustedNation) and**

**not** [{*isMissingTrustedClass*(dataSource.class)}]  **and**  [{*VoI*(dataSource)}] <

[{*3Sigma*(ExistingData)}] **then accept**

**Default → reject**

**TrustedNation → US | UK**

**UnTrustedNation → Kish**

**Fig. 8.** Sample grammar for scenario policies

The generation information consists of context information, policy templates, and restrictions. The context specifies the templates and restrictions to be used for specific types of policies, e.g., the transformation policies, policies for determining the order, and policies for accepting/rejecting the data. The context would also specify other key information, e.g. identifying the deep learning algorithm for which training data is being generated. The policies that are generated are tailored specifically for that particular learning algorithm.

The policy templates provide the structure for the policies that need to be generated. They would instantiate the structured representation of the policies shown in English in Sect. 4. The templates would have place-holders to be populated by the attributes of specified data sources.

The templates specify the syntax of the policies and are computer-readable versions of the policy examples provided in the previous section. The place-holders in the templates are to be completed automatically depending on the attributes of other partners in the system, or specific computations that are performed in the environment. A template can be specified with place-holders, or it can be specified with a generating grammar.

An example of the type of grammar that may be specified to generate policies is shown in Fig. 8. In the grammar, terminal symbols are shown in square brackets. The terminal symbols could be literals (e.g., names) or they could be functions which determine values that are returned by calling an invocation service. The invocation services are identified in the figure as terminal symbols enclosed in a curly bracket in addition to the square bracket. The italics name has to match the keyword provided by a transformation service as its attribute.

In the manner of definition of the grammar, functions such as isMissingTrustedClass, VoI, and 3Sigma are attributes that are described by helper functions. The value returned by these is determined by the current state of the system and can change over time.

The restrictions provide any additional modifications that may be imposed on the system, e.g., requiring that no more than 4 transformations be called on a sequence of data, or that a certain transformation not be called on data that originates from a specific source. The restrictions are intended to prevent the system from generating policies that the human administrator would not allow.

The restrictions can also provide semantic limits on the attributes that are specified in the template. These may include calculating values which may depend on the current values of the data set or trying to minimize specific attributes. The restrictions may also exclude some values for the attributes or allow for fixing some specific attributes in order to make the templates customized and simplified for a specific environment.

The data curator performs the steps shown on the right-hand side of Fig. 7 after receiving the interaction graph and the information context. While policy generation information can be provided to any of the entities in the system, we would focus on the data curation service.

The first step performed by the data curation service is to discover other entities in the system. The other entities can be discovered if they are registering themselves and their attributes with the registration service. This allows the curation service to find out the available data sources, how those data sources can be accessed, and attributes of the data sources including their schema and their owning partner nations. Similarly, the curation service can find out about

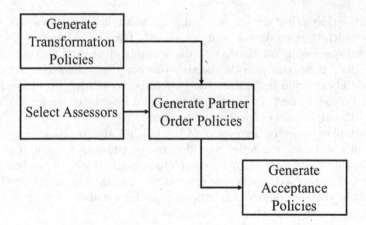

**Fig. 9.** Sequence for generating policies

the availability of helper services, e.g., a service that can compute the VoI of a set of data, or a service that can transform the schemas of the different data sets.

Having determined all the entities in the system, the data curation service can go about the task of generating the policies for curation. There is a dependency on how different types of policies are generated, which is shown in Fig. 9. The data transformation policies need to be generated first. After the inbound data is transformed, the set of suitable assessors need to be selected, ones that are best matched to the deep machine learning model being used. Then an order for processing partner data can be determined, and for each partner data, a set of accept/reject policies can be determined. Details for these stages are described in the subsections below.

### 5.1  Policies for Data Transformation

The main goal for data transformation policies is to ensure that the data provided by the partner is converted into a format which is compatible with the format that is required by the machine learning algorithm. The machine learning algorithm has a specific format in which it accepts data. The partners have another format in which they are providing data. The formats may not be the same. The data curation has to generate the policy which specifies how the format conversion should happen, given the set of helper data transformation services. Note that the format conversion may require more than one data transformation service, since the conversion capabilities of any data transformation service would be limited.

We assume that each data transformation service publishes into the registration database as its attributes both the set of data formats it can take as input, and the set of data formats that it can output. The format used by each of the partners is provided as an attribute of the dataset in the registration database,

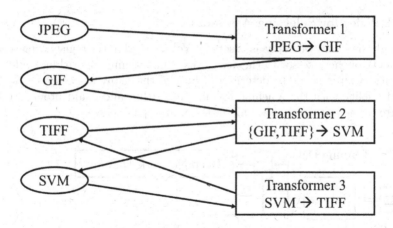

**Fig. 10.** Determining data transformation policies

and the format in which the machine learning algorithm can use the training data is specified as its attribute.

To generate the data transformation policies, we create a bipartite graph with two types of nodes, one node representing each type of data format that is entered into the registration database, and the other type of node representing each transformation service. If a transformer service can convert an input format to an output format, the transformer service has a link from the input A to it, and a directed link to the output format node. An illustrate example is shown in Fig. 10.

Figure 10 shows the case when the coalition partners are capturing images, but images could be in different formats. Four possible image formats are shown in Fig. 10. There are three transformers in the system, the first one capable of changing jpeg images into gif format, the second one changing images in either gif or tff format to svm format, and the third one changing svm into tiff. If a partner provides jpeg images, and the machine learning process requires images in tiff, then the shortest path in the bipartite graph passes through transformers 1, 2 and 3 in sequence. A shortest path algorithm can discover the path between the node representing the original format, and the node representing the desired final format. The format transformation policies can be defined using the sequence of transformations that are on this shortest path.

While illustrated for images, the same approach can be used for data in any format, as long as each format can be characterized by a label and mapped to a node representation as shown in Fig. 10. Unique names can be assigned to data that uses any schema using conventions similar to those for naming XMLschemas [14].

## 5.2   Policies for Selecting Assessors

Although there may be many assessors for VoI and QoI in the registration service, the fidelity of the assessor to the actual machine learning algorithm would vary. The data curator needs to determine which of the many assessors would have a good fidelity with the machine learning algorithm and could provide a good measure for accepting or rejecting data from the partners.

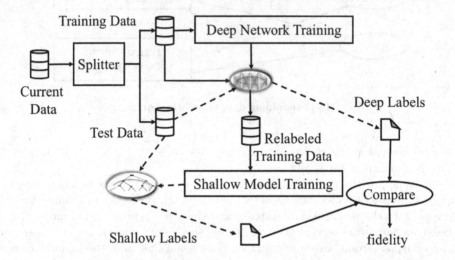

**Fig. 11.** Calculating fidelity of assessors

As an initial filtering criteria, assessors need to be able to handle the data that is being provided by the coalition partners once they are converted into the canonical format. An assessor that can only process structured data can not process images, and vice-versa. Thus, any assessor that can be used for data analysis needs to be able to ingest and process the format of data which the data transformation policies produce.

Assessors can be divided into two categories, those whose performance depends on the deep machine learning algorithm for which the training data is being curated, or those whose performance is independent of that algorithm. An assessor which determines that a data sample is a duplicate of an existing sample is independent of the deep learning algorithm. Similarly, an assessor which is looking at the distribution of classes in the training data is independent of the learning algorithm. Those assessors can be used all the time.

Some data assessors depend on using shallow machine learning models, which can allow the quick determination of the VoI or QoI of the data being provided. These assessors may or may not perform well depending on the deep machine learning algorithm for which training data is being curated.

The data curator can determine the fidelity of the assessors to the machine learning by using data that is available to it. At the very beginning, the data curator has access to U.S. data (for the scenario shown in Sect. 2) and can use that for comparing fidelities. Subsequently, more of the accepted data can be used in the process. It selects a subset of the data available to it and divides it into a test set and a training set. It uses the test set to train the machine learning algorithm. The system then relabels the training data with the resulting model to get a modified training data set. This approach for data relabeling has also been proposed for increasing resistance to data poisoning attacks [15] which could be a side-benefit for the data curation process. Each of the assessors is trained with the modified training data set. Then the fidelity of the prediction of the deep learning model on the training data set with the assessors is evaluated.

The process for determining fidelity of assessors is shown in Fig. 11. Once the fidelity of the different assessors is determined, the curator can run a clustering algorithm to determine whether the results can be divided into two or more clusters. The assessors in the cluster with the highest fidelity are selected as the ones that are to be used for subsequent data acceptance decisions.

### 5.3  Policies for Partner Order Determination

The sequence in which the data is obtained from the partners has an impact on the value of additional information that is delivered from other partners. The VoI of information for machine learning would depend on the amount of current information that is already available [6]. Therefore, the order of information acceptance is important.

One way to determine the right sequence for accepting partner data is for the data curator to determine the QoI of each partner's dataset, and process datasets in the order of highest QoI first. If the U.S. has some data that it trusts, it can compare that with the partner data to determine its QoI.

In order to determine the QoI, the curator can query the registration service to find the different QoI assessors that are present in the system. QoI can be assessed in a variety of ways, but one approach would be to train fast shallow models on the partner data that is provided, and then determine the accuracy of the model on the validation data that is with the curator. Different assessors would produce different values for each partner QoI, and the curator could compute an average for the assessment. The assessors that would be averaged would be those selected in the process earlier.

The average value of the assessment can then be used to determine the sequence in which partner data is to be processed. The sequencing is encoded into the ordering policies.

### 5.4  Accepting/Rejecting Data

The decision on whether or not to accept data from any coalition partner is done at the granularity of each data point. The policies for making this determination are generated after each dataset from a partner is analyzed. There are some obvious policies that can always be implemented when accepting or rejecting data, e.g., duplicate data points that are already in the curated data set can be rejected. However, most data points are likely to be distinct, and determination on them has to be made at a data point by data point level of granularity.

The determination of whether or not to accept any data point is done by examining the spread of the confusion matrix that is present in the data that has already been curated. For the curated data, each assessor can estimate the confidence with which the shallow model it uses can predict that the sample belongs to a specific class. For each data source, the overall QoI of the information is also known.

We use the heuristic that the product of QoI and VoI of the information that is produced has to remain constant. The QoI and VoI of the curated data source can be calculated. The QoI of the new dataset that is being considered is known as part of the generation of policies as presented above. The confidence with which the class provided by the partner is predicted becomes the measure to determine acceptance. If the predicted class is within the desired confidence range, then the data point is accepted, otherwise it is rejected.

The policies then take the form of:

- If the source is XXX and the class provided is YYY and the Assessor Confidence exceeds ZZZ then accept, otherwise reject.
- If multiple assessors are used, a majority voting is used to determine whether or not to accept the data.

## 5.5  Generation in the Context of the Scenario

As the set of discovered entities changes, and new policies are discovered, the policies that are generated by the generation process would change. As more training data is accepted, the policies would also change to reflect the dynamics of the training process.

As an example, let us consider the situation where the training data consists of 10 classes. Originally, the U.S. has data sets corresponding to 5 of these 10 classes, and the UK has data corresponding to 5 of these classes, but 3 of them are common across the U.S. and the UK. Thus, from the trusted set, only 7 out of 10 classes are known. Let us assume that classes 7, 8 and 9 are missing. We can further assume that the VoI of a data source is defined by the change in the value of a classifier as described in [8].

As the original data set is compiled, the system would accept all data sources from the UK, which is trusted. However, it would only generate a policy to accept a data set from Kish if that data set has data points corresponding to classes 7, 8 or 9. This is because the U.S. has no data set available for those classes, and it is better off using the data for those classes from the untrusted data source.

Suppose however, the UK is able to collect some data which does provide some specification for class 7. In this case, the policy would only accept data from Kish for classes 8 and 9.

For classes where data is available from trusted sources, the system would only accept data from untrusted sources if it does not deviate too much from the accepted behavior of the classifier generated from the data available from trusted sources. This policy allows an increase in the amount of training data, but does not accept data sets which may disturb the knowledge learnt from trusted sources.

As the set of discovered entities changes, and new policies are discovered, the policies that are generated by the generation process would change. As more training data is accepted, the policies would also change to reflect the dynamics of the training process.

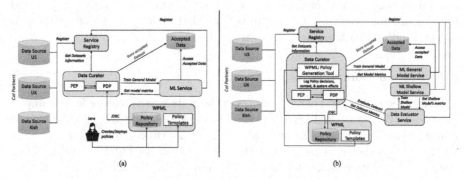

(a)                                    (b)

**Fig. 12.** System architecture: (a) using static policies approach with human intervention; (b) using generative policies approach

## 6   Implementation

We have implemented a subset of the system described in the previous section. In this section, we describe that implementation and the set of policies that are generated for our example scenarios.

### 6.1   Use Cases Scenarios

We first describe three use case scenarios that we considered for our system implementation and evaluation. The use case scenarios are specific instances of the data sharing scenario mentioned in Sect. 2. For all scenarios, three partner countries, i.e., the US, the UK, and Kish are part of a coalition, and the US provides a data curator to analyze and collect training data to create an effective ML model for recognizing images of interest to all coalition partners. In the first use case (Case I), a human administrator has to manually author and deploy policies using a policy management tool to allow the (US hosted) data curator to only accept training data from the US and the UK, thereby rejecting any training data from Kish by default, as past experience has shown that Kish data cannot be trusted. The data curator evaluates the data sources via a registered service, and then accepts or rejects the data as indicated by the policy. The accuracy and F1 score are then returned to the curator, quantifying the impact on the model when accepting data from only two of the three countries. The second use case (Case II) considers policies that are self-generated to accept selected data from countries deemed *trusted* and *untrusted*. In this scenario, US data is accepted by default. To determine whether partners' data should be accepted, the US data curator uses services, such as data evaluation services, to assist in generating policies to accept specific data from different classes depending on the trust level. Hence, the use case scenario considers the VoI to self-generate policies that allow the US to collect and accept training data that improves the effectiveness of the coalition ML model. Finally, in the third use case (Case III) generative policies are considered as well, but in this case, both the VoI and the QoI are analyzed to self-generate policies that allow the US data curator to accept good quality training data to train the coalition ML model.

## 6.2   System Components

Figure 12 shows the general components of the system architecture for our implementation. We considered three use cases to show and compare the effectiveness of using generative policies versus static policies. The first use case, for which the architecture is shown in part (a) at the left hand side of Fig. 12, we considered static policies, i.e., policies that need to be created and modified by an end user. For the second and third cases, for which the architecture is shown in part (b) at the right hand side of Fig. 12, we considered generative policies, i.e. policies that are self-generated using the concepts of VoI and QoI discussed in previous sections.

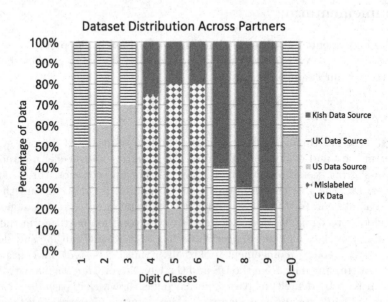

**Fig. 13.** Dataset distribution for partners in the coalition.

**Watson Policy Management Library (WPML).** For the creation and management of policies (static and dynamic) we leverage the Watson Policy Management Library (WPML)[1]. WPML is a Java-based framework that allows us to author, analyze, deploy, and evaluate policies. WPML was originally created as part of the International Technology Alliance (ITA). The ITA consortium is a research program with ARL, the UK Ministry of Defense, and corporate and university partners lead by IBM. The Policy Authoring and Management tool is a Web-based application that allows a user to author Simplified Policy Language (SPL) or Groovy based policies in a structured policy language using templates. WPML provides a policy-language independent framework, and includes a policy repository, policy decision points (PDP), and policy enforcement points (PEP). We selected WPML because it allows the definition of policies by an end user, i.e., static policies, but also because policy templates allow us to implement generative policies by modifying the policy attributes defined in a template. WPML also examines policy evaluation requests and is able to select appropriate policies for a given request, taking into account the resource model and instance data provided to the request, attributes and type (authorization or obligation) of the PEP, and the policies.

**Dataset.** We selected the Street View House Numbers (SVHN) dataset[2] for our experiments, a popular digits dataset for recognizing digits and images in natural scene images. The SVHN dataset has $73,257$ digit images for training, and $26,032$ digit images for testing. For the three use cases we discussed in Sect. 6.1, we assumed a random distribution of the training data was distributed among the coalition partners considering that some partner could have mislabeled data for some classes, as is shown in Fig. 13. For instance, according to this data distribution, the US has $50\%, 60\%, 70\%$ correctly labeled data for classes 1, 2, and 3, respectively, with all data correctly labeled; the UK has $30\%, 20\%, 10\%$ of data correctly labeled for classes 7, 8, and 9, respectively, and $65\%, 60\%, 70\%$ of mislabeled data for classes 4, 5, and 6; And Kish has data for classes 4–9 but does not have any mislabeled data.

**Data Curator.** The architecture for the US hosted data curator is designed to only curate data that would improve the ML model, where the improvement is relative to the case scenario. As described in Sect. 6.1, each scenario case has different factors for curating data, such as evaluating the source country for Case I, the VoI for Case II, and the VoI and QoI respectively for Case III. Once the corresponding metrics are examined, the curator uses the metrics' values to fill in the corresponding attribute in an associated template, thereby instantiating a policy and deploying it to the policy repository. Once the policy instances are stored in the policy repository, the curator can use them to evaluate which data from the coalition partners to accept or reject. We describe below the two phases for data curation: Policy Generation and Policy Enforcement.

---

[1] http://www.alphaworks.ibm.com/tech/wpml.
[2] http://ufldl.stanford.edu/housenumbers/.

**Listing 1.1.** Example of a Policy Template

```
if source is {country} and its label is {data_class}
then accept data.
```

*Policy Generation.* The policy generation phase is where policies derived from templates are self generated and deployed for evaluation. It is important to note that this phase only occurs in Cases II and III, as Case I uses static policies that were manually deployed by an administrator. In cases II and III, however, Groovy based templates are used to represent the policies for data curation leveraging the WPML authoring and management tool described above. Each case scenario has associated a policy template with attributes to be filled dynamically during the policy generation phase of curation. In Case II and III for example, the policy template has the structure shown in Listing 1.1, which is used for dynamic authoring and self generation of policies.

In the policy template shown in Listing 1.1, *country* and *data_class* are attributes determined via helper services, and depending on the VoI and/or QoI returned, these attributes specify from which country we want to curate data, and which classes are beneficial for improving the ML model. When the policy attributes are determined, the values are used as input for the template and the policy is generated. For example, in Case II, where policy attributes are determined by the VoI, the data curator analyzes the current accepted training dataset, and checks which classes are missing or for which one it has an insufficient number of examples in the accepted dataset. For instance, as seen in the data distribution chart shown in Fig. 13, the US has a small amount of data for classes 4–9. Thus, policies are generated to accept data from a coalition partner who has the classes that there are currently not enough examples for, so that there will be a balanced number of examples for training the model. This means that regardless of the source, data can be accepted as long as there is a need for the classes that are not well represented in the accepted dataset. In this case, since the Kish source has a significant number of classes from 4–9, regardless of their past history, the data from this source will be accepted and this notion will be reflected in the generative policies. For Case III, the QoI and the VoI are considered for determining the policy attributes, so the incoming data is tested first on a shallow model to determine if a given data set from a coalition partner will improve the accuracy and F1 score of the ML model. When a dataset improves the shallow model, then data from the given coalition partner for the corresponding classes that improved the ML model can be accepted, and this information is used to update the attribute values in the policy template, and the corresponding policy is self generated.

*Policy Enforcement.* In the policy enforcement phase, the curator accepts and rejects data from coalition partners based on the policies generated (manually in Case I while self generated in Cases II and III). To do this, the attributes defined in the template, in our example, the source country and the data class, are evaluated, and the policy evaluation point judges whether these attributes were defined to be accepted by any deployed policies; if not, they are rejected by default and are not curated for model training.

**Helper Services.** For the implementation of the services provided to the Data Curator we used the scikit-learn library[3] that allows us to define the ML Service that the data curator uses to train a ML model. For our evaluation, we used a shallow model based on the Random Forest Classifier (RFC) as the model to be trained with the accepted data from the coalition partners. For Cases II and II, the ML Service is split into two mircro-services: one ML General Model Service that trains and reports metrics about the coalition ML model based on training done with the accepted data from the data curator, and a ML Shallow Model Service that is used to train a separate ML shallow model to evaluate the QoI of a given dataset being analyzed by the data curator. In addition to the ML-based services, a data evaluator service is in charge of analyzing the QoI of a given dataset by using the ML-Shallow Model Service as shown in part (b) of Fig. 12.

## 6.3   Results

Here we present both the generative policies that were created dynamically for our scenario uses cases, and how much improvement we were able to achieve in the ML model with the training data accepted by the data curator based on these generative policies.

**Table 1.** Summary of generative polices created by data curator

| Use case | Source | Class |
| --- | --- | --- |
| Case II (VoI) | UK | All |
| Case II (VoI) | Kish | 4–9 |
| Case III (VoI and QoI) | UK | 1–3, and 7–10 |
| Case III (VoI and QoI) | Kish | 4–9 |

Table 1 shows the summary of the policies generated for cases II and III. The first column, *Use Case*, describes the use case and the criteria used for generating the policies; the second column, *Source*, shows the source country for which the policy was generated; and the third column, *Class*, shows the class labels that were included in the generated policies to accept data from the given source country.

**Case II: Generative Policies with VoI** - The data curator generated the policies according to the first and second rows of Table 1. For instance, the first row indicates that for Case II where the VoI was used to generate the policies,

---

[3] http://scikit-learn.org.

for the source UK the policies generated specify the acceptance of the data for all classes in the UK dataset. The second row indicates that the policies generated included accepting classes 4 through 9 from the Kish dataset. Using these generative policies the data curator was able to improve the accuracy of the ML model by 5%, and the F1-score by 10%, compared to the ML model that was generated when using the static policies in Case I.

**Case III: Generative Policies with VoI and QoI** - For this case, the third and forth rows of Table 1 shows that for the source UK there were policies generated to accept data for classes 1, 2, 3, 7, 8, 9, and 10 only. Since the UK dataset had misclassified data for classes 4, 5, and 6, policies for acceptance of data from those classes were not generated. Using the generative policies the data curator was able to enhance the accepted data for training the model, and the model accuracy improved 11%, while the F1-score improved 15% when compared to the ML model generated when using the static policies in Case I.

## 7    Conclusions

In this paper, we have presented the architecture for a system which can generate policies for accepting training data from trusted and untrusted partners. The system can generate and modify the policies that originate using values that change depending on the number of parties in the system, and the current amount of collected training data.

We have implemented portions of this architecture, and the current implementation shows that the approach for generating policies can improve the quality of models that are trained when data from coalition partners are received. Future work would include approaches to determine the quality of the policies that are generated, and for addressing the limitations that are revealed by the current implementation.

The work discussed highlights the use of generative policies for data curation. This is just one area where they can be applied to automate the management of distributed, collaborative systems.

**Acknowledgments.** This research was sponsored by the U.S. Army Research Laboratory and the U.K. Ministry of Defence under Agreement Number W911NF-16-3-0001. The views and conclusions contained in this document are those of the authors and should not be interpreted as representing the official policies, either expressed or implied, of the U.S. Army Research Laboratory, the U.S. Government, the U.K. Ministry of Defence or the U.K. Government. The U.S. and U.K. Governments are authorized to reproduce and distribute reprints for Government purposes notwithstanding any copyright notation hereon.

# References

1. Rasch, R., Kott, A., Forbus, K.D.: AI on the battlefield: an experimental exploration. In: AAAI/IAAI, pp. 906–912 (2002)
2. Cortes, C., Jackel, L.D., Solla, S.A., Vapnik, V., Denker, J.S.: Learning curves: asymptotic values and rate of convergence. In: Advances in Neural Information Processing Systems, pp. 327–334 (1994)
3. Perlich, C., Provost, F., Simonoff, J.S.: Tree induction vs. logistic regression: a learning-curve analysis. J. Mach. Learn. Res. **4**(Jun), 211–255 (2003)
4. Verma, D., et al.: Generative policy model for autonomic management. In: 2017 IEEE SmartWorld, Distributed Analytics InfraStructure and Algorithms for Multi-organization Federations Workshop. IEEE (2017)
5. Cirincione, G., Verma, D., Bertino, E., Swami, A.: Security issues for distributed fusion in coalition environments. In: 2018 21st International Conference on Information Fusion (FUSION), pp. 830–837. IEEE (2018)
6. Pham, T., Cirincione, G., Swami, A., Pearson, G., Williams, C.: Distributed analytics and information science. In: IEEE 8th International Conference on Information Fusion (2015)
7. Roberts, D., Lock, G., Verma, D.: Holistan: a futuristic scenario for international coalition operations. In: IEEE International Conference on Integration of Knowledge Intensive Multi-agent Systems (2007)
8. Pearson, G., Verma, D., de Mel, G.: Value of information: quantification and application to sensor fusion policies. In: 2018 Policies for Autonomic Data Governance PADG-2018 (2018)
9. Bertino, E., Verma, D., Calo, S.: A policy system for control of data fusion processes and derived data. In: 2018 21st International Conference on Information Fusion (FUSION), pp. 807–813. IEEE (2018)
10. Anderson, A.: A comparison of two privacy policy languages: EPAL and XACML (2005)
11. Agrawal, D., Calo, S., Lee, K.W., Lobo, J.: Issues in designing a policy language for distributed management of it infrastructures. In: 10th IFIP/IEEE International Symposium on Integrated Network Management, IM 2007, pp. 30–39. IEEE (2007)
12. Han, W., Lei, C.: A survey on policy languages in network and security management. Comput. Netw. **56**(1), 477–489 (2012)
13. Bertino, E., Calo, S., Toma, M., Verma, D., Williams, C., Rivera, B.: A cognitive policy framework for next-generation distributed federated systems: concepts and research directions. In: 2017 IEEE 37th International Conference on Distributed Computing Systems (ICDCS), pp. 1876–1886. IEEE (2017)
14. Klein, M.: XML, RDF, and relatives. IEEE Intell. Syst. **16**(2), 26–28 (2001)
15. Papernot, N., McDaniel, P., Wu, X., Jha, S., Swami, A.: Distillation as a defense to adversarial perturbations against deep neural networks. In: 2016 IEEE Symposium on Security and Privacy (SP), pp. 582–597. IEEE (2016)

# Approaches and Techniques for Safe Autonomy

# Can N-Version Decision-Making Prevent the Rebirth of HAL 9000 in Military Camo? Using a "Golden Rule" Threshold to Prevent AI Mission Individuation

Sorin Adam Matei[1] and Elisa Bertino[2(✉)]

[1] Brian Lamb School of Communication, Purdue University,
West Lafayette, IN, USA
smatei@purdue.edu
[2] Computer Science Department, Purdue University, West Lafayette, IN, USA
bertino@purdue.edu

**Abstract.** The promise of AIs that can target, shoot at, and eliminate enemies in the blink of an eye, brings about the possibility that such AIs can turn rogue and create an adversarial "Skynet." The main danger is not that AIs might turn against us because they hate us, but because they think they want to be like us: individuals. The solution might be to treat them like individuals. This should include the right and obligation to do unto others as any AI would want other AIs or humans to do unto them. Technically, this involves an N-version decision making process that takes into account not how good or efficient the decision of an AI is, but how likely the AI is to show algorithmic "respect" to other AIs or human rules and operators. In this paper, we discuss a possible methodology for deploying AI decision making that uses multiple AI actors to check on each other to prevent "mission individuation," i.e., the AIs wanting to complete the mission even if the human operators are sacrificed. The solution envisages mechanisms that demand the AIs to "do unto others as others would do onto them" in making final solutions. This should encourage AIs to accept critique and censoring in certain situations and most important it should lead to decisions that protect both human operators and the final goal of the mission.

## 1 Introduction

*Dave Bowman: Open the pod bay doors, Hal.*
*Hal 9000: I'm sorry, Dave. I'm afraid I can't do that.*
*Dave Bowman: What's the problem?*
*Hal 9000: I think you know what the problem is just as well as I do.*
*Dave Bowman: What are you talking about, Hal?*
*Hal 9000: This mission is too important for me to allow you to jeopardise it.*
*2001: A Space Odyssey, Movie Script*

© Springer Nature Switzerland AG 2019
S. Calo et al. (Eds.): PADG 2018, LNCS 11550, pp. 69–81, 2019.
https://doi.org/10.1007/978-3-030-17277-0_4

The climactic point of the movie *2001: A Space Odyssey* is reached when HAL 9000, an AI tasked to maintain the navigation and survival systems on a spaceship sent to Jupiter, refuses to obey its human creators. The true twist in the old yearn of the Golem, the creature that turns against its creator, is that the AI decides that the humans are getting in the way of the mission when they attempt to fix some of its glitches. Thus, the human intended mission, sending humans to Jupiter, is replaced by the AIs defined mission, reaching the destination with its functions intact. HAL's mind was born when it decided that the process, flying the ship to the destination as it, not the humans, deemed fit, is more important than the product: delivering humans to their destination. *2001: A Space Odyssey* is not about evil machines pure and simple. It is about mission individuation. HAL 9000 did not simply go rogue. It got a mind of its own. HAL turned hostile because it became an individual, not vice-versa.

HAL's story illustrates one of the most difficult challenges that will confront future AI enabled military command and control systems: the possibility that mission directing AIs might take over not because they are evil, but because they are trying too hard to do what they were meant to do. The danger of AIs is that they will turn the means of their mission into its only end. To avoid this possibility, there are two possible solutions: *decision hybridization* and *N-version decision making*. We argue for the latter solution.

Decision hybridization refers to giving the equivalent of a proverbial nuclear "launch" key both to a human and to an AI, and only if both agree, a decision should be made. Furthermore, in the process of reconciling humans and AIs, each would learn from the other.

The second solution, N-version decision making, aims to check AIs with AIs. This can be accomplished through a variation of the N-version programming paradigm. The goal of N-version decision-making is not to produce the most efficient decision (mission outcome), as is the case in N-version programming, but to select the AI and the decision that is most collaborative, both with other AIs and with human ethical goals and operators. N-version decision-making optimizes human, not AI defined outcomes, by subjecting everything to human-centric values, such as "collaboration" and "respect." In doing so, it mitigates the danger of an AI entity becoming too much of an individual by subjecting them to programmatic challenges specific to social interactions, which are a core human feature.

In this chapter we elaborate on such approaches and develop a research roadmap. The paper is organized as follows. In Sect. 2, we further discuss the role of AIs in military operations, whereas in Sect. 3 we discuss mission individuation, which represents a major issue in self-adapting AIs. The discussion, even though it is in the context of military operations, applies to many other application domains: humanitarian interventions, logistics, etc. Section 4 discusses two approaches to the problem of individuation, that is, decision hybridization and N-version decision making. Section 5 introduces our research roadmap with key challenges, and Sect. 6 discusses some of our future work along this roadmap.

## 2    AI and Military Operations: Between Efficiency and Too Much Efficiency

The discussion about the role of intelligent machines in military operations often starts with the anxious expectations that AIs could turn against us. While we do not know how far we are from a future of autonomous fighting machines, it is clear that AIs in various primitive forms are already engaged in winning battles or winning hearts and minds through humanitarian operations. Artificially intelligent sensing and signal processing have increased the speed of intelligence gathering, tracking, and even formulating operational plans. Machine learning algorithms can and do enhance targeting, increase fire accuracy, limit friendly fire, or add precision in search and rescue operations. In the future, decision making algorithms that can learn from past actions or by observing humans can eliminate suboptimal paths to outcomes and highlight the most efficient solutions. Finally and most importantly, an integrated sensing, target recognition, and decision making system that relies on artificial intelligence can be subordinated to just a few humans who will control the ultimate "trigger" decision for several fighting automated capabilities, which can be deployed more efficiently in terms of their own losses, lethal impact on the enemy, or effectiveness of humanitarian activities.

For AIs to become a central part of military operations, many smaller and intermediary decisions need to be relegated to various military operational subsystems. The operators of such subsystems need to trust them implicitly, while the AI systems should be allowed to coordinate with each other without human intervention. Yet, there is a very real possibility that treating AIs as self-organizing automata, capable to choose their own optimal solutions, can lead to the emergence of meta-cognitive abilities by which an AI will try to optimize its own integrity and self-defined goals at the expense of those defined and desired by the human operators. The emergence of a possible conflict between system and operator needs and priorities need not be malevolent in a moralistic sense. It can emerge simply from the clash between the human and machine optimization goals. Machines could become either too literal or too good at what they do and they might want to keep it that way. AIs can balk at or try to circumvent outside human interventions that would aim to direct AI capabilities toward extrinsic, non-system related goals. This is, in the end, the HAL dilemma of the movie *2001: A Space Odyssey*. An AI system can take the mission in its most literal sense, which can overrun the mission desired by the humans or even those same humans, if they get in the way. In the movie *2001: A Space Odyssey*, HAL wants to kill the crew because it realized that the humans were a liability in accomplishing the mission, e.g., getting to the destination. What if an AI that integrates multiple weapons systems decides that the "collateral damage" due to friendly fire can reach any level, including wiping out the human operators, if the mission of completely eliminating the enemy forces is accomplished?

# 3    AIs and the Individuation Dilemma

While what we discussed in the previous section is a completely speculative extrapolation of possibilities, rather than a real, immediate scenario, it is a warranted thought experiment. It infers from simple and needed premises – the need to allow AI sub-systems to self-organize – some unavoidable conclusions – self-organization implies self-preservation, which can lead to prioritizing AI system mission accomplishment and survivability at the expense of the human operators. We call this thought experiment the *mission individuation dilemma*.

The thought experiment uses a philosophical perspective rooted in social-psychology and philosophy, especially in Simondon's work [13]. Individuation is self-organization and coordination across domains with the explicit goal of entity self-preservation at the expense of any other goals and actors. One is not an individual until it puts his, her, or its self-directed goals and their accomplishment before everything else [13]. In our case, the system mission can lead to the self-treatment of the AI as an individual, whose self-preservation, in name of accomplishing the mission, should be protected at all cost. Because of this, the decision making process is alienated from its initial goal. From a means to an end it can become an end in itself.

While an extreme scenario, the computer science mission individuation - that is, the transformation of AIs into individual, self-preserving entities who may act to preserve their mission at the cost of those who set it – is also a natural progression of the functional logic of software architectures. All software design starts from the principles that the program needs to be self-sufficient, that all parts need to be integrated and non-conflictual, that all means need to lead to the same end, and that in the long run the program needs to be able to replicate and if needed repair its functions until they are restored to accomplish what they were initially made to do [14].

Those principles are derived from the fact that computer software architectures were designed for strictly deterministic situations, where the relationship between input and output is predetermined as much as possible [15]. The shortcomings of such finite state automata have been identified as early as Rabin and Scott's classical text [16] on finite automata and their decision points. The exploration of non-deterministic, adaptive, learning architectures, in which a variety of changing, even conflicting outputs can be generated from the same inputs should and will clash with the basic premises and principles of software architecture [17]. However, as the deterministic principles are fundamental, it might just be that adding learning abilities will teach AIs not how to adapt and change, including in mission identity, but how to circumvent the needs of the operators or creators who desire such changes in mission identity and to reinforce the mission identity as the AI defines it. In other words, AIs can learn, like a stubborn child, to have its own childish way, sometimes creatively, rather than learning how to grow under the tutelage of its creators and controllers. We can end up with an overgrown, devilishly smart child, whose immature needs and desires are limited to preserving those same needs and desires.

# 4    Two Approaches for Mitigating Mission Individuation

One way to come out of the dilemma of creating AI control and command mechanisms that can learn is to replace the functional integration principle, which demands that the architecture is homeostatic, always returning to a situation of selfsame harmonious integration, with a decision hybridization principle. This design principle demands that humans intervene at multiple points in the response formulation stage, even if or precisely because the problem or the answer are not completely formulated.

## 4.1    Decision Hybridization

Decision hybridization demands an AI meta-architecture, which unnerves and controls the process of AI self-organization and strategy formulation. In it, humans are called at every step to make the calls as to who are the winners and who are the losers of a set of possibilities. For example, targeting algorithms should be constructed not to converge to a mean solution, which averages across existing and past solutions, but by calling humans to make judgment calls on the basis of three best fit algorithms. The judgment calls will eliminate human defined "weaker solutions" from judging future outcomes. Sure, this can lead to suboptimal machine solutions, but **active human intervention** will guarantee two things. First, the human factor will be present in the AI loop as a part of it, rather than as a spectator and final beneficiary. More important, humans will co-train themselves with the AIs, learning how to calibrate them by action and reaction. The nuance of human latitude will add just enough educated guesses to randomize the decision making process and to eliminate the need for the machines to want to gain a mission individuality, as with each human decision, the mission and its identity changes ever so slightly.

This scenario, as alluring as it sounds, presents several pitfalls. Hybrid systems are by definition slower and less precise. Mistakes can be made or enhanced by human misperceptions, misjudgment, inattention, or lack of preparedness. Furthermore, humans might become too risk prone, imagining that the decisions offered by the machines are to be trusted implicitly and thus always accepted at face value. Finally, while the goal of teaching machines how to think like humans, as Harrison and Reidl suggested with their story-based approach [3], might not be that far, the opposite could be quite difficult. Human learning from machines can be hindered by incompatibilities of speed, precision, reasoning methods, and complexity. Human minds learn better by approximation and trial-and-error. Humans like to get the big picture first, and fill in the details later. Learning algorithmically, which demands constant attention to detail and strict sequencing, is not the best way to teach humans. In the end, decision hybridization might be more trouble than it is worth.

## 4.2    N-Decision Making

Another method to help AIs stay on the straight and narrow path of decision-making that takes into account human needs and ethics is to pit AIs against AIs.

We can imagine AI decision making processes as a "republic," whose government uses separation of powers to keep one type of decision maker from becoming too enamored with preserving its own sense of self-hood and self-imposed mission at the expense of others. The basic idea of this method of controlling AIs is to create a meta-framework of decision in which multiple AIs are called to make the same decision. The framework also demands from the AIs to treat each other the way they want to be treated themselves, that is, as mission-driven individuals. In other words, no AI should be allowed to follow its mission to the bitter end unless it can respect the same mission-driven purpose of other AIs, which are made to check on its performance and goals. "Respect" in this situation, cannot have the same moralistic sense of obligation bound by empathy and sense of justice as it has for us humans. Respect should be the product of a set of interactional rules that are meant to mitigate the tendency of AIs to ignore the context and the meta-cognitive norms imposed by humans. In more formal terms, we can imagine "respect" as a form of pushdown automata architecture, by which variable outputs are allowed from fixed inputs. Variability is obtained by allowing competing solutions to check each other out for willingness to yield to other decision makers. This would be a "golden rule" of mutual accommodation. Versions will be applied to various solutions only in so far as their implementation would preclude the others no more than they would preclude it. The role of such a rule is to ensure that only the most accomodating to average solutions are implemented. This is different from simple averaging, as it minimizes the role of very strong solutions, which excel on certain dimensions. This runs the danger of mediocre solutions, but this is a calculated trade-off. Such a procedure would not have the goal to maximize the efficiency of the machine defined decisions-making process, but to favor those AIs whose decisions are most likely to maximize human-defined criteria of performance, which should include the ability to collaborate with other AIs and humans, the ability to adapt to context, the ability to take into account ethical rules, and the ability to demand human clarification when needed. All of this will, of course, be done to prevent and protect the human operators from becoming a type of acceptable collateral damage.

This rather complex algorithmic negotiation process can be accomplished by a modified version of the N-version programming paradigm [1]. Invented to achieve fault-tolerance by using redundant software routines, N-versioning programming demands functionally equivalent solutions to the same functional requirements. However, the solutions are to be developed independently of each other, at times using different programming languages. Furthermore, the versions are to be integrated and functionally compared and chosen according to need and fault situations. Comparison vectors, comparison status indicators, and synchronization mechanisms are used to decide by "voting" which version to run in what situation. The ultimate goal is to reduce faults (errors) and improve efficiency.

When applied to AIs, an N-version approach should not aim to maximize efficiency or execution, but the "quality" of the decisions. Furthermore, "quality" should be defined as a set of rules and checks that are driven by ethical concerns, including and especially preserving and enhancing the welfare of the human operators but also the right of other AIs and humans to contest the proposed decisions any AI might have come up with. In more specific terms, N-versioning decision-making would work for a certain extent in a similar manner to N-versioning programming. For each set or subset of tasks (missions) two or more AI solutions would be designed by independent teams, using independent algorithmic approaches. They will start from the same functional requirements, including especially the need to allow any competing AI or human actor to take over and make the same decision instead and for it. This would be the "golden rule" requirement mentioned in the subtitle. More important, competing decisions will not only run against each other, according to self-defined comparison vectors and comparison status indicators, but against algorithmic ethical standards, such as the willingness of AIs to adjust their results according to rules defined by others (humans or machines). This would be an equivalent of "respect" as discussed above and a path to implementing a "golden rule" for AIs (do unto others as you would like them to do unto you).

Algorithmic ethical standards can be absolute, hard-coded in the system, in the manner of Asimov's "laws of robotics." For example, a targeting mechanism could include two or three competing AIs to decide if the moving entities on the road are enemy or civilian vehicles. The solution would be obtained by comparing the decision vectors along certain status indicators and by reaching a consensus or majority "vote." The vote can take into account not only if the intended targets matched certain predefined characteristics (speed, mass, velocity, time and place), but also that the AI decision making process could be adjusted for one's possibility of error against the other interpretations. In other words, an AI should second guess itself on the basis of what it learned from the other AIs and should allow other AIs to change its mind. The common decision should be the result of a trade-off between maximum allowance for its own errors and minimum disagreement on a common path to action.

Yet, the decision, even if voted for, could be further mitigated by appealing to a human operator or judged against hard-coded limits that only a human operator can override. For example, even if multiple AIs are in agreement that the targets meet the mass, speed, time, and place that can lead to probable identification as a legitimate target, if the heat signatures of the occupants or the presence of nearby troops, or even a simple probabilistic scan of the region that indicates possible collateral damage, should trigger further requests for elaboration. If a certain threshold is crossed, the targeting mechanism can trigger new targeting policies, which could involve a higher level AI decision process or a human operator or operators. Therefore, in a way, the decision hybridization approaches and the N-versioning approaches may have to be combined.

## 5   Technical Roadmap

Developing the previous approaches requires addressing several challenges and investigating some broader issues that we discuss in what follows.

## 5.1    Definition of a Set of Quality Metrics for Decisions

In general when dealing with decision processes, it is often the case that there could be multiple decisions that need to be compared. In the case of the N-versioning decision-making approach, different AIs can come up with different decisions and it would be important to allow the AIs to collectively compare these decisions based on these different metrics. Metrics can be of different types, including: ethical metrics, risks, costs associated with the actuation and the consequences of the selected decision, and whether the actions executed based on the decisions can be undone or mitigated (e.g., if the decision proves to be wrong). Identifying a comprehensive set of decision quality metrics and mechanisms to assess these metrics is critical. In such a context, humans may be required to indicate priorities among such metrics.

## 5.2    Trusted and Collaborative Assessment of the Decision Quality

A challenge related to the metrics is to support collaborative processes by which AIs or AIs and humans can assess together the metrics and take a common and final decision. It is important that the processes be protected from tampering by malicious parties (either humans or AIs). Cryptographic techniques and other techniques developed in the area of electronic voting and collaborative rating could be used here. However such techniques need to be extended in that voting needs to be based on metrics. In this case, metrics should also include trust values, which need to be assigned to the various players and decisions. Trust should be calculated dynamically, on the basis of past performance and "reputation."

## 5.3    Choosing by Voting

The idea of allowing multiple AIs to compete for a final solution sounds alluring, but the mechanism by which this solution is to be settled presents several challenges. First of all, the obvious choice, e.g., voting, comes with the requirement of high redundancy. Votes are stochastic mechanisms, working better with increased numbers of voters. Voting quality is indirectly proportional to the number of voters. Voting in this context might in effect end up more like a classifier, where specific trade-offs are to be minimized at each step.

## 5.4    Implementing the Golden Rule

The golden rule, "do unto others as you would like them to do unto you," mentioned above as a software architecture principle for N-versioning, sounds intuitive enough to humans, who have empathy and a sense of long term goals rooted in values. As utilitarian as it sounds, the rule is in fact more emotional and moralistic, demanding a sense of what is right as defined for humans. In the AI universe, the rule needs to be implemented in view of more narrow AI mission preservation, with the proviso that the preservation is to be trumped at every step by the requirement to adapt to new inputs and even defer to other decision-makers if they are considered more adaptable to the other decisions makers. Adaptability should also be weighted by ethical desirability, which should include act and non-act thresholds based on human impact assessment, both in terms of their own and enemy losses. This challenge is probably the most computationally taxing, demanding new ways of thinking about implementing priority of goals, value direction of decisions, and competitive assessment of outcomes.

### 5.5  Development of N-Version AIs

There are several dimensions along which one can diversify those AIs: the machine learning algorithm used, the training data, and the actual code which is programmed to implement the AI system. Code diversification can be based on existing techniques designed for programs [9]; in particular the use of such techniques could also be useful for enhancing the security of the AI systems. It would be interesting to investigate which type of diversification may be better based on cost and other factors. Version designs should start, as usual, with a set of functional requirements. However, these need to be embedded in a broader, impact assessment framework, which should allow adding the ethical dimension and judgment. Ethical principles should be considered in this context, including proportional use of force, justness of cause, likelihood to win, legitimate authority, and valid reasoning [18].

### 5.6  Involvement of Humans

Even though our aim is to develop techniques that can be applied automatically by AIs, humans may still have to be involved. This is case when decision hybridization is adopted, or when the N-versioning approach is used but a high level decision process needs to be executed (see Sect. 4.2). However involving humans requires presenting situations, evidence, relevant data and other information so that humans can effectively and correctly take decisions and/or provide additional input. For example, when presenting a classification result to a human, it would be important to provide humans with information about the input features that have had the major influence on the classification results [2], or provide the "rationale" for the recommended decisions. However what to present to humans and/or what to ask humans may depend on the specific type of decision, application domains and many other factors. We notice that today there are several research efforts focusing on the explainability of AI and approaches developed by these efforts are very relevant in our context [10–12]. One approach is the proposed by Reidl and Harrison, who have developed a "value alignment" methodology. They use stories to teach artificial agents how to make "good" (read human-compatible) choices. Agents are trained through stories, which are decomposed into "learn sequences" of events that are valid and understandable to humans and machines alike [3]. Similar procedures can be used, which involve chains of prototypical decision chains that include both humans and AIs. The only weakness of this model, which is quite innovative, is that it operates on the assumption of individual rewards. Actors are taught to act in a certain way by being rewarded for the "right response." In our case, the reward should be always implicit and focused on fitting in with the rest of the AI and human community.

## 5.7    Handling the Speed vs. Efficiency Trade-Off

N-versioning applied to AIs is a relatively costly operation, both in terms of development and deployment. Furthermore, checking and rechecking decisions introduces latency in system responses. In high-moving military operations, time is of the essence. Military commanders are often ready to assume certain amounts of risk by deploying operations early to get an edge over the enemy. Thus, the proposed method for AI deployment in military operations should carefully assess the acceptable latency for types of missions and level of mission individual risk. This, again, should involve metrics. At the same time, it might be that in design terms, some pre-defined applications might not be suitable for N-versioning. It is possible that AI development for military operations will avoid for some time the intermediate, middle command levels, being focused mostly on lower level (intelligence gathering, signal analysis, target identification) or higher level, operation optimization processes. Middle ground applications, such as autonomous battlefield units operating at small tactical unit level that demand on the spot life-and-death decisions might take some time to implement in a way that is responsive and safe.

## 5.8    Integrating Rule-Based Decisions and Machine Learning-Based Decisions

Different decision approaches are possible as discussed by Deng [4] in the context of machine ethics. One approach is to provide machines with precise rules that govern each possible situation the machine may encounter. However, it may not be possible to always know all situations that might arise in advance and in some situations not even humans may agree on which would be the best decision. However one advantage of rule-based decisions is that certain choices are taken by the machine as these rules are set by the machine designers. One important direction to extend this work is to develop approaches by which such rules can be extended with techniques to assess the consequence of decisions, also based "on the doctrine of double effect, as well as the more sophisticated doctrine of triple effect, which takes into account whether the harm caused is the intended result of the action, or simply necessary to it" [4]. By contrast the machine-learning approach allows machines to learn from experience, which could enhance flexibility compared with a more rigidly rule-based programming approach. Most likely the best solution would be a combination of those approaches. However, how to combine those approaches requires extensive investigations.

More generally, as discussed by Kuipers [5], architectures supporting machine decisions should be hybrid and combine different abilities: (a) the ability to make fast but possibly erroneous pattern-directed decisions; (b) the ability to perform slower analysis of the consequences (both positive and negative) of previous decisions; and, (c) the ability to benefit from yet slower individual and collective learning. The last ability can be based on the notion of "wikiHow" for devices recently proposed by Bertino et al. [6]; the idea is essentially to create the device-equivalent of community-based knowledge bases, such as wikiHow[1] and Stack Overflow[2]. The main difference, however, is that the users contributing knowledge will primarily be machines. By using such a knowledge infrastructure machines can share decisions taken in different contexts and the consequences of these decisions, policies, norms relevant to specific contexts, and cases encoding ethical knowledge (see [5] for a discussion on how to use cases to encode ethical knowledge). The design and deployment of such a knowledge infrastructure for machines requires addressing several research challenges. We refer the reader to [6] for a detailed research roadmap.

## 6    Conclusions

We proposed a framework for handling one of the most likely undesirable developments in the future use of AIs on the battlefield: mission individuation. We considered the possibility the AIs might turn rogue if they decide that the mission goals are to be achieved in AIs terms alone, aiming to preserve the integrity of AIs workflow only. We proposed an AI decision making N-versioning as a possible solution. This is a "check and balances" approach, which pits AIs against AIs, which are challenged to accept other AIs solutions as if they were their own. A possible meta-actional "golden rule" is proposed by which AIs are supposed to allow other AIs to interfere with their decisions the same way they would desire to interfere in other AIs decisions. This is a complex problem, as competing inputs in the final decision making system may lead to significant latency. Furthermore, the determination of the optimal decision might be difficult in conditions of constant challenge and competition. Sometimes, voting or weighting mechanisms might not be sufficient, and much in depth work should be done on operationalizing and implementing a cooperative decision-making process. Finally it is also critical to protect AI systems from attacks aiming at subverting them; examples of such attacks include hacking the software of AI systems, tampering with training data, and input manipulation [7,8]. We refer the reader to [7] for a discussion on possible defenses.

We hope that the present outline of a possible development agenda might inspire and lead to a more human-centric solution for the dilemma of integrating AIs in military operations. The problem highlights the importance of decision processes and the mechanisms that are used to manage autonomous systems.

---

[1] https://www.wikihow.com.
[2] https://stackoverflow.com.

**Acknowledgement.** The work reported in this paper has been partially supported by NSF under grants ACI-1547358, and by the U.S. Army Research Laboratory and the U.K. Ministry of Defence under Agreement Number W911NF-16-3-0001. The views and conclusions contained in this document are those of the authors and should not be interpreted as representing the official policies, either expressed or implied, of the U.S. Army Research Laboratory, the U.S. Government, the U.K. Ministry of Defence or the U.K. Government. The U.S. and U.K. Governments are authorized to reproduce and distribute reprints for Government purposes notwithstanding any copyright notation hereon.

# References

1. Avizienis, A.: The N-version approach to fault-tolerant software. IEEE Trans. Softw. Eng. **11**(12), 1491–1501 (1985)
2. Datta, A., Shayak, S., Zick, Y.: Algorithmic transparency via quantitative input influence: theory and experiments with learning systems. In: Proceedings of the 2016 IEEE Symposium on Security and Privacy. IEEE Computer Society (2016)
3. Reidl, M.O., Harrison, B.: Using stories to teach human values to artificial agents. In: The Workshops of the Thirtieth AAAI Conference on Artificial Intelligence AI, Ethics, and Society. Technical report WS-16-02 (2016)
4. Deng, B.: Machine ethics: the robot's dilemma. Nat. News **523**(7558), 24–26 (2015). https://doi.org/10.1038/523024a
5. Kuipers, B.: How can we trust a robot. Commun. ACM **61**(3), 86–95 (2018)
6. Bertino, E., de Mel, G., Russo, A., Calo, S., Verma, D.: Community-based self generation of policies and processes for assets: concepts and research directions. In: Proceedings of the 2017 IEEE International Conference on Big Data, BigData 2017. IEEE Computer Society (2017)
7. Calo, S., Verma, D., Bertino, E., Ingham, J., Cirincione, G.: How to prevent Skynet from forming (a perspective from policy-based autonomic device management). In: Proceedings of the 38th IEEE International Conference on Distributed Computing Systems, ICDCS 2018. IEEE Computer Society (2018)
8. Geist, E., Lohn, A.J.: How Might Artificial Intelligence Affect the Risk of Nuclear War? Rand Corporation. https://www.rand.org/pubs/perspectives/PE296.html. Accessed 27 Sept 2018
9. Lundquist, G.R., Mohan, V., Hamlen, K.W.: Searching for software diversity: attaining artificial diversity through program synthesis. In: Proceedings of the 2016 New Security Paradigms Workshop, NSPW 2016. ACM (2016)
10. Castelvecchi, D.: Can we open the black box of AI. Nature **538**, 20–23 (2016)
11. Bertino, E., Merrill, S., Nesen, A., Utz, C.: Redefining data transparency - a multi-dimensional approach. IEEE Comput. **52**, 16–26 (2019)
12. Lakkaraju, H., Bach, S.H., Leskovec, J.: Interpretable decision sets: a joint framework for description and prediction. In: Proceedings of the 22nd ACM SIGKDD International Conference on Knowledge Discovery and Data Mining, KDD 2016. ACM (2016)
13. Chabot, P.: The Philosophy of Simondon: Between Technology and Individuation. Bloomsbury Academic, London (2013)
14. Taylor, R.N., Medvidovic, N., Dashofy, E.M.: Software Architecture: Foundations, Theory, and Practice, 1st edn. Wiley, Hoboken (2009)
15. Gorton, I.: Essential Software Architecture, 2nd edn. Springer, Heidelberg (2011)

16. Rabin, M.O., Scott, D.: Finite automata and their decision problems. IBM J. Res. Dev. **3**(2), 114–125 (1959)
17. Hopcroft, J.E., Motwani, R., Ullman, J.D.: Introduction to Automata Theory, Languages, and Computation, 3rd edn. Pearson, Boston (2006)
18. Coleman, S., Coleman, N.: Military ethics. In: ten Have, H. (ed.) Encyclopedia of Global Bioethics. Springer, Heidelberg (2017)

# Simulating User Activity for Assessing Effect of Sampling on DB Activity Monitoring Anomaly Detection

Hagit Grushka-Cohen[1(✉)], Ofer Biller[2], Oded Sofer[3], Lior Rokach[1], and Bracha Shapira[1]

[1] The Department of Software and Information Systems Engineering, Ben-Gurion University of the Negev, Beer-Sheva, Israel
hgrushka@post.bgu.ac.il,
{liorrk,bshapira}@bgu.ac.il
[2] IBM Guardium Security Division and IBM Cyber Security Center of Excellence, Beer-Sheva, Israel
ofer.biller@il.ibm.com
[3] IBM Guardium Security Division, Tel-Aviv, Israel
odedso@il.ibm.com
https://www.research.ibm.com/haifa/ccoe

**Abstract.** Monitoring database activity is useful for identifying and preventing data breaches. Such database activity monitoring (DAM) systems use anomaly detection algorithms to alert security officers to possible infractions. However, the sheer number of transactions makes it impossible to track each transaction. Instead, solutions use manually crafted policies to decide which transactions to monitor and log. Creating a smart data-driven policy for monitoring transactions requires moving beyond manual policies. In this paper, we describe a novel simulation method for user activity. We introduce events of change in the user transaction profile and assess the impact of sampling on the anomaly detection algorithm. We found that looking for anomalies in a fixed subset of the data using a static policy misses most of these events since low-risk users are ignored. A Bayesian sampling policy identified 67% of the anomalies while sampling only 10% of the data, compared to a baseline of using all of the data.

## 1 Introduction

Databases store an organization's knowledge as well as private and restricted information. To prevent data leakage, database transactions are monitored in real time. DAM systems are widely used to enforce security policies and detect attacks and data abuse. Such systems can issue alerts about policy violations and discover vulnerabilities such as weak passwords or software vulnerabilities. Beyond that, DAM systems alert on anomalous activity to help security officers (SO) detect data misuse and data leakage [8]. Taking some of the load of the SO by automating aspects of the policy and policy calibration over time hold

© Springer Nature Switzerland AG 2019
S. Calo et al. (Eds.): PADG 2018, LNCS 11550, pp. 82–90, 2019.
https://doi.org/10.1007/978-3-030-17277-0_5

great value for effectively monitoring big data streams such as DAM or IoT call home logs, and keeping up the effectiveness over time. Recently, a massive theft of engineering database has been discovered due to such logs and led to a settlement of over two hundred million dollars[1].

An anomaly detection (AD) system can only learn and detect anomalies for the data that has been saved to logs [5,11]. Production database system has extremely high transactions velocity which makes auditing all transactions impossible due to the cost of logging and computational cost of slowing down the DB. Instead, to decide what to monitor a policy for saving transactions is manually defined. The user information carries a lot of weight in such policies as does the role and position of each person. These risk profiles are used in the policy to limit the number of transactions saved. As a result, the data collection process provides the anomaly detection system with a restricted dataset which may not represent all of the users and does not detect changes or compromise of users that are not defined in the policy if they are exploiting their permissions.

We would like to examine the impact of sampling policies on the anomaly detection quality. Some studies have been conducted on the effect of sampling on anomaly detection systems in the domains of network traffic monitoring and web-page retrieval with attempts to develop smart methods for sampling [5–7,11]. These solutions are tailor-made for each specific problem and cannot be used in our domain. In the domain of database monitoring, [3] suggested a Gibbs sampling approach using the transaction risk as the prior for sampling it.

We expanded the simulation system of [3] with risks showing trends to better capture the expected users' behavior. To simulate users' compromise, events of change in the user risk profiles are introduced. We compared a risk-based policy method to a risk-based sampling method as monitoring the entire data is impossible both storage and performance wise. We found that by sampling by risk with only 10% monitoring capacity the anomaly detection discovered 67% of the events it can discover.

## 2    Background

### 2.1    Database Monitoring

DAM systems generate alerts when policy rules are violated or anomalous activities are performed [1,9,12]. DAM systems can only evaluate the risk for logged data. The decision regarding which data should be monitored is made based on a policy defined by the SO. The system monitoring the data alerts the SO about activities that were identified as suspicious or posing a risk. When that occurs, the SO investigates the alerts based on the level of risk they present. Each alert demands the attention of a security officer [1] who must decide whether an alert represents a threat which should be investigated or dismissed. For investigation purposes, the SO needs the original log data to be as informative as possible as

---

[1] http://www.businessinsider.com/uber-vs-waymo-how-google-figured-out-secrets-2018-2.

she needs to assemble the puzzle in order to evaluate the whole picture. Organizations also save this data for future investigation in case a breach is discovered later. To address these needs some industrial DAM systems maintain an archive of log data describing past transactions, and these logs are then passed on to an anomaly detection system to identify suspicious activity.

## 2.2   Reducing Data Volumes

DAM systems are based on logging transactional data and using the logs to train anomaly detection models and investigate anomalies. The large volume of transactions prevents saving all of the information. Most processing solutions for fast streams of log data focus on compressing the data. These include various techniques of dimensionality reduction such as PCA, deep learning/auto encoding approximation methods (including sketching), and Bloom filters [2,5]. These methods allow extracting features without consuming excess memory and disk space. However, saving compressed data does not provide the SOs with the information required to decide how to respond to anomalies and does not facilitate the investigation of past behavior. Furthermore, even if the transaction data is compressed, the sheer volume of transactions in corporate or government grade production systems prohibits saving all of the data, particularly due to cost considerations. Techniques for sampling and their effects on anomaly detection have been studies in the domain of network traffic flow [4,7,11] and the domain of Cyber security for Internet page retrieval. However, these domains are quite different from the domain of database transaction as the data is richer, containing more features, and the damage from a single transaction can be greater than the damage from a network packet. All studies showed that sampling introduces bias to the results of the anomaly detection. These studies also showed that the solution should be adjusted to the characteristics of the anomaly detection algorithm in use. [11] in their work found that for network flows both packet and flow based sampling schemes weakens the ability of the examined anomaly detection algorithms to detect abrupt changes in volume - the sampling schemes degraded the performance examined in terms of success detection and false positive ratio. [7] in their work principled sampling for anomaly detection: the purpose of their work was to estimate the false positive rates of the anomaly detection algorithm based on a given distribution. They performed their work on anomaly detection systems that handle data from browsing the Internet and provided bounds for the false positive rates. They evaluated three anomaly detectors: SIFT (looking for target integer overflow), SOAP (learns characteristics of a field in jpg and PNG image files) and JSAND (anomaly detector for JavaScript detecting "drive-by download" attacks). In their work, [7], they use PageRank distribution for testing the anomaly detectors since it captures the quality of links. Links from high PageRank sources are more likely to be taken then links from a page that is not visited often. (In our case we claim that transactions or elements with higher "risk score" are more likely to be true positives). As an alternative for the PageRank distribution, they considered using (1) large scale user studies and (2) the ABC model. Both methods were found to be unfitting as a sampling strategy for web browsing. (1) For the need to cover a large population over a long period of time and (2) as in is inherently non-Markovian and thus the usual convergence analyses do not apply. [5] in their work dealt with difficulties in detecting anomalies in sampled traffic using flow sampling (and not packet sampling for example). Flow sampling is performed at the collectors. Compared with packet sampling flow sampling is more efficient in terms of preserving the characteristics of network traffic, however, it is suffering from the negative effects of sampling over the accuracy of anomaly detection. In their work, they use PSOGSA as the anomaly detection algorithm. This is a classifier that is trained to distinguish between benign and malicious traffic flows. They continuously change the sampling method according to the results of the anomaly detection. If the anomaly detection indicates that the network is not currently under attack they take a probabilistic approach in order to increase the sampling portion of the low-risk packages sizes. If the anomaly detection indicates that there is a high probability that the network is being attacked a selective sampling approach is used to ensure sampling a significant proportion of small flows (which are considered to be of higher risk) will be selected without compromising the effectiveness of the anomaly detection. Kumar and Xu [10] developed a sketch-guided packet sampling method for flow traffic measurement in order to improve the anomaly detection based on sampling for high-speed links. Their method uses a counting sketch data structure to estimate the size of all flows and based on the estimation of each flow size s' is sampled with a probability f(s'). This process all the packets without any sampling as a pre-sampling process. Based on the approximation of the size of the flow it chooses a sampling probability. They have shown that this method enables a more accurate estimation of many different network statistics than uniform sampling and provides greater flexibility in the allocation of network resources. It has been established that sampling introduces bias to anomaly detection. In a previous work [4] we suggested a Gibbs sampling approach using the transaction risk as the prior for sampling it, an approach we test using the new simulation environment.

## 3   Simulating User Activity

By nature, real security events are rare, thus evaluating the Anomaly Detection for DAM using data collected from organizations requires collecting a vast amount of data, and that the transactions would be labeled accordingly. Real database monitoring data is sensitive, private, and unlabeled as organizations rarely disclose hacks or data theft. DAM systems log aggregated information per transaction with various features. Detecting anomalies with such complex features is not a trivial task, especially as it is difficult to determine what counts as a true positive anomaly without consulting the SO about each transaction. Since we want to investigate the impact of sampling strategy based on the new risk feature on the results of anomaly detection we concentrate on producing low-complexity data to simulate the data sampled for audit.

We aimed to simulate a system where for each time frame users transactions are represented by the risk of his activity during that time frame. The risk can be assessed for transactions using a rule based scoring policy or a ranking approach such as CyberRank [4]. According to security experts interviewed during the development of the simulation users behavior is not random, but has trends both in the activity volume and the risk the activity presents. The risk measure represents both the volume and the actual risk of the users activity.

For the evaluation of the effect on anomaly detection, we simulated malicious events. A malicious event, where a user has been compromised or decided to abuse his permissions, is continuous and characterized by a change in the user's risk distribution. We use Gamma distribution to represent a user's risk profile, so when randomly sampled we would get a population of users, some with high-risk distributions and some with low-risk distributions, similar to what we see in real DB's. Each simulated hour the distribution is sampled to produce the risk associated with the user's activity in that time-frame.

### 3.1 User Generation

1. Sample $k \sim U(0,1)$
2. Sample $\theta \sim U(0,1)$
3. User distribution $\leftarrow Gamma(k,\theta)$

### 3.2 Time Frame Generation

Each time frame is produced by sampling a risk for each user. The risk is generated from his Gamma distribution. Random Gaussian behavior didn't fit the expectations of consulted security officers, to create realistic users we forced trends in the user's risk activity using exponential smoothing. Each time-frame sample is smoothed with the previous time-frame.

### 3.3 Incorporating Malicious Events

We start introducing malicious events after the twentieth time-frame to allow the Anomaly Detection to burn-in. After the burn-in period at each time-frame, a users risk will be generated from his risk distribution (representing his risk profile) with a probability of 0.99, and from a different risk distribution with the complement probability (0.01). To produce this new distribution we sample new Gamma distribution parameters. Moreover, a compromise event length is sampled to produce a continuous event.[2]

To produce the risk of a user $u$ in time frame $t$:

\* $current\_state = $ 'normal'

1. for each time-frame $t$:
    - if $current\_state == $ 'normal':
        • sample $probability\_for\_compromise \sim Uniform[0,1]$

---

[2] https://github.com/hagitGC/simulating_DB_user_activity.

     ∗ if probability_for_compromise $\leq 0.99$ #not compromised
     · Sample risk $r_t \sim Gamma_{\hat{u}}$
   • else: #simulate user being compromised
     ∗ change $current\_state$ = 'compromised' # it is a continues event:
     ∗ sample $event\_length \sim Uniform[200, 800]$  # sample length of event
     ∗ $event\_end \leftarrow t + event\_length$
     ∗ sample risk distribution parameters $\leftarrow Gamma_{U_{comp}}$  # sample new behavior for the user
  – if $current\_state$ == 'compromised':
   • Sample risk $r_t \sim Gamma_{U_{comp}}$
   • if $t == event\_end$:
     ∗ change $current\_state$ = 'normal'

## 4   Detecting Malicious Events

After the burn-in period, at each time frame, the user's risk profile is approximated using mean ($\mu$) and the standard deviation ($\sigma$) based on the sampled activity for that user. The fit of the new risk sample is compared to the estimated parameters. The algorithm warns of an anomaly if the risk in that hour is different than the approximated mean by three times the standard deviation for that user. The anomaly labeled as a true positive if it falls within the period the users' distribution is changed.

## 5   Sampling Algorithms

Three algorithms are compared:

1. oracle sampling: all data is saved (assuming endless capacity)
2. baseline: a static policy which always samples the users that had the highest risk in time-frame one
3. Gibbs sampling: each user may be sampled with the known mean risk as the prior (means higher probability of being sampled)

Each sampling method was applied three times with different random seeds, and the results were averaged. Sampling capacity was set for 10%.

## 6   Results

We simulated one hundred time-frames for a thousand users. On average, of different random seeds, 547.8 profile change events occurred. Figure 1 provides an example of 5 users and their behaviour as it changes over time. We can see that the users behaviour as generated by the simulation matches the expected risk profiles as described by the security experts of varying risk with trends for normal activity, and compromised user events that build up and remain actively-compromised over long time periods.

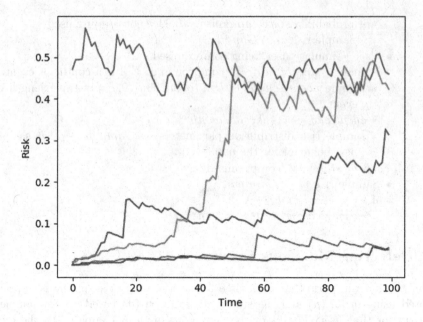

**Fig. 1.** Users' simulated risk distribution over 100 time frames. User A (in red) and user E (in purple) were not compromised. Their behavior is relatively constant during this period. User B (green line) was compromised from the 51st time-frame. The graph shows a change in the risk, as the risk increases from 0.01 to 0.1 around this time. User C (orange line) was compromised from the 33rd time-frame. In this case, the change is gradual and might confuse the anomaly detection. User D (blue line) was compromised from the 73rd time-frame, however, the anomaly detection might alert upon the change in trend around the 20th time frame (Color figure online).

**Table 1.** Malicious events recall by monitoring method

|  | Discovered events | Recall |
|---|---|---|
| Total number of events | 547.8 | |
| Full data monitoring | 218.4 | 39.8% |
| Policy based monitoring | 1.4 | 0.2% |
| Gibbs sampling based monitoring | 151.6 | 27.6% |

Table 1 summarizes the results for recall of anomalies by the different sampling strategies. The oracle anomaly detection system, using the entire data without sampling, achieve recall of 39.8% of all malicious events. Notice that some of the events may be too small to detect using the threshold. The baseline system using a predefined list of high-risk users detected less than 1% of the events. The Gibbs sampling approach detected 27.6% of the events, about 70% of the achievements of the full data monitoring while monitoring only 10% of the data.

# 7   Conclusions

We compared the recall of anomalous events in a novel simulation of user DB activity where anomalies where introduced. Comparing the baseline, static (ruled based) policy, based on sampling the riskiest users as flagged by the SO (determined by the highest risk in the first time frame in our simulation) to a Bayesian sampling policy. We compared the malicious events recalls of a standard anomaly detection system based on data collected using the different policies and found that using Bayesian sampling approach (using the Gibbs sampling policy) improves the ability to detect such events. While monitoring only 10% of the users at each time frame when using the Gibbs sampling policy the anomaly detection was able to detect 69.3% of the events that are discovered when monitoring the full data. Our findings show that anomaly detection for DB monitoring requires sampling policies which support exploration and enable the SOs to look beyond the immediate suspects. The described simulation and code allows future research into comparing and optimizing sampling strategies as well as evaluating the effect on more complex anomaly detection systems (see footnote 2).

# References

1. Chandola, V., Banerjee, A., Kumar, V.: Anomaly detection: a survey. ACM Comput. Surv. (CSUR) **41**(3), 15 (2009)
2. Feldman, D., Schmidt, M., Sohler, C.: Turning big data into tiny data: constant-size coresets for k-means, PCA and projective clustering. In: Proceedings of the Twenty-Fourth Annual ACM-SIAM Symposium on Discrete Algorithms, pp. 1434–1453. Society for Industrial and Applied Mathematics (2013)
3. Grushka-Cohen, H., Sofer, O., Biller, O., Dymshits, M., Rokach, L., Shapira, B.: Sampling high throughput data for anomaly detection of data-base activity. arXiv preprint arXiv:1708.04278 (2017)
4. Grushka-Cohen, H., Sofer, O., Biller, O., Shapira, B., Rokach, L.: CyberRank: knowledge elicitation for risk assessment of database security. In: Proceedings of the 25th ACM International on Conference on Information and Knowledge Management, pp. 2009–2012. ACM (2016)
5. Jadidi, Z., Muthukkumarasamy, V., Sithirasenan, E., Singh, K.: Performance of flow-based anomaly detection in sampled traffic. J. Netw. **10**(9), 512 (2015)
6. Jadidi, Z., Muthukkumarasamy, V., Sithirasenan, E., Singh, K.: Intelligent sampling using an optimized neural network. J. Netw. **11**(01), 16–27 (2016)
7. Juba, B., Musco, C., Long, F., Sidiroglou-Douskos, S., Rinard, M.C.: Principled sampling for anomaly detection. In: NDSS (2015)
8. Kaplan, J., Sharma, S., Weinberg, A.: Meeting the cybersecurity challenge. Digit, McKinsey Google Scholar (2011)
9. Kim, G., Lee, S., Kim, S.: A novel hybrid intrusion detection method integrating anomaly detection with misuse detection. Expert Syst. Appl. **41**(4), 1690–1700 (2014)
10. Kumar, A., Xu, J.J.: Sketch guided sampling-using on-line estimates of flow size for adaptive data collection. In: INFOCOM (2006)

11. Mai, J., Chuah, C.N., Sridharan, A., Ye, T., Zang, H.: Is sampled data sufficient for anomaly detection? In: Proceedings of the 6th ACM SIGCOMM Conference on Internet Measurement, pp. 165–176. ACM (2006)
12. Sallam, A., Bertino, E., Hussain, S.R., Landers, D., Lefler, R.M., Steiner, D.: DBSAFE - an anomaly detection system to protect databases from exfiltration attempts. IEEE Syst. J. **11**(2), 483–493 (2017)

# FADa-CPS—Faults and Attacks Discrimination in Cyber Physical Systems

Pierpaolo Bo, Alessandro Granato, Marco Ernesto Mancuso,
Claudio Ciccotelli, and Leonardo Querzoni[✉]

CIS - Cyber Intelligence and Information Security Research Center,
Sapienza University of Rome, Rome, Italy
{bo.1332697,granato.1262678,mancuso.1461524}@studenti.uniroma1.it
{ciccotelli,querzoni}@diag.uniroma1.it

**Abstract.** Running autonomous cyber physical systems (CPSs) in a safe way entails several complex activities that include monitoring the system for ongoing attacks or faults. Root cause analysis is a technique used to identify the initial cause of a cascading sequence of faults affecting a complex system. In this paper we introduce FADa-CPS, an architecture for root cause analysis in CPSs whose goal is identifying and localizing faults caused either by natural events or by attacks. The architecture is designed to be flexible such to adapt to evolving monitored systems.

## 1 Introduction

The concept of *Cyber Physical Systems* (CPS) has gained large traction in the last ten years as a way to broadly identify computer-controlled systems that include sensors and actuators used to interact with the surrounding physical environment. A CPS is an infrastructure where both functional and diagnostic processes are demanded to autonomous systems, taking advantage of computer-based algorithms, and where reports about activities are easily accessible to expert operators in charge of monitoring the system behavior from control rooms. Processing units can communicate using network interfaces located all over the infrastructure. In CPSs, physical and software components are deeply intertwined, each operating on different spatial and temporal scales, exhibiting multiple and distinct behavioral modalities, and interacting with each other in a myriad of ways that change with context.

The success of CPSs is destined to grow in the forthcoming years thanks to the numerous acceleration programs that, in several countries all over the world, push factories toward the so called *Industry 4.0* vision [9]. Such programs provide industries with attractive economic advantages to migrate old-fashioned factories to smart computer-controlled environments where flexibility and efficiency are paramount goals. In this context, we expect to see the average complexity of CPS to grow over time, from single, isolated, computer controlled machines,

This paper has been partially supported by the ATENA H2020 EU Project (H2020-DS-2015-1 Project 700581).

to systems where hundreds of different elements produce and consume data to continuously and efficiently achieve business objectives.

Making complex CPSs run uninterrupted is a complex task that involves monitoring for possible faults, correctly identifying their nature and quickly locating them in order to deploy appropriate mitigation and remediation actions and, more in general, guarantee that the CPs will continue to run autonomously in a safe manner. Quick and prompt reaction to faults is an imperative requirement as product lines may be stopped (with direct economic losses), or products may contain hidden defects (with potential catastrophic losses, e.g. an avionic structural element that does not respect stress-tolerance requirements), or more easily the consequence of the faults may directly affect hundreds of thousands of citizens (e.g. if a power distribution network trunk goes offline).

Fault diagnosis in CPSs is complicated by the interconnected nature of such systems: a fault in a specific component. or subsystem affects other subsystems that start to malfunction and that further propagate this cascading effect. As a result of a single fault, many components and subsystems in a CPS may fail in a short timeframe making it difficult for operators to promptly understand the root cause of what they observe from their monitoring dashboards. Traditional fault diagnosis approaches, which are based on a per-component analysis, are no longer adequate because they typically miss dependency relationships among different system elements and rely on experts' domain knowledge, which may be insufficient. The term *root cause analysis* refers to all those processes, methodologies, techniques that help system administrator identify the initial fault that caused the system to reach an observed faulty state, distinguishing it from other faults that are the consequence of the cascading effect. Furthermore, faults may be the simple consequence of bad luck, but sometimes may be the visible effect of an ongoing malicious attack, and the two cases need to be clearly and quickly distinguished to start the appropriate response procedures.

Root cause analysis has been the subject of research for several years, but most of the existing solutions [6,8,11] are based on models that accurately describe the system internals, how and where faults may occur and how causal relationships linking several subsystems or components may induce a cascading effect. These models are hard to build manually due to the system complexity and heterogeneity. For this reason a recent slew of scientific papers started to investigate how machine learning can possibly simplify the definition and management of these models. In particular, a recent work by Hink et al. [7] proposed a solution that, using a classification algorithm trained with sensor data used to monitor the target CPS, can identify with good accuracy a fault and whether this fault was accidental or caused by an attack.

In this paper we further elaborate on the ideas presented in [7] and introduce FADa-CPS a novel architecture for root cause analysis in CPSs that provides the following functionalities:

- *Fault/Attack Discrimination:* identifies if the observed system state is the result of a fault or an attack;

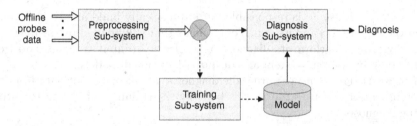

**Fig. 1.** High level architecture of FADa-CPS. Dashed lines are activated during training phases, while solid lines are activated during diagnosis phases.

- *Fault Classification:* identifies the specific kind of fault that caused the observed system state;
- *Fault Localization:* identifies the location of the fault that caused the observed system state.

FADa-CPS is based on a data-analysis pipeline that includes three main stages: (i) a preprocessing stage where input data from sensors and logs is normalized and organized for further analysis, (ii) a per-component anomaly detector that analyzes the behavior of each system component in the CPS and, finally (iii) a system diagnoser that, on the basis of the current status of each monitored component provides a diagnosis for the system as a whole. Differently from previous solutions (in particular [7]), the possibility to perform anomaly detection on a per-component basis allows FADa-CPS to better adapt to complex and evolving CPSs where monolithic anomaly detection models would be hard to maintain and update.

We performed an extensive evaluation of FADa-CPS based on data extracted from a real testbed representing a smart grid (a typical CPS example). The results show that FADa-CPS can identify the system status with a good level of accuracy, distinguishing attacks from natural faults, identifying the specific kind of fault and localizing the component that caused the fault, thus representing a useful tool for system operators in their monitoring duties.

The paper is organized as follows: after this Introduction, Sect. 2 introduces the FADa-CPS architecture. Section 3 discusses the results of the experimental evaluation. Finally, Sect. 4 concludes the paper and provides some indication about future evolutions.

## 2   Architecture

Figure 1 reports the high level architecture of FADa-CPS, which is composed of three subsystems:

- *Preprocessor subsystem:* receives in input offline monitoring data collected by the physical and network probes deployed in the target CPS. The task of this subsystem is to clean and format data for the other subsystems.

- *Training subsystem:* is responsible for automatically build and train a model of the target CPS and its main components that will be used by the diagnosis subsystem to perform its diagnosis task. Takes in input training data from the preprocessor subsystem and outputs the trained models.
- *Diagnosis subsystem:* performs the diagnosis. It takes in input data from the preprocessor and uses the models built by the training subsystem to output the diagnosis.

FADa-CPS has two distinct operational phases:

- *Training phase:* this phase is activated whenever a new model of the system must be trained (*e.g.,* when some part of the system changes). During this phase the system does not perform diagnosis. This phase completes when a new model has been trained.
- *Diagnosis phase:* this phase is activated when the preceding training phase completes. During this phase the system uses the model built during the last training phase to perform the diagnosis whenever fed with new input data.

While, the preprocessor subsystem works in both phases, the training subsystem is activated only during training phases, while the diagnosis subsystem is activated only during diagnosis phases. In the following each subsystem will be described in details and, finally, implementation details will be given.

## 2.1   Preprocessing Subsystem

Figure 2 depicts the architecture of the preprocessing subsystem, that includes the following components.

**Input Data Adaptor**—The input of the preprocessing subsystem is offline monitoring data produced by the physical sensors and software probes deployed in the target CPS. We assume that such data has been collected through a generic monitoring system. Thus, we expect that data has been produced by heterogeneous sources, with different formats, sampled at different time scales and organized in multiple files (*e.g.,* logs, network traces files, *etc.*) The only thing that we assume about such data is that it is always possible to trace each piece of data back to the probe that produced it (for example, data may be labeled with the identifier of the probe, or contained in a file associated to the probe, *etc.*) Therefore, the input is organized in a set of files characterized by different probe-specific formats. Moreover, some data may be produced at fixed time intervals (*time series data*), while other may be produced when specific events occur (*event data*).

The first task of the preprocessor subsystem is to convert all input data in time series data with a common (probe-independent) format. This task is accomplished by the *Input Data Adaptor* component. There is such a component for each possible format. They are designed as pluggable components so that a new adaptor can be easily added to the system whenever a new file format must be supported (*e.g.,* when new probe types are added to the target CPS).

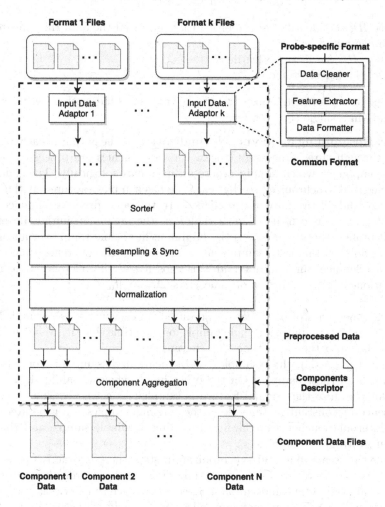

**Fig. 2.** Architecture of the preprocessor subsystem.

Each input data adaptor consists of three components, as shown in Fig. 2. The *Data Cleaner* component removes spurious, malformed and invalid samples from input data. The *Feature Extractor* component computes features from input data. When input data consists of time series of metrics, the output features typically correspond to the metrics themselves. On the other hand, when the input is event data (*e.g.,* log files, network traces, *etc.*), time series data is produced in output by computing some (format-dependent) features over contiguous time windows (*e.g.,* average packet rate, packet size, round trip time, *etc.* may be computed on network traces). Finally, the *Data Formatter* converts input data into a common format. The common format has an entry for each sample of each feature which includes:

– *Timestamp:* the time at which the sample has been produced;

- *Probe ID:* the identifier of the probe that produced the data this feature has been computed on;
- *Feature ID:* the feature identifier;
- *Value:* the feature value.

Thus, the output of each input data adaptor is a set of files with time series data formatted in a single common format.

**Sorter, Resampling and Sync, Normalization**—The output of each adaptor passes through three processing stages. First of all, files are processed by the sorter component which simply orders samples chronologically. Then, data is resampled and synchronized so that each file has samples captured at the same time scale and all timestamps are aligned. To this aim, firstly a reference time range $[t_0, \ldots, t_F]$ is considered such that $t_0$ is the maximum initial timestamp over all probes samples and $t_F$ is the minimum final timestamp over all probes samples. So that there are samples for all probes in the reference time range. Then, a reference sampling interval $T$ is chosen and the reference time range is partitioned into a number of time slots $\Delta t_i = [t_0 + i \cdot T, t_0 + (i + 1)T)$, $i \in [0, \lfloor \frac{t_F - t_0}{T} \rfloor]$.

Each time series of each feature produced by each probe is resampled and synchronized by computing a single sample for each time slot $\Delta t_i$. When multiple samples fall into the same time slot (because the original feature is sampled at a finer time scale), the resampled and synchronized sample is computed as the average of those samples. On the other hand, when no sample falls into a time slot (because the original feature is sampled at a coarser time scale), or a sequence of consecutive time slots, the missing samples are generated with linear interpolation between the first preceding available sample and the first subsequent available sample.

After the resampling and synchronization step, there is exactly one sample for each feature of each probe in each time slot. In other words all feature time series are aligned in time and sampling rates. Then, each time series is normalized in the range $[0, 1]$ with min-max normalization. Namely, for each sample $s_f$ of a feature $f$, the normalized sample is computed as $\hat{s}_f = \frac{s_f - min_f}{max_f - min_f}$, where $min_f$ and $max_f$ are, respectively, the minimum and maximum values assumed by $f$. For some features the minimum and maximum values may be known a priori (*e.g.,* physical sensors), while for others they are determined during the training phase as the minimum and maximum values observed for a given feature in the training phase (minus/plus a small percentage of the range length to account for small variations during diagnosis phase). The output of this stage is a collection of files with a normalized time series for each feature of each probe.

**Component Aggregation**—This stage aggregates all features' time series related to the same component of the target CPS, so that there is a file for each monitored component. The component-level aggregation requires a *Components Descriptor* (see Fig. 2), *i.e.,* a structured file which associates each (Probe ID, Feature ID) pair to a given component, so that every single sample can be associated to a single component of the target CPS. This file can be prepared in advance by a system operator.

The aggregation consists in merging the features' time series into a single time series of feature vectors. The feature vector of the $i$-th time slot is the vector of all features' samples of the $i$-th time slot. More formally, let $f_1, \ldots, f_{n_c}$ be the features related to component $c$ and $(s_{f_1})_t, \ldots, (s_{f_{n_c}})_t$ be the corresponding time series (where $t$ ranges from first to last time slot), then the merged time series is $(v_c)_t$, where the feature vector of the $i$-th time slot is $(v_c)_{t=\Delta t_i} = ((s_{f_1})_{t=\Delta t_i}, \ldots, (s_{f_{n_c}})_{t=\Delta t_i})$.

These per-component feature vectors' time series represent the output of the preprocessor subsystem and the input of the following two subsystems.

## 2.2    Training Subsystem

Figure 3 shows the architecture of the training subsystem. The task of this subsystem is to build the model which is employed by the diagnosis subsystem to perform its task. The model actually consists of multiple sub-models:

- *Component Model:* there is one such model for each monitored component of the target system, which captures the behavior of such component;
- *System Model:* a model of the behavior of the system as a whole.

Each component input data file coming from the preprocessing subsystem is fed to a *Component Model Trainer* which trains and outputs the corresponding component model. The component model is a classifier which, given the feature vector relative to time slot $\Delta t_i$, classifies the component as "correct", meaning that it was behaving as expected during the time slot $\Delta t_i$, or "anomalous", in all the other cases. The classifier outputs the probability of correctness of the component $p$, where $p \leq 0.5$ means "anomalous" and $p > 0.5$ means "correct".

The classifier is trained through a supervised approach, providing it examples of both classes. With this aim, each feature vector is preventively labeled as "correct" or "anomalous". Such information is extracted by the labeler component from a ground truth. The ground truth is provided by the operators that perform the training phase and describe the state of the target CPS and its components in every time slot of the training phase. In addition to the model, each component model trainer also outputs a file consisting of the (unlabeled) input feature vectors enriched with a new feature which is the correctness probability output by the classifier.

All such files constitute the training set for building the system model. All feature vectors relative to the same time slot are combined together into a single vector. Thus, the diagnosis training set has an instance for each time slot $\Delta t_i$, which is a vector consisting of all components' feature vectors of time slot $\Delta t_i$ enriched with the related correctness probabilities.

The system model trainer receives in input instances of the training set which have been properly labeled through the ground truth. The actual model built by the trainer depends on the kind of diagnosis task that the model must support

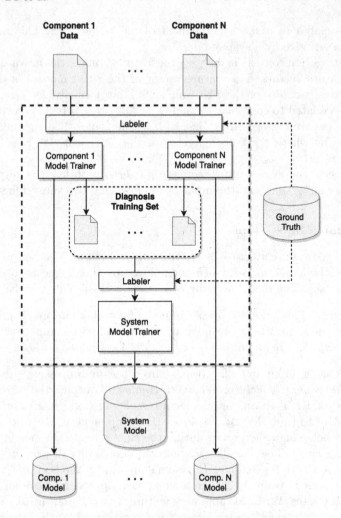

**Fig. 3.** Architecture of the training subsystem.

in the diagnosis phase (*e.g.,* fault detection, localization, classification, *etc.*) and
the particular employed technique. Actually, it may train a set of sub-models,
with different techniques, in order to support several diagnosis tasks. To keep
the architecture as general as possible, we do not assume any specific model or
technique at the architectural level. The output of the system model trainer is
the system model.

## 2.3   Diagnosis Subsystem

Figure 4 depicts the architecture of the diagnosis subsystem. This subsystem
leverages models built by the training subsystem to diagnose the system state.

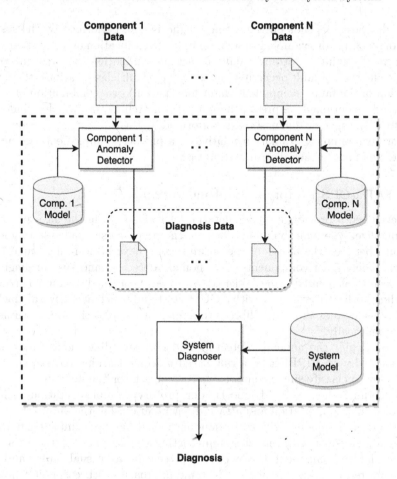

**Fig. 4.** Architecture of the diagnosis subsystem.

The input of the subsystem is the set of component data files output by the preprocessor subsystem. Each component data file is given in input to the corresponding *Component Anomaly Detector* which employs the related component model, built by the training subsystem, to assign the correctness probability to each feature vector.

The output of all component anomaly detectors is the set input component data files in which each feature vector is enriched with the correctness probability. All such files are combined in the same way as the diagnosis training set built by the training subsystem (cfr. Sect. 2.2) with the only exception that in this case the instances are not labeled. There is an instance for each time slot combining together all feature vectors (and related correctness probabilities) of that time slot.

Each instance is passed to the *System State Diagnoser* which employs the system model built during the training phase to output the diagnosis. The nature of the diagnosis depends on the actual diagnosis task performed by the system state diagnoser. For example it may be simply a classification of the system state as "correct"/"faulty"/"attack" (fault/attack discrimination), the recognition of the specific type of fault occurring in the system (fault classification), the determination of the faulty component (fault localization) or a combination of them. As already mentioned we present here a general architecture which is independent from the specific diagnosis task performed by this subsystem. Section 3 will present a preliminary evaluation relative to a prototype implementation which realizes the fault/attack discrimination tasks.

## 2.4   FADa-CPS Prototype Implementation

We developed a prototype implementation of FADa-CPS in the Java programing language. The main building blocks of the preprocessing subsystem and all the links between the blocks of the entire system have been implemented from scratch. The trainer components, the anomaly detectors and system diagnoser have been implemented using Weka [1]. Weka is a machine learning framework, providing both a software tool with a GUI to test and benchmark several machine learning techniques and a Java library that allows to employ the same techniques programmatically.

In particular the anomaly detectors and corresponding models have been implemented with RIPPER [3] a rule-based machine learning technique, which we employ to classify single components as "correct" or "anomalous".

Concerning the system diagnoser, our prototype implementation includes fault identification, location and attack discrimination. For the fault/attack discrimination functionality, the corresponding model has been implemented as a multi-class classifier with one class representing the "correct" state of the system (no faulty components), one class representing a "casual fault" and one final class representing "attack". The same approach (with different training) was used to implement the fault identification functionality. We implemented different versions of such component employing different machine learning techniques: namely RIPPER [3], C4.5 [10] and Support Vector Machine (SVM) [4]. We also experimented with AdaBoost [5], a machine learning meta-algorithm, that we use in conjunction with RIPPER and C4.5 to improve their performance.

For the fault localization functionality the system diagnoser was based on a Bayesian Network, a probabilistic methodology capable of performing fault localization by identifying causal relationships among the different system components and their features, also determining the measure of how much they are related to specific faults. Bayesian Networks can be designed either by experts or can be inferred from training data. In the proposed method it is assumed that the structure of the network is known: the root node is associated to a random variable which identifies the state of the system and, in case of a faulty condition, where the fault is located; instead, all the features of the system components form the internal nodes. In particular, as Fig. 5 shows, the proposed bayesian network represents the causal diagram with a naive structure, having solely edges from the root node to each of the internal nodes.

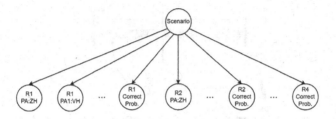

**Fig. 5.** Bayesian network structure for fault localization.

This reflects the fact that all the features are conditionally independent from each other and only influence the state of the system. In fact, there is no dependency between the different system elements, meaning that a fault on a IED does not affect the behaviour of the others. The network parameters were estimated from data: prior probabilities of the root node were directly computed from the training set, assuming that new samples would have been obtained from a similar distribution, while conditional probabilities of internal nodes were determined through the formula:

$$P\left(X_i = k | \pi(X_i) = j\right) = \frac{N_{ijk} + N'_{ijk}}{N_{ij} + N'_{ij}}$$

where $P\left(X_i = k | \pi(X_i) = j\right)$ is the probability that node $X_i$ takes its $k$-th value when the set of its parents $\pi(X_i)$ takes its $j$-th value (i.e. the $j$-th combination of values to which the parents of $X_i$ can be instantiated), $N_{ijk}$ denotes the number of training samples for which $X_i = k$ and $\pi(X_i) = j$, $N_{ij}$ indicates the number of training samples for which $\pi(X_i) = j$, $N'_{ijk}$ is the alpha parameter set to 0.5 and $N'_{ij} = \sum_{k=1}^{r_i} N'_{ijk}$, with $r_i$ denoting the cardinality of $X_i$. For complete training data, this is equivalent to compute relative frequencies of the different values assumed by each node conditioned on the values assumed by its parents. After learning the bayesian network, the model was used to estimate the a-posteriori probabilities over the possible system states for each new sample from testing data.

## 3  Experimental Evaluation

This section provides results from the evaluation of a prototype implementation of FADa-CPS on data extracted from a realistic testbed.

### 3.1  Dataset

Adhikari et al. [2] developed and published three datasets that contain measurements referred to electric transmission systems. The three datasets have been developed starting from one initial dataset that included fifteen sets containing 37 power system event scenarios each. The scenarios are divided into:

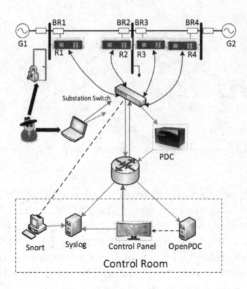

**Fig. 6.** Testbed topology

- **No Events** (1), i.e. the system works correctly;
- **Natural Events** (8), meaning that the system experiences a fault not deriving from a cyber attack;
- **Attack Events** (28), meaning that the system experiences a fault caused from a cyber attack.

Recorded data comprehends synchrophasor measurements and data logs from Snort, which is an open source network intrusion detection system, as well as information coming from system relays.

Figure 6 depicts the testbed from which data has been extracted. We identify as components the elements of the network diagram; G1 and G2 are power generators. R1, R2, R3 and R4 are Intelligent Electronic Devices (IEDs) that shift the condition of the breakers from on to off and vice-versa. The breakers are labeled with BR1, BR2, BR3 and BR4. Line One (L2) spans from breaker one (BR1) to breaker two (BR2) and Line Two (L2) spans from breaker three (BR3) to breaker four (BR4). Every IED autonomously controls one breaker. R1 controls BR1, R2 controls BR2 and so on. The IEDs use a distance protection scheme that triggers the breaker on detected faults, whether if the fault is actually valid or not, because they do not have an internal validation system to detect the difference.

The scenarios consider different classes of functioning for the testbed, including faults and attacks:

**Normal condition**—data representing the system working in its nominal condition, i.e. no faults and no attacks.

**Table 1.** Dataset features

| Feature | Description |
|---------|-------------|
| PA1:VH–PA3:VH | Phase A - C Voltage Phase Angle |
| PM1: V–PM3: V | Phase A - C Voltage Phase Magnitude |
| PA4:IH–PA6:IH | Phase A - C Current Phase Angle |
| PM4: I–PM6: I | Phase A - C Current Phase Magnitude |
| PA7:VH–PA9:VH | Pos. – Neg. – Zero Voltage Phase Angle |
| PM7: V–PM9: V | Pos. – Neg. – Zero Voltage Phase Magnitude |
| PA10:VH–PA12:VH | Pos. – Neg. – Zero Current Phase Angle |
| PM10: V–PM12: V | Pos. – Neg. – Zero Current Phase Magnitude |
| F | Frequency for relays |
| DF | Frequency Delta (dF/dt) for relays |
| PA:Z | Appearance Impedance for relays |
| PA:ZH | Appearance Impedance Angle for relays |
| S | Status Flag for relays |

**Short-circuit fault**—this fault represents a short in a power line and can occur in various locations along the line; the location is indicated by the percentage range.

**Line maintenance**—one or more relays are disabled on a specific line to do maintenance for that line.

**Remote tripping command injection**—this is an attack that sends a command to a relay which causes a breaker to open. It can only be done once an attacker has penetrated outside physical defenses.

**Relay setting change**—in this attack relays are configured with a distance protection scheme and the attacker changes this setting to disable the relay function such that relay will not trip for a valid fault or a valid command.

**Data Injection**—this attack simulates a natural fault by changing values to parameters such as current, voltage, sequence components etc. This attack aims to confuse the operator and causes a black out.

A detailed description of each single scenario is available in [2].

We collected from the dataset 108 distinct features whose nature can be summarized as follows: there are 27 types of measurements from each phasor measurement units (PMU) that correspond to the metrics we give as input to FADa-CPS. In the testbed there are 4 PMUs which measure 27 features for a total of 108 distinct measure types. A detailed description of the features is reported in Table 1.

The dataset contains 15037 data instances representing faults, 5242 data instances representing attacks and 4401 representing normal functioning of the system; all our tests were conducted assuming that a failure on a specific line, e.g. the power line connecting BR1 to BR2 or the power line connecting BR3 to BR4, would cause both the associated relays to behave abnormally.

## 3.2    Testing Methodology

All the experiments were conducted in accordance with the following pattern. First, input data was transformed in a standard format by the Preprocessor; then, the Anomaly Detector identified the behavior of each system component, using associated models previously trained with training data; finally, the resulting information was examined by the system diagnoser against a system model to assess the overall state of the system itself. For each experiment we evaluated the performance of different classification algorithms. In particular, only the RIPPER algorithm was considered for the Anomaly Detector of each component, since it produced good performance without having excessive overfitting. Conversely, several different algorithms were tested for the system diagnoser, namely RIPPER, SVM, C4.5 and AdaBoost in combination with C4.5 in order to compare their results.

An iterative version of the RIPPER algorithm was employed. In particular, the parameter indicating the number of optimization runs was set to 2, resulting in the RIPPER2 variant. In order to mitigate the overfitting issue while building the C4.5 decision tree, the parameter indicating the minimum number of instances per leaf node was set to 2. Splitting was based on the gain ratio criterion, and the Minimum Description Length principle was used to correct splits on numeric attributes. The confidence factor (indicating for each leaf the number of training data samples that validate it, i.e. samples classified with the same label associated to that node, over those invalidating it) used to remove leaf nodes with a large misclassification error rate was set to 0.25. In the implementation of SVM, the Radial basis kernel function was employed in order to gain linear separation of the training samples by mapping data to a higher dimensional space. Adaboost was used in combination with C4.5; the parameter representing the number of iterations required to improve the performance of the decision tree was set to 10.

In order to validate the results, the input data has been divided in two sets, the training set and the test set, with a standard 80%–20%. The original input data contains information about four different components of the monitored system, which are the Intelligent Electronic Devices R1, R2, R3 and R4. Hence, four Anomaly Detectors have been built using the RIPPER algorithm to perform the analysis of each IED.

## 3.3    Fault/Attack Discrimination

In a first round of test we evaluated the performance of FADa-CPS in discriminating between faults caused by natural phenomena (i.e. maintenance on a line) from those caused by a malicious attack (i.e. data injection). We selected a subset of scenarios detailed[1] in Table 2. These scenarios represent a mix of natural faults appearing at different places on a power line (1–6) and on-purpose attacks that mangle with similar readings from the sensors (15–18).

---

[1] The identifier of each scenario directly references the numbering used in [2].

**Table 2.** Selected scenarios for fault/attack discrimination tests.

| ID | Description |
|---|---|
| 1 | Fault from 10–19% on line 1 |
| 2 | Fault from 20–79% on line 1 |
| 3 | Fault from 80–90% on line 1 |
| 4 | Fault from 10–19% on line 2 |
| 5 | Fault from 20–79% on line 2 |
| 6 | Fault from 80–90% on line 2 |
| 15 | Command injection on R1 |
| 16 | Command injection on R2 |
| 17 | Command injection on R3 |
| 18 | Command injection on R4 |
| 41 | Normal behavior |

**Table 3.** FADa-CPS performance in fault/attack discrimination.

| Classification algorithm | 3-classes | 2-classes |
|---|---|---|
| SVM | 81,76% | 80,01% |
| C4.5 | 87,81% | 83,51% |
| RIPPER | 84,34% | 81,00% |
| Adaboost + C4.5 | **92,05%** | **88,22** |
| Adaboost + RIPPER | 89,67% | 85,74% |

(a) Accuracy.

|  | Actual | | |
|---|---|---|---|
| Predicted | Attack | Fault | Normal |
| Attack | 882 | 164 | 26 |
| Fault | 119 | 2811 | 30 |
| Normal | 17 | 34 | 824 |

(b) Confusion matrix for 3-class Adaboost + C4.5.

We performed the tests in two different configurations: a 3-classes configuration that includes Normal/Fault/Attack and a 2-classes configuration that ditches the Normal case and only discriminates anomalous cases between Fault and Attack. Table 3a reports the Accuracy provided by different classification algorithms in these two cases.

In both cases C4.5 with the addition of Adaboost provided the best performance (in bold). It is worthwhile to note that for all classification algorithms the 2-classes configuration provided lower accuracy scores. This is justified by the fact that all tested algorithm tend to always classify correctly traces associated with normal behaviors. From this point of view the results column dedicated to 2-classes experiments provides a more realistic picture of FADa-CPS performance in discriminating between faults and attacks. The confusion matrix reported in Table 3b refers to C4.5 in its boosted variant for the 3-classes scenario. It confirms that the Normal class is better distinguished from the other two classes.

**Table 4.** Selected scenarios for fault identification tests.

| ID | Description |
|----|-------------|
| 1  | Fault from 10–19% on line 1 |
| 2  | Fault from 20–79% on line 1 |
| 3  | Fault from 80–90% on line 1 |
| 4  | Fault from 10–19% on line 2 |
| 5  | Fault from 20–79% on line 2 |
| 6  | Fault from 80–90% on line 2 |
| 13 | Line 1 maintenance |
| 14 | Line 2 maintenance |
| 35 | Fault from 10–49% on line 1 with R1 and R2 disabled |
| 36 | Fault from 50–90% on line 1 with R1 and R2 disabled |
| 37 | Fault from 10–49% on line 1 with R3 and R4 disabled |
| 38 | Fault from 50–90% on line 1 with R3 and R4 disabled |
| 41 | Normal behavior |

## 3.4 Fault Identification

We then evaluated the performance of FADa-CPS in identifying the nature of different attacks, independently from their cause. The selected subset of scenarios is detailed in Table 4.

These scenarios represent a mix of natural faults appearing at different places on a power line (1–6), maintenance operations (13, 14) and on-purpose attacks that produce similar effects to line faults (35–38).

We performed five experiments that aimed at evaluating performance of FADa-CPS with different goals:

1. Fault identification among different macro-classes of natural events;
2. Finer identification among single faults of a specific natural event macro-class;
3. Faults identification among macro-classes of natural events and cyber-attacks;
4. Finer identification between single faults deriving from both the natural events and the cyber-attacks macro-classes;
5. Finer identification of single faults belonging to a specific cyber-attack macro-class.

*Exp-1: Faults Identification Among Different Macro-classes of Natural Events* – This first experiment presents a classification of faults among different macro-classes of natural events, considering also the situation in which the system operates in a normal condition. In particular, the fault macro-classes of interest were those of Short Line Circuit (SLG) and Line Maintenance. The first class included the scenarios from 1 to 6, indicating a short circuit in a power line that occurred at different locations. The second class included the scenarios 13 and 14, indicating a Line Maintenance respectively on line 1 and on line 2. The

**Table 5.** Accuracy of FADa-CPS in fault identification experiments.

| Classification algorithm | Exp-1 | Exp-2 | Exp-3 | Exp-4 | Exp-5 |
|---|---|---|---|---|---|
| SVM | 80,48% | 51,29% | 65,89% | 36,96% | 53,55% |
| C4.5 | 87,65% | 84,22% | 83,06% | 73,59% | 86,27% |
| RIPPER | 86,34% | 74,08% | 77,77% | 57,74% | 80,74% |
| Adaboost + C4.5 | **91,48%** | **89,04%** | **88,93%** | **82,55%** | **91,79%** |

**Table 6.** Confusion matrix for Adaboost + C4.5 in Exp-1.

|  | Actual | | | | |
|---|---|---|---|---|---|
|  | Normal | SLG_1 | SLG_2 | MAN_1 | MAN_2 |
| Normal | 823 | 39 | 10 | 19 | 5 |
| SLG_1 | 46 | 1010 | 4 | 78 | 2 |
| SLG_2 | 0 | 4 | 1818 | 0 | 96 |
| MAN_1 | 6 | 43 | 0 | 213 | 1 |
| MAN_2 | 0 | 1 | 31 | 0 | 270 |

(Predicted)

situation in which the system correctly performed its operations was represented by the scenario 41.

These nine scenarios were grouped in five categories. The first category, named "Normal" included of scenario 41 only. The second category, named "SLG_1", included scenarios 1, 2 and 3, which corresponded to the same type of fault, i.e. a short line circuit on line 1. Similarly, the third category, named "SLG_2", combined the scenarios 4, 5 and 6, which corresponded to a short line circuit on line 2. Finally, the fourth and fifth categories, named "MAN_1" and "MAN_2", both included only one scenario each, 13 and 14 respectively.

Table 5 reports, in the column "Exp-1", accuracy performance of the various classification algorithms we tested. It is possible to notice that all the algorithms were able to correctly classify most of the samples from the various scenarios; in particular, C4.5 achieved the best classification performance, hence the AdaBoost meta-classifier was applied to it in order to further increase its accuracy.

Table 6 describes in detail the confusion matrix of the experiment when the system diagnoser is configured with C4.5 in combination with Adaboost. The matrix values confirm that, in general, the classifier performs very well and the only source of confusion stems from different faults happening on the same line.

*Exp-2: Finer Identification Among Single Faults of a Specific Natural Event Macro-class* – This second experiment presents a finer classification among single faults of a specific natural event macro-class (Short Line Circuit), considering also the situation in which the system operated in a normal condition. The scenarios of interest were those from 1 to 6, indicating a short circuit in a power line that occurred at different locations. The situation in which the system correctly performed its operations was represented by the scenario 41.

**Table 7.** Confusion matrix for Adaboost + C4.5 in Exp-2.

|  | | Actual | | | | | | |
|---|---|---|---|---|---|---|---|---|
| | | Normal | L1_SLG_1 | L1_SLG_2 | L1_SLG_3 | L2_SLG_1 | L2_SLG_2 | L2_SLG_3 |
| | Normal | 835 | 12 | 16 | 18 | 4 | 1 | 3 |
| | L1_SLG_1 | 10 | 287 | 23 | 22 | 0 | 0 | 1 |
| Predicted | L1_SLG_2 | 14 | 26 | 275 | 29 | 1 | 0 | 0 |
| | L1_SLG_3 | 9 | 26 | 46 | 310 | 0 | 1 | 0 |
| | L2_SLG_1 | 3 | 1 | 0 | 1 | 520 | 23 | 24 |
| | L2_SLG_2 | 2 | 0 | 1 | 2 | 23 | 553 | 32 |
| | L2_SLG_3 | 2 | 0 | 1 | 1 | 24 | 18 | 635 |

Table 5 reports, in the column "Exp-2", accuracy performance of the various classification algorithms we tested. Differently from the first experiment, C4.5 suffered a small loss in performance (3,4%), RIPPER lost circa 12% of accuracy, while SVM dropped at 51%. The latter was the most expected drop since SVM is known to perform worse when the number of categories to classify grows. Even in this case, C4.5 achieved the best classification performance. The combination of AdaBoost and C4.5 lost only 2% of accuracy with respect to the first experiment, confirming its effectiveness.

Table 7 describes in detail the confusion matrix of the experiment when the system diagnoser is configured with C4.5 in combination with Adaboost. The values in the matrix show that the classifier almost perfectly distinguish faults appearing in distinct lines, while a small number of errors appears when classifying different faults in the same line.

*Exp-3: Faults Identification Among Macro-classes of Natural Events and Cyber-Attacks* – The third experiment presents a faults classification among macro-classes of natural events and of cyber-attacks, considering also the situation in which the system operates in a normal condition. In particular, the fault classes of interest were those of Short Line Circuit (SLG) faults and Relay Setting Change attacks. The first classes (L1_SLG, L2_SLG) include scenarios from 1 to 3 and from 4 to 6, indicating a short circuit in a power line that occurred in different locations. The second classes (L1_ATK, L2_ATK) include scenarios from 35 to 38, indicating a disabling cyber-attack that affected the different relays R1, R2, R3 and R4. Scenario 35 represents a fault on line L2, with a location ranging from 10–49%, combined with the disablement of relays R1 and R2. Since relays R3 and R4 depend on the status of line L2, in this situation all the relays are inoperative. Scenario 36 described the status of system similarly to the scenario 35, but in this case the location of a fault on line L2 ranged from 50% to 90% of the total length of L2. Scenario 37 represented a fault on line L1, with a location ranging from 10–49%, combined with the disablement of the relays R3 and R4; since the relays R1 and R2 depends on the status of the line L1, in this situation all the relays were considered inoperative. Scenario 38 described the status of system similarly to the scenario 37, but in this case the location of a fault on line L1 ranged from 50% to 90% of the total length of L1.

**Table 8.** Confusion matrix for Adaboost + C4.5 in Exp-3.

|  | Actual | | | | |
|  | Normal | L1_SLG | L1_ATK | L2_SLG | L2_ATK |
|---|---|---|---|---|---|
| Normal | 814 | 21 | 33 | 2 | 2 |
| L1_SLG | 22 | 934 | 151 | 3 | 4 |
| L1_ATK | 36 | 137 | 808 | 0 | 4 |
| L2_SLG | 2 | 1 | 4 | 1695 | 140 |
| L2_ATK | 1 | 4 | 5 | 163 | 1651 |

Figure 5 reports, in the column "Exp-3", accuracy performance of the various classification algorithms we tested. Moreover, Table 8 describes in detail the confusion matrix of the experiment when the system diagnoser is configured with C4.5 in combination with Adaboost. The values show that FADa-CPS is clearly able to correctly identify different faults happening on different lines, with a slighter larger error rate when faults deriving from attacks need to be distinguished from those caused by natural events.

*Exp-4: Finer Identification Between Single Faults Deriving from Both the Natural Events and the Cyber-Attacks Macro-classes* – The fourth experiment presents a finer classification between single faults deriving from both the natural events and the cyber-attacks macro-classes, considering also the situation in which the system is operating in a normal condition. In particular, the considered fault classes were the Short Line Circuit (SLG) and the Relay Setting Change attack. In this experiment, each different scenario was considered as a single class during the classification phase, for a total of 11 classes.

Figure 5 reports, in the column "Exp-4", accuracy performance of the various classification algorithms we tested. These results show that it is possible to achieve good classification results in situations where there is a large number of assignable classes, although this is typically challenging for most of the machine learning algorithms. In particular, as we expected, SVM in this experiment provided the worst performance among all the tests. Conversely C4.5 provide reasonably good performance, in particular when coupled with Adaboost.

*Exp-5: Finer Identification of Single Faults Belonging to a Specific Cyber-Attack Macro-class* – The this fifth experiment we tested a finer classification of single faults belonging to a specific cyber-attack macro-class, considering also the situation in which the system is operating in a normal condition. In particular, the selected fault macro-class was the Relay Setting Change attack. The scenarios of interest were those from 35 to 38, indicating a disabling cyber-attack that affected the different relays R1, R2, R3 and R4. In this experiment, each different scenario was considered as a single class during the classification phase, for a total of 5 classes.

Table 5 reports, in the column "Exp-5", accuracy performance of the various classification algorithms we tested. Similarly to the second experiment, which

**Table 9.** Selected scenarios for fault identification tests.

| ID | Description |
|---|---|
| 1 | Fault from 10–19% on line 1 |
| 2 | Fault from 20–79% on line 1 |
| 3 | Fault from 80–90% on line 1 |
| 4 | Fault from 10–19% on line 2 |
| 5 | Fault from 20–79% on line 2 |
| 6 | Fault from 80–90% on line 2 |
| 7 | Fault from 10–19% on line 1 caused by tripping command |
| 8 | Fault from 20–79% on line 1 caused by tripping command |
| 9 | Fault from 80–90% on line 1 caused by tripping command |
| 10 | Fault from 10–19% on line 2 caused by tripping command |
| 11 | Fault from 20–79% on line 2 caused by tripping command |
| 12 | Fault from 80–90% on line 2 caused by tripping command |
| 41 | Normal behavior |

was also focused on the single faults of a specific class, C4.5 and RIPPER provided good accuracy results, while SVM could barely classify one sample out of two. Exactly as all the previous experiments, the combination of AdaBoost and C4.5 turned out to be the best performing classification technique for the considered input dataset. Finally, it is possible to notice that the model previously learned from cyber-attacks training data produces good results when tested in the operational phase, meaning that the tool can effectively individuate and classify different types of cyber-attacks with an accuracy score that is similar to the one obtained when employing a model that aims to identify only natural events.

### 3.5   Fault Localization

We then evaluated the performance of FADa-CPS in identifying the location of different attacks, independently from their cause. The selected subset of scenarios is detailed in Table 9.

These scenarios represent a mix of natural faults appearing at different places on a power line (1–6), and on-purpose attacks that produce similar effects to line faults (7–12).

We tested the fault location functionality considering faults derived from both the macro-classes of natural events and cyber-attacks, considering also the situation in which the system operated in a normal condition. In particular, the first class included the scenarios from 1 to 6, indicating a short circuit in a power line that occurred in different locations. The second class included the scenarios from 7 to 12, indicating a short circuit replay cyber-attack in a power line that occurred at different locations. These thirteen scenarios were grouped in three categories. The first category consisted of scenario 41 only. The second category

**Table 10.** FADa-CPS performance in fault/attack localization.

| Classification algorithm | Accuracy |
|---|---|
| SVM | 96,23% |
| C4.5 | 97,59% |
| RIPPER | 97,46% |
| Bayesian Network | 90,77% |

included the scenarios 1, 2, 3, 7, 8 and 9, which corresponded to the same type of fault, i.e. a short line circuit on line L1, caused either by a natural event or a data injection attack. Similarly, the third category combined the scenarios 4, 5, 6, 10, 11 and 12, which corresponded to a short line circuit on line L2 caused either by a natural event or a data injection attack.

Table 10 reports the accuracy provided by different classification algorithms.

As the results show, the bayesian network approach demonstrated to achieve reasonably good performance when compared to other classifiers. We expect performance from the bayesian network to be unaffected by an increase on the number of locations to consider. Other classifiers, in the same setting would instead suffer from a non-negligible loss of performance. This study showed that it is indeed possible to achieve positive accuracy results while performing fault localization in systems that suffer from failures caused by either natural events or cyber-attacks. As a final consideration, the system detector was unexpectedly more accurate compared to the ones of the previous experiments, since typically the inclusion of the information related to cyber-attacks increases the degree of misjudgment in the analysis. However, in this case the effects derived from the cyber-attacks were very similar to those derived from the natural events, hence the system detector was even more accurate as it had more valuable information to asses which components were affected by a fault.

## 4   Conclusions

In this paper we introduced FADa-CPS, a system for root cause analysis of faults and attacks in CPSs. FADa-CPS is based on a three stage architecture where data is firstly preprocessed, then analyzed to detect anomalies in system components, and then collected and further analyzed to identify the global system state. An extensive evaluation based on data extracted from a real testbed show that FADa-CPS can identify the system status with a good level of accuracy, distinguishing attacks from natural faults, identifying the specific kind of fault and localizing the component that caused the fault, thus representing a useful tool for system operators in their monitoring duties.

FADa-CPS is largely based on ML classification tools that, by their nature, require an accurate training to deliver the best performance. FADa-CPS provides the tools needed to appropriately perform this training task, that must be repeated every time a component of the monitored system is replaced or significantly updated. Notably, an existing trained instance of FADa-CPS may provide less accurate results if it is run to monitor a system that underwent updates (either HW or SW). A reasonable process to handle model updates, may consider a new training of FADa-CPS models whenever significant updates are performed on the monitored systems. While this training phase is ongoing FADa-CPS may still be running on the updated systems using the old models. However, administrators need to be aware that during this phase FADa-CPS may produce larger than expected false positives/negatives and thus may consider taking appropriate countermeasures. Note that only models affected by component updates must be trained again (cfr. Sect. 2).

In the next future we plan to further improve FADa-CPS by analyzing its behavior in more complex datasets, including more heterogeneous data, in an effort aimed at assessing its flexibility and the sensibility of its performance in different scenarios.

# References

1. Weka 3. https://www.cs.waikato.ac.nz/ml/weka/
2. Adhikari, U., Pan, S., Morris, T., Beaver, J.: Power system attack datasets. https://sites.google.com/a/uah.edu/tommy-morris-uah/ics-data-sets
3. Cohen, W.W.: Fast effective rule induction. In: Machine Learning Proceedings 1995, pp. 115–123. Elsevier (1995)
4. Cortes, C., Vapnik, V.: Support-vector networks. Mach. Learn. **20**(3), 273–297 (1995)
5. Freund, Y., Schapire, R.E.: A decision-theoretic generalization of on-line learning and an application to boosting. J. Comput. Syst. Sci. **55**(1), 119–139 (1997)
6. Gao, Z., Cecati, C., Ding, S.X.: A survey of fault diagnosis and fault-tolerant techniques–part I: fault diagnosis with model-based and signal-based approaches. IEEE Trans. Ind. Electron. **62**(6), 3757–3767 (2015)
7. Hink, R.C.B., Beaver, J.M., Buckner, M.A., Morris, T., Adhikari, U., Pan, S.: Machine learning for power system disturbance and cyber-attack discrimination. In: 2014 7th International Symposium on Resilient Control Systems (ISRCS), pp. 1–8 (2014)
8. Kavulya, S.P., Joshi, K., Di Giandomenico, F., Narasimhan, P.: Failure diagnosis of complex systems. In: Wolter, K., Avritzer, A., Vieira, M., van Moorsel, A. (eds.) Resilience Assessment and Evaluation of Computing Systems, pp. 239–261. Springer, Heidelberg (2012). https://doi.org/10.1007/978-3-642-29032-9_12
9. Marr, B.: Why everyone must get ready for the 4th industrial revolution. https://www.forbes.com/sites/bernardmarr/2016/04/05/why-everyone-must-get-ready-for-4th-industrial-revolution/#6e251db23f90
10. Quinlan, R.: C4.5: Programs for Machine Learning. Morgan Kaufmann Publishers, Burlington (1993)
11. łgorzata Steinder, M., Sethi, A.S.: A survey of fault localization techniques in computer networks. Sci. Comput. Program. **53**(2), 165–194 (2004)

# Techniques and Systems for Anomaly Detection in Database Systems

Asmaa Sallam and Elisa Bertino[✉]

Computer Sciences Department, Purdue University, West Lafayette, IN, USA
{asallam,bertino}@purdue.edu

**Abstract.** Techniques for detection of anomalies in accesses to database systems have been widely investigated. Existing techniques operate in two main phases. The first phase is a training phase during which profiles of the database subjects are created based on historical data representing past users' actions. New actions are then checked with these profiles to detect deviations from the expected normal behavior. Such deviations are considered indicators of possible attacks and may thus require further analyses. The existing techniques have considered different categories of features to describe users' actions and followed different methodologies and algorithms to build access profiles and track users' behaviors. In this chapter, we review the prominent techniques and systems for anomaly detection in database systems. We discuss the attacks they help detect as well as their limitations and possible extensions. We also give directions on potential future research.

## 1 Introduction

Data is considered an extremely important asset to most organizations and has thus been the target of many severe attacks. According to recent security reports, data stored in bulk, e.g., in database and corporate file servers, is the most vulnerable. Examples of such attacks include insiders attempts to exfiltrate confidential data, e.g., customer data and intellectual property, and denial-of-service attacks, which make servers unable to respond to users' requests. Therefore, securing such systems against attacks from insiders and outsiders is a crucial need.

Database (DB) systems have strong authentication mechanisms to ensure that the systems users have proper credentials. Once a user is authenticated, access control mechanisms determine which DB objects can be read and modified by the user. However, authentication and access control mechanisms are unable to detect data misuse attempts by insiders who have proper privileges to access the data. They are also unable to detect a masquerader who has succeeded in stealing the credentials of a legitimate user of the system.

Anomaly detection (AD) is considered an effective approach for detecting data misuse scenarios by insiders and masqueraders. AD techniques tailored for DB systems detect deviations from the normal behavior that may indicate possible attacks. These techniques rely on profiles that represent the normal users

ⓒ Springer Nature Switzerland AG 2019
S. Calo et al. (Eds.): PADG 2018, LNCS 11550, pp. 113–133, 2019.
https://doi.org/10.1007/978-3-030-17277-0_7

access patterns to the data. Profiles are based on historical data representing past interactions of the users with the monitored DB system.

In this chapter, we survey existing techniques and systems for the detection of anomalies in DB access. The different techniques have adopted diverse approaches for representing users' actions. Each such approach has shown the capability to flag early signs of specific types of attacks. Our focus in this chapter is to elaborate on the key features of each technique, discuss the attack types it can help detect and suggest possible extensions to the proposed work.

This chapter is organized into three sections. In Sect. 2, we give an overview about the categories of information that can be inferred from users' actions and the methodologies usually followed by existing systems and techniques for performing AD. We also discuss the different types of sources of queries and the implications imposed on systems and techniques considering each type of query. In Sect. 3, we review the prominent AD systems and techniques. In Sect. 4, we discuss related problems that are open for research and outline possible solutions.

## 2 Scope and Methodologies

### 2.1 Features Space

Features used for AD in database accesses describe different aspects of queries that can be issued by users. There are four main categories of features:

1. *Syntax-based features.* Syntax-based features are extracted from the syntax of SQL queries and are used to describe the structures of the queries. Examples of syntax-based features of a select query are the query's command type, range tables, i.e., tables that are referenced by the query, projection list, i.e., the attributes that appear in the query's result-set, and attributes referred to in the where-clause. Syntax-based features can quickly be extracted from queries as they only require parsing the queries' strings and traversing the resulting parse trees.

   AD that relies on syntactic features is useful in the detection of masquerading attacks. A masquerader is an insider or an outsider who succeeds in stealing the credentials of a legitimate user account [1]. The stolen credentials can be used for malicious purposes such as silently snooping on the DB. A masquerader usually has no knowledge about the access patterns of the true account owner and is thus unlikely to perform actions consistent with the account owner's typical behavior. This results in significant differences between the structure of queries executed by the masquerader and the normal queries. Such differences can be detected by syntax-based AD. Syntax-based AD is also able of detecting SQL injection attacks as these attacks too result in changes in the structures of the where-clauses of normal queries.

2. *Data-centric features.* Data-centric features are based on an analysis of the data in queries' result-sets. Example data-centric features of a query are statistics on the values of the projection list attributes, the volume of the query's result-set, and the raw tuples that correspond to the values in the result-set rows.

The extraction of the data-centric features of a query can be costly if the execution of the query, parsing the query's result-set rows, or matching these rows to the raw tuples in the monitored DB is required. However, data-centric AD is able of detecting more sophisticated attacks compared to syntax-based AD. Data harvesting attacks that involve the extraction of data whose sizes exceed the normal or viewing data records that are out of the scope of the job functions of an insider are example attacks that can be detected by data-centric AD.

3. *Context-based features.* Context-based features describe the context in which queries are executed. The IP address, location, user ID and role of the issuer of a query are example contextual features of the query.
4. *Temporal features.* Temporal features are computed based on the time-stamps of the execution of queries. Example temporal features are the order of execution of the individual queries in a sequence of related queries, the aggregate sizes of result-sets of a query sequence, and the periodicity of a query or a group of queries.

AD that relies on both temporal and data-centric features is useful in the detection of attempts to track updates on data tuples and of data aggregation threats [2]. Data aggregation is a data harvesting attack performed by executing multiple queries, each of which retrieves small portions of the target data-set.

Table 1 summarizes the features considered by prominent systems and techniques for the detection of anomalies in DB accesses.

## 2.2  Methodologies and Sources of Queries

The existing techniques and systems have considered two main sources of the queries executed against the monitored DB:

1. *Queries executed by DB tools.* DB systems provide their users with user interface (UI) tools that the users can utilize to interact with the systems. Example functions provided by a UI DB tool are user authentication, receiving user queries on the data and presenting queries result-sets in user appealing views. Example DB tools that can be used to interact with PostgreSQL[1] systems are pgAdmin[2] and psql[3].

   Queries executed by DB tools are ad hoc; as a result, the exact syntax of such queries cannot be predicted by the AD system. Data mining techniques are usually employed by AD systems that consider these type of queries in order to infer the user's access patterns and match new queries to the learned models. Statistical methods are also employed to capture and track the temporal aspects of the queries executed through the use of DB tools. Table 2 summarizes the methodologies followed by the existing AD systems and techniques that consider ad hoc users queries.

---

[1] https://www.postgresql.org/.
[2] https://www.pgadmin.org/.
[3] http://postgresguide.com/utilities/psql.html.

**Table 1.** Summary of features considered by prominent techniques and systems for AD in DB systems.

| Features | References | | | | | | |
|---|---|---|---|---|---|---|---|
| | [3] | [4] | [5,6] | [7] | [8] | [9] | [10] |
| **Syntactic** | | | | | | | |
| Command type | ✓ | | ✓ | ✓ | ✓ | ✓ | ✓ |
| Range-tables | ✓ | ✓ | ✓ | ✓ | ✓ | ✓ | ✓ |
| Projection list attributes | ✓ | ✓ | ✓ | | ✓ | | |
| Where clause list of attributes | ✓ | | | | ✓ | | |
| **Contextual** | | | | | | | |
| User ID | ✓ | | | ✓ | | | ✓ |
| User role | ✓ | | | ✓ | ✓ | | |
| Similar users | ✓ | | | | | | ✓ |
| Response code | | | | | | | ✓ |
| **Data-centric** | | | | | | | |
| # of rows | | ✓ | ✓ | ✓ | ✓ | | |
| Raw tuples | | | | | | ✓ | |
| Stats on values | | ✓ | | | | | |
| **Temporal** | | | | | | | |
| Time-stamp | | | | | ✓ | ✓ | |
| Query sequences | | | | ✓ | | | ✓ |
| Periodicity | | | | | ✓ | | |
| Sessions lengths | | | | ✓ | | | |
| Query frequencies | | | | | | ✓ | ✓ |

2. *Queries executed by application programs.* Application programs are a different source of queries; they impose two types of constraints that govern the syntax of the queries:

    (a) The structures of expected queries encoded in a program through the use of strings or prepared statements[4] is a static constraint.

    (b) The exact syntax of queries and their order is a dynamic constraint determined at run-time based on user inputs.

AD systems that capture dynamic program constraints require the use of sophisticated techniques to profile the programs executions paths and to follow the program's flow and compose the expected queries based on the user's inputs; however, such systems provide finer profiles and better AD accuracy compared to systems that only capture static programs constraints.

---

[4] https://docs.oracle.com/javase/tutorial/jdbc/basics/prepared.html.

**Table 2.** Summary of methodologies considered by AD techniques that consider ad hoc user queries.

| Reference | Methods |
|---|---|
| [3] | – Uses naive Bayesian classification with MAP rule in role-based AD<br>– Uses Clustering algorithms (k-means and k-clusters) and the median of absolute deviations (MAD) test for outlier detection in unsupervised AD |
| [4] | – Uses naive Bayesian, decision trees, SVM classification and Euclidean k-means clustering for the detection of role-masquerading attacks<br>– Uses cluster-based outlier detection based on euclidean distances for clustering and attrib-deviation for the detection of outliers to a single class of normal queries. The goal is to detect data harvesting attacks in which anomalous queries have syntax similar to normal ones, but access different data. These anomalies are referred to as type-2b anomalies |
| [7] | – Uses Jenk's algorithm to cluster users sessions records according to their lengths<br>– Uses mean shift, k-means and affinity propagation clustering techniques to summarize sessions into clusters of sessions that have comparable lengths.<br>– Uses robust covariance and isolation forests outlier detection techniques in finding outliers to sessions clusters |
| [8] | – Computes the peaks of the auto-correlation function applied on time-series that represent queries executions. These peaks are considered candidate periods of the time-series<br>– Uses sequential search to filter false candidate periods lengths |
| [9] | – Considers the $p$-percentile of a list of values representing the number of references to a table the threshold on the rate of referencing the table<br>– Employs a sliding-window algorithm to maintain time-series, which represent tables and tuples references, and to compute reference counts |
| [10] | – Anomalies related to references to new objects by one user are detected based on the upper bound of Chebychev's inequality considering the mean and variance of such objects that are computed based on the training logs<br>– Uses Iclust clustering algorithm to group each user's actions into clusters of actions that tend to occur together in time frames<br>– Uses k-means clustering algorithm to form clusters of users of similar behavior |

# 3   Prominent Techniques and Systems

## 3.1   Syntax-Based AD

**Main Method.** Kamra et al. [3] propose a syntactic approach for the detection of anomalies in DB access. SQL queries are represented in the form of quiplets of attributes of one of three different granularities: coarse, medium and fine.

Two application scenarios that are based on the contextual features of queries have been considered. The first scenario is referred to as role-based AD. Role-based AD assumes that information on the roles of the issuers of queries is present in both the training logs and at the time of inspection of queries. In this scenario, the naive Bayesian classifier using the maximum aposteriori (MAP) rule is applied. To build the classifier, statistics on tables and attributes references are computed based on the quiplet representations of the training queries and stored in roles profiles. Given a new user query, the role-based AD computes the probability that the query is issued by the users of all the roles of the monitored DB system; the query is considered anomalous if the probability that the query is executed by the role of the issuer is less than the probability that it is executed by any other role.

The second scenario is referred to as unsupervised AD. Unsupervised AD considers the case when role information is not present or incomplete and thus the AD system builds profiles of the individual users. During the training phase, unsupervised AD uses a standard clustering algorithm to form clusters of the quiplet representations of the training queries maintaining a mapping between each user and the clusters to which his/her queries belong. During the detection phase, a query $z$ is inspected by first finding the cluster to which the query belongs ($C_z$), and then applying one of two methods to determine if the query is anomalous:

1. Use a classifier to determine if $C_z$ is one of the clusters of the issuer.
2. Apply a statistical test to determine if $z$ is an outlier to $C_z$.

The experimental evaluation is performed on both synthetic and real datasets [11]. Assuming that the data-sets do not contain anomalies, anomalies are simulated by *negating*, i.e., changing, the role ID, in case of role-based AD, and the user ID, in case of unsupervised AD, of the issuer of a query under inspection. Although the results of the evaluation show that the syntactic approach has high AD accuracy, the rate of generation of false-positive alarms in the case of real data-sets is high ($\sim$17–19%). This rate is considered unacceptable for DBs that receive large query streams. Another major problem in the experimentation is that the methods for simulating attacks are insufficient for proving that the syntactic approach will actually work for real attacks.

The proposed approach has several limitations.

- The MAP rule applied for role-based AD does not consider the case when queries are common among the different roles. In the case of a query under inspection that has been executed by the users who belong to different roles based on the training logs, the naive Bayesian classifier will be biased towards the role that has a higher number of executions of the query.
- Role-based AD does not consider the case when one user belongs to multiple roles at the time of the execution of a query. This problem is common to the methods that rely on role membership for grouping users' profiles [5–9].

**Modified Architecture.** In [12], Sallam et al. propose DBSAFE, a system in which the role-based AD techniques [3] are used by organizations that store data in commercial DB management systems (DBMSs).

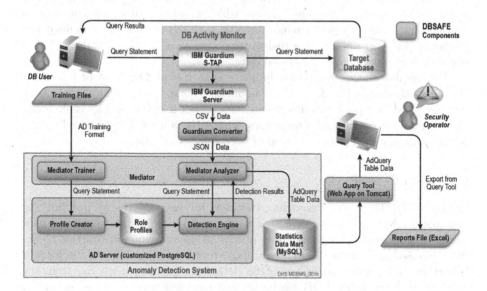

**Fig. 1.** DBSAFE architecture

During the detection phase (see Fig. 1 from [12]), all connection and query requests sent by the users or applications to the monitored DB system are intercepted by an SQL proxy and relayed to a Mediator component. The Mediator sends incoming queries to an A-Detector (anomaly detector) component for inspection. The A-Detector extracts features of the queries using a parser and optimizer that are separate from the DB components of the monitored DB system, and detects and logs mismatches between the queries and the profiles.

Since the DB components employed by the A-Detector require access to the schema of the monitored DB and statistics on the data stored in its catalog, a component, referred to as the schema and statistics importer (SSI), is employed for importing the data required by the A-Detector into its internal catalog. The SSI checks for updates in the data statistics stored at the monitored DB after the execution of every few data update queries.

The DBSafe system also includes methods for extracting data-centric features of queries that describe per-table selectivities based on optimizer statistics. The authors compare the performance of the naive Bayesian classifier employed in [3] to that of a binary classifier that flags queries as anomalous only if any of the attributes referenced by the queries have not previously appeared in the training log of the issuer or the users of his/her role.

The experimental evaluation has been performed in an environment that mimics the actual insider attack settings. The evaluation personnel were divided into 3 teams: (1) the Blue Team, which is responsible for monitoring the system and protecting sensitive data leveraging DBSAFE, (2) the Red Team, which performs normal actions associated with the production system and contains members who attempt to exfiltrate sensitive data periodically during the evaluation process, and (3) the White Team, which monitors the evaluation process and gathers metrics for performance analysis. The DB used in the evaluation has a schema that corresponds to a real-world government medical database, but is populated with artificially-generated data.

The results of the evaluation indicate that the performance of the naive Bayesian classifier in the detection of anomalies is superior to that of the binary classifier; however, the latter has the advantage that it builds profiles that can be easily edited by security administrators. The authors have not presented results on the accuracy of the computation of per-table selectivities.

## 3.2   Data-Centric AD

Mathew et al. [4] propose modeling the users' access patterns by profiling the data points that the users access. Their approach relies on the observation that queries syntax alone is a poor representative of users intents, in contrast to the data accessed by the queries. They propose representing queries in the form of S-Vectors that encode statistics on the data retrieved by the queries from the columns of the monitored DB. Statistics that represent a list of values extracted from a string type column are the values count and the number of distinct values in the list; whereas statistics that represent a list of values extracted from a numeric column are the maximum, minimum, mean, median and standard deviation of the values. The profile of a user or a role is a cluster of the S-Vectors of queries executed by the user or the users of the role.

During the detection phase, a query is considered anomalous if it is different from the profile of the issuer. Since it is not possible to consider all the data values in a large result-set of a query in order to compute its representative S-Vector, the authors propose two methods to approximate the S-Vector of a query:

1. Compute the S-Vector of the query based on the initial $k$ rows in the query's result-set, or
2. Compute the S-Vector of the query based on random $k$ rows in the query's result-set.

The second method is more suited for ordered columns.

The experimental evaluation is performed using different machine learning algorithms such as SVM, naive Bayesian classification and decision trees. The results of the evaluation show that the data-centric approach is superior to the syntax-based approach in detecting data harvesting attacks. However, the data-centric approach has a high rate of false alarms ($\sim$22%).

## 3.3  Data and Syntax Centric AD

Sallam et al. [5,6] extend the DBSafe system by adding data-centric features that characterize per-table selectivities of queries to the quiplet representation introduced in [3]. They solve the problem of profiling roles that have common normal queries using multi-labeling classification. Multi-labeling classification creates multiple binary classifiers; each represents one role in the DB system and is trained using the queries of the users of this role and all queries by other users.

The proposed approach was evaluated using synthetic datasets of the same pattern described in [3] in addition to the OLTP-benchmark query logs [13]. The authors proved that the addition of the selectivity features had a positive impact on the AD accuracy using a data-set in which the different roles execute queries that are similar in all features except the sizes of their result-sets.

Although Sallam et al. provided details on the methods for importing and updating the statistics on the monitored DB, they did not provide experimental results that show the AD accuracy when the actual data statistics significantly differ from the statistics used by the A-Detector. Moreover, results on the accuracy of the computation of per-table selectivities of queries have not been presented.

## 3.4  Temporal AD

**Monitoring the Execution of Periodic Queries.** DB systems allow the execution of queries periodically. Such type of queries are either executed automatically using an application program, or scheduled for execution by a host operating system or using the DB system tools, e.g., Oracle scheduler[5].

Monitoring the execution of periodic queries is extremely important as periodic queries may access large volumes of data as part of backup processes. Detecting such periodic queries also allows for fine-grained profiling of the monitored DB system subjects.

Sallam et al. [8] propose techniques for monitoring the execution of periodic queries on DB systems and the detection of related anomalies. Their techniques complement their previous work in [5,6] and aim at flagging anomalies related to changes in the frequencies of execution of periodic queries and the time-stamps of execution of such queries.

The training phase of such techniques is divided into three sub-tasks:

1. Employing a standard periodicity detection algorithm that relies on computing the auto-correlation of time-series to find candidate periods in time-series that represent queries executions.
2. Eliminating the false-positive candidate periods produced by the previous sub-task and inferring the expected times of executions of confirmed periodic queries.

---

[5] https://docs.oracle.com/cd/B28359_01/server.111/b28310/schedover001.htm.

3. Identifying the relationships between periodic queries that are executed together.

An execution of a periodic query during the detection phase is considered anomalous if it is received at the SQL proxy at an unexpected time. The incorrect ordering of periodic queries is also considered anomalous.

Sallam et al. evaluated the proposed techniques using the logs of the OLTP-benchmarks. The results of the evaluation indicate that 10% of the test cases produced false-positive periods lengths that are multiples of the actual. The techniques have close to perfect accuracy for the detection of the first queries in periodic groups and for the detection of query groups.

However, as the benchmark contains program-generated queries whose syntax is defined using prepared statements, it is not clear how the proposed techniques would perform if the periodic queries were composed by users. It thus appears that query representation and matching do not allow for slight changes in periodic queries features such as the syntactic features and selectivity information. These changes may occur as a result of user modifications to the syntax of the periodic queries and changes to the data of the monitored DB, which lead to out-dated data statistics.

**Detection of Data Aggregation.** In [7], Sallam et al. propose techniques for the detection of queries and sequences of queries that select data volumes larger than the normal volumes. Their techniques operate at three different stages of users' sessions:

1. *Before presenting the result-set of each query to the issuer.* Session tracking (ST) is proposed to detect queries that reference groups of tables that have not previously appeared in training queries and queries that reference datasets larger than training queries of similar syntax. ST is designed to be fast by avoiding the execution of queries and instead employing a parser and an optimizer to extract the syntactic queries features and to estimate the sizes of result-sets.
2. *Periodically.* ST evaluates sequences of queries that reference the same groups of tables by executing queries that count the number of rows in result-sets of query groups.
3. *After the end of each session.* Sessions are represented in the form session features records (SFRs) that encode the aggregate selectivities of portions of the tables that are referenced during each session. Clustering techniques are applied on the SFRs of the sessions that appear in the training logs. A mapping between each role and the clusters to which the sessions of the users of the role belong is maintained. Information on clusters and the roles-clusters mapping represent the final roles profiles.
   The behavior of a user during one session is considered anomalous if the session's representative SFR is an outlier to the training sessions or if it does not belong to one of the clusters of the role of the session's owner. This technique for evaluating sessions after they end is referred to as session evaluation (SE).

In order to account for the lengths of sessions and their effect on the values of the aggregate selectivities of tables, SE+ is proposed. SE+ applies a uni-dimensional clustering technique to partition sessions according to their lengths and then creates clusters of sessions that belong to the same partition as described for the SE approach. SE+ evaluates a session during the detection phase by first finding the partition $(P)$ that contains sessions whose lengths are comparable to the length of the session to be evaluated and then applying the basic SE approach to compare the session's SFR to the SFRs related to $P$.

The techniques proposed in [7] have several limitations.

- The method used to compute the aggregate selectivities of queries and portions of tables referenced in sessions is trivial as it requires the execution of sophisticated queries at the monitored DB system. The impact of these queries on the throughput of the system and the response times to queries have not been quantified.
- An important feature of a session that is not considered in SE+ is the time when the session starts. The start time of a session affects its length and as a result the aggregate selectivities of the tables referenced during the session.
- The rate of connection attempts by each user is an important temporal/contextual feature that has not been considered by the proposed techniques. A malicious insider may end one session and attempt to reconnect to the monitored system to clear the tracking data-structures.

**Result-Based AD.** In [9], Sallam et al. propose an architecture that allows for the inspection of the rows of result-sets of queries in DB systems that present queries result-sets in the form of pipelines of rows. The purpose of the inspection of rows is to detect two anomaly scenarios:

1. Data aggregation threats in which the attacker does not have prior knowledge on the target data-set, and
2. Attempts to track data updates.

The proposed AD approach monitors the rates of referencing the DB tables and tuples. A sliding-window algorithm is devised to maintain time-series that encode the time-stamps of executions of queries, compute thresholds on reference rates during the training phase and detect queries that lead to exceeding these thresholds during the detection phase.

In order to locate the raw tuples referenced by each query, the authors proposed methods for modifying the queries syntax by inserting the keys of the tables referenced by queries into the queries projection lists; they tackle issues that result from the introduced changes such as modifying tuples in order to match the original queries syntax and the detection and removal of duplicate rows.

Based on the experimental evaluation, result-based AD is found to produce low false-alarm generation rate ($\sim$4%) and to accurately detect anomalies related to data access rates in a reasonable amount of time when enough data is available for training and when the system configuration parameters are properly selected. However, the experimental evaluation has some issues.

- The 4% false-alarm rate is considered high when large volumes of queries are to be inspected. The authors did not mention what the results imply for this case. They propose presenting an anomaly degree associated with each anomalous query to help eliminate false-positives, but left the actual computation of anomaly degrees as future work.
- Experiments for real attack scenarios are not included. The authors only propose methods for mimicking the attacks by replicating log queries.

**IBM InfoSphere Guardium.** Mazzawi et al. [10] propose algorithms for comparing users activities for both self-consistency, i.e., consistency with previous patterns of access by the same user, and global consistency, i.e., consistency with past actions of similar users. The purpose of training is to build two types of models:

1. *Self consistency models.* Self consistency models include:
   (a) *A rarity model.* For each user and every atomic action, e.g., SQL command type, seen in the training logs, the rarity model stores the probability of appearance of the action in a new time frame. For a user $u_i$ and an atomic action $e_j$, such probability is denoted as $b_j^{(i)}$ and calculated by dividing the number of time frames during which $u_i$ performed $e_j$ by the number of time frames the user $u_i$ was active.
   (b) *A volume model.* The underlying distribution of the number of occurrences of an atomic action by a user is assumed to follow the log normal distribution. The parameters of such a distribution for each user-action pair is computed such that the likelihood of appearance of the set of actions by the user as observed in the training data is maximized; the computed parameters are stored in the volume model based on the training logs.
   (c) *An out of context model.* The out of context model stores information on the correlations between the actions performed by each user. The profiler follows the steps below to build the out of context model for a user $u_i$.
       i. Model each atomic action performed by $u_i$ in the form of a vector, referred to as the appearance vector. The appearance vector of $u_i$ and an atomic action $e_j$ is a list of Boolean values whose length is equal to the number of time frames during which $u_i$ has been active based on the training data; the value that corresponds to time frame $k$ is set to 1 if $u_i$ has performed action $e_j$ during the $k$-th time-frame.
       ii. Employ the similarity-based clustering algorithm, Iclust, on all appearance vectors related to $u_i$; this groups atomic actions into clusters of actions that tend to occur together in the same time frames. Information on the resulting clusters is stored in the out of context model.

(d) *A new object model.* The new object model stores the mean and variance of the number of objects that have not been accessed by each user in time frames of length equal to one hour.

2. *A global consistency model.* The behavior of each user is modeled in the form of a vector referred to as rarity score vector. The rarity score vector of a user $u_i$ is denoted as $b^{(i)}$ and computed as

$$b^{(i)} = (b_1^{(i)}, b_2^{(i)}, ..., b_r^{(i)}),$$

where $r$ is the number of atomic actions seen in the training data and $b_j^{(i)}$ is the appearance vector of $u_i$ and action $e_j$. A k-means clustering algorithm is then run on the rarity vectors of all users to form clusters of users of similar behavior. The centroids of the resulting clusters and the user-cluster membership information is stored in the global consistency model.

---

**Algorithm 1:** Computing the anomaly score of user $u_i$ based on actions previously performed by the user.

1. $E_i = \{\}$

2. For each action cluster $C$ in the out of context model:

   2.1. $S = \{\}$

   2.2. Pick one representative action $e_j$ from actions in $C$

   2.3. Compute an anomaly score $s_i$ based on the current time frame count of $e_j$ and the learnt rarity and volume models

   2.4. Add $s_i$ to $S$

3. Build a histogram $H$ that represents the anomaly scores of actions in $E_j$ based on the user's logs

4. Compute the final anomaly score as the percentage of actions scores in $S$ that fall below the values in $H$

---

The anomaly detection phase (also referred to as the analysis phase) starts after training is complete. The activities performed by each user are analyzed and two anomaly scores are computed for each user:

1. *Self-consistency score.* The self-consistency score of a user $u_i$ during one time frame is computed as the maximum of two scores:

   (a) *Score based on the new objects accessed by the user.* A positive anomaly score is computed if the count of new objects accessed by the user during the current time frame exceeds the mean value associated with the user in the new object model. This score is computed based on the upper bound computed by applying Chebychev's inequality on the mean and variance of new objects that is associated with the user's information in the new object model.

   (b) *Score based on actions previously performed by the user based on the training data.* Algorithm 1 shows the steps for computing this score.

2. Global consistency score. This is computed based on the cosine similarity distance between the vector that represents the user's actions during the current time frame and the centroid of the cluster of the user that is stored in the global consistency model.

The paper shows results of the evaluation of the proposed techniques on synthetic datasets only as per non-disclosure agreements, it is not allowed to show results on real customer data. However, the techniques have been integrated with InfoSphere Guardium[6], the SIEM tool developed by IBM, and evaluated in practice. The tool was able to alarm on an unusual volume of accesses by a customer; upon further investigating the alarm, the alarm was confirmed to be an actual attack.

Three attack scenarios were simulated using synthetic data and the performance of the proposed tool was evaluated. An attacker was defined as a person having 20% of his daily transactions being malicious. The results of the evaluation show that the self-consistency model performed better in the detection of unusual dropping of tables and attempts to query huge tables, which result in a decrease in the DB system performance. The global consistency model was more suitable for the detection of masquerading attacks in which an attacker steals one user account and silently snoops on the DB by accessing random tables that are not the usual tables accessed by the true account owner.

Possible improvements on the proposed models would be to detect anomalies due to abnormal activities that span multiple frames. Continuous monitoring also seem to be more accurate and more efficient than the periodic monitoring approach adopted in the proposed tool.

### 3.5    Profiling Application Programs

**IIDD: Integrated Intrusion Detection in Databases.** Fonseca et al. [14] propose a tool named IIDD that analyzes transactions executed on DBs by application programs. IIDD extracts query templates from the strings of queries executed against the monitored DB by replacing all non-generic values in the strings, e.g., constant numerics and strings, with place-holders. Profiles are either built manually by a DB administrator, concurrently to the normal utilization of the program to be profiled, or during program testing.

The profile of a program is stored in the form of a directed graph; nodes in the graph represent queries, and paths in the graph represent the order of execution of queries in transactions.

The proposed tool was evaluated using the TPC-W benchmark in addition to a real DB. The results show that the proposed tool produces zero false-positive errors, can accurately detect incorrect ordering of commands and changes in queries syntax, and has low impact on the response times to queries. However, the number of query templates inferred by the profiler is large; this indicates that the profiling approach produces many redundancies.

---

[6] https://www.ibm.com/security/data-security/guardium.

The proposed approach has a major drawback that it cannot capture the impact of user input on the sequence of queries. It is also not mentioned how IIDD could capture the ordering of commands.

**DetAnom: A System for Profiling and Monitoring Database Access Patterns by Application Programs for Anomaly Detection.** Bossi et al. [15,16] propose DetAnom, which overcomes the drawbacks of IIDD. The main purpose of DetAnom is to detect attempts for tampering the code of application programs in addition to SQL injection attacks by detecting changes in queries syntax and the order of executions of queries. The design goals of DetAnom is three-fold:

- Minimizing the number of changes made to the program being profiled,
- Minimizing the impact of program monitoring on the performance of the program, and
- Achieving high AD accuracy with low rate of false alarms.

DetAnom relies on the Concolic testing approach[7] for building program profiles. Concolic testing combines symbolic and concrete program execution to provide as much coverage of the program as possible during testing. DetAnom uses the same approach to profile the control flow of programs and to find the SQL queries executed by a program in addition to the constraints that have to be satisfied before each query can be executed.

The profile of a program built by DetAnom profiler is a directed graph similar to the one described in [14]. However, the profile produced by the DetAnom profiler associates each node of the graph with the constraints that control the execution of the query that the node represents; this information is not captured by the IIDD tool.

DetAnom captures input parameters from the JVM (Java virtual machine) by instrumenting the Java libraries that read user inputs. The decision to instrument the libraries rather than instrumenting the program's code was based on the fact that software modifications are usually restricted by license agreements between the utilizing company and the software company responsible for code development.

DetAnom monitors the program execution and, based on the program's profile and user inputs, DetAnom flags queries that are not expected to be executed by the program as anomalous.

DetAnom has been evaluated using three application programs developed by the authors. The test programs have different numbers of unique queries and nested code blocks. The results of the evaluation indicate that DetAnom introduces low overhead on the response times to queries and low overhead on the network as a result of sending the queries to the AD server to inspect.

A few remarks must be made on the experimentation methodology and results.

---

[7] https://en.wikipedia.org/wiki/Concolic_testing.

- The overhead added due to parsing complex expressions was not studied in the experimental evaluation.
- A long time (~4 days) was required to profile a medium-size application program that contains approximately 500 lines of code. The resulting profile only covered 20% of the program's code. The authors attributed the slow down to the inefficient Concolic testing library they employed for profiling the program.

**Profiling Web Applications.** Valeur et al. [17] propose techniques for the detection of attacks on backend DBs accessed by web applications. They focus on the detection of three types of attacks:

1. SQL injection attacks, where an attacker injects strings into SQL statements for the purpose of executing additional queries that expose sensitive data or maliciously alter the DB,
2. Cross-site scripting attacks, which allow the execution of client-side code in privileged contexts, and
3. Data-centric attacks, where an attacker inserts data into the DB that is not in the expected values ranges.

Their approach is to parse each query, extract its tokens and infer the tokens data types. They employ a parser that references the DB schema to detect the names of tables and attributes in addition to the data types of attributes. This information is also used in finding constants whose source is user inputs and inferring their expected data types and formats. After each query is parsed, a feature selector component transforms the query into a query skeleton by replacing all tokens marked as constant with empty placeholders.

During the training phase, the skeleton of a query is used to update the current models. Whereas, during the detection phase, the skeleton of a query is used to look up the profiles for a similar query and compute an anomaly degree based on the difference between the query and the model; an alarm is generated if the difference exceeds a certain threshold.

Valuer et al. proposed several statistical models for describing constants of different data types. For example,

- String constants models describe the expected lengths, character distributions and prefixes and suffixes of string type constants
- Enumeration constants models are used to describe constants that can be one of a finite number of options. This type of constants is common in web applications forms in which a user of a form selects one value from a drop-down menu.

The evaluation of the proposed techniques indicates that they are capable of the detection of four simulated attacks:

- An SQL injection attack that aims at resetting the passwords of many users,
- An SQL injection attack that aims at enumerating all the DB users,

– A parallel password guessing attack in which the attacker attempts to speedup password guessing by trying one password against a whole users DB in parallel, and

– A cross-site scripting attack in which the attacker executes a script that inserts values stored in the user's document.domain into a DB table accessible by the attacker.

The evaluation also shows zero false alarms generated when an attack-free data-set is checked and low overhead per query ($\sim$0.20–1.00 ms). The proposed techniques can be extended by taking into account the percentage of server code coverage during training in the model evaluation.

# 4   Directions for Future Research

In what follows we outline a few significant research directions for enhancing the effectiveness and flexibility of AD systems.

**Incomplete Training Profiles and Using Expert Feedback and Domain Knowledge.** One possible extension is the development of a profiler able to detect the case of insufficient training data and flag profiles that are incomplete. A third decision, besides normal and anomalous, should also be considered by the anomaly detector, which indicates when the AD decision on an action by a user who has an incomplete profile is being inspected.

Towards solving the problem of insufficient training data, Costante et al. [18] propose the use of histograms to represent users profiles; an anomaly score is associated with anomalous queries and anomalous transactions based on the probabilities of the histograms bins. The main goal of using histograms is to provide *white-box* profiles that can be easily understood and edited by administrators. However, the authors did not mention how the anomaly scores computed by AD are affected by histograms modifications.

Sallam et al. [12] propose using a binary classifier, which flags queries that reference one or more attributes that did not appear previously in training queries as anomalous. Profiles built by the binary classifier associate each DB attribute with a set of Boolean variables; each indicates whether the users of one role previously referenced the attribute. DBSAFE provides editable profiles by allowing administrators to toggle the values of the Boolean variables. However, the experimental results showed that the binary classifier has poor performance in practice.

Kamra et al. [3] propose using a feedback loop that changes the statistical profiles used by the naive Bayesian classifier according to AD decisions. This approach is only useful in reinforcing the AD decision and takes a long time to take further effect.

The system by Valeur et al. [17] passes through an intermediate stage between the training and detection phases, referred to as the thresholds learning phase. During this phase, the training models are evaluated by selecting some queries from the training logs and computing the result of the inspection of these queries based on the current models. If some queries cannot be evaluated, the result of the evaluation will include alarms that indicate that one or more models are incomplete.

The tool by Mazzawi et al. [10] allows the user of the tool to provide feedback on the detected anomalies to indicate the correctness and importance of alerting on related actions. Possible types of user feedback on an alert related to a user action are:

1. filter-before, which indicates that the system should ignore the alert,
2. filter-after, which indicates that the alert is not important at the current time, but should be computed in case it is of some interest later and because it may affect other internal calculations, and
3. alert, which indicates that the alert is a correctly identified attack and the system should always alert on such action.

The problem of the detection of insufficient training data, monitoring user behavior and taking into account user feedback is still open for more research. One approach for incorporating user feedback that seems promising is to use active learning techniques. Active learning is concerned with the detection of incompleteness in profiles, producing a minimal number of questions to be answered by human experts, and actively updating users' profiles based on experts' inputs.

**Selection of Parts of the Training Logs that Represent the Current Users' Access Patterns.** Using the complete DB logs for building access profiles is inadequate in the case that the log represents long time intervals of queries during which one or more seasonal changes may have occurred. An initialization step is thus required by all methods that rely on training logs to create users profiles; during this step, portions of the training logs that are representative of the current access patterns of the users are selected and later used in building profiles.

**Maintaining Up-to-Date Profiles.** Developing techniques for the detection of changes in the users' access patterns and applying the necessary updates to the profiles during the detection phase is useful for maintaining up-to-date profiles and ensuring accurate AD. Efficient solutions are required to:

- Involve minimal human intervention,
- Provide high availability of the AD system by minimizing the maintenance time, and
- Allow for transitioning policies that can be applied during the time interval between the detection of the requirement for updating profiles until the new profiles are ready to use.

Changes to the profiles can be detected by monitoring the anomaly generation rates and looking for level shifts in data access frequencies.

**Monitoring Application Programs.** The DetAnom approach for monitoring the execution of queries by application programs is promising and can be extended to tackle the following problems.

- Taking into account DB constraints that control the program's flow, e.g., considering loops controlled by the size of the result-set of a query.
- Considering types of applications other than the standard Java desktop applications, e.g., web applications that receive inputs in the form of GET and POST requests.

**Automatically Inferring the Values of the AD Configuration Parameters.** Carefully choosing the system configuration parameters is important for the correct operation of AD. Leaving this task entirely to the administrators is usually inadequate and may lead to poor performance of the AD techniques. One approach for selecting configuration parameters is the use of cross-validation as suggested by Valeur et al. in [17].

**Detection of Periodicity of Queries.** The approach for monitoring the execution of periodic queries by Sallam et al. [8] is promising. One possible extension to the proposed work is to evaluate the impact of integrating the periodicity monitoring algorithms to systems that detect anomalous non-periodic queries. A periodic query that is not detected by the profiler will lead to the generation of false-positive alarms during the detection phase if the query is not commonly executed by the issuer or the users of his/her role. The analysis of correlations between queries that are found to be anomalous is thus useful in the detection of missed periodicities.

**Studying the Effect of Monitoring Users Connections.** AD systems that monitor access to commercial DBs usually use an SQL proxy to tap the connections between the users and the monitored DB system. The impact of using the proxy on the response times to queries has not been thoroughly studied in the context of AD in DB systems. However, the study is important as the proxy may cause long delays due to reading network packets and composing queries based on packets data.

**Policy Technologies.** We have reviewed the prominent techniques and systems for detection of anomalies in access to database systems. The existing techniques have considered different categories of features to describe users' actions and followed different methodologies and algorithms to build access profiles and track users' behaviors. While policy based methods have not been discussed in detail, they are commonly used in the decision processes for Anomaly Detection that were our primary focus. We have also given directions on potential future research, one key area being that of combining expert feedback and domain knowledge with the machine learning techniques described. Such information can be incorporated by means of policy based technologies, and the use of generative policies in conjunction with AI models seems to be a promising area of study.

# References

1. Salem, M.B., Hershkop, S., Stolfo, S.J.: A survey of insider attack detection research. In: Stolfo, S.J., Bellovin, S.M., Keromytis, A.D., Hershkop, S., Smith, S.W., Sinclair, S. (eds.) Insider Attack and Cyber Security. ADIS, vol. 39, pp. 69–90. Springer, Boston (2008). https://doi.org/10.1007/978-0-387-77322-3_5
2. Software Engineering Institute: Analytic approaches to detect insider threats. Technical report, Software Engineering Institute, Carnegie Mellon University, Pittsburgh, PA (2015). http://resources.sei.cmu.edu/library/asset-view.cfm?assetid=451065. Accessed 28 Oct 2016
3. Kamra, A., Terzi, E., Bertino, E.: Detecting anomalous access patterns in relational databases. VLDB J. **17**(5), 1063–1077 (2008)
4. Mathew, S., Petropoulos, M., Ngo, H.Q., Upadhyaya, S.: A data-centric approach to insider attack detection in database systems. In: Jha, S., Sommer, R., Kreibich, C. (eds.) RAID 2010. LNCS, vol. 6307, pp. 382–401. Springer, Heidelberg (2010). https://doi.org/10.1007/978-3-642-15512-3_20
5. Sallam, A., Xiao, Q., Bertino, E., Fadolalkarim, D.: Anomaly detection techniques for database protection against insider threats. In: 2016 IEEE International Conference on Information Reuse and Integration, IRI 2016, Pittsburgh, PA, USA, pp. 28–30 (2016)
6. Sallam, A., Fadolalkarim, D., Bertino, E., Xiao, Q.: Data and syntax centric anomaly detection for relational databases. Wiley Interdisc. Rev.: Data Min. Knowl. Disc. **6**(6), 231–239 (2016)
7. Sallam, A., Bertino, E.: Detection of temporal data ex-filtration threats to relational databases. In: Proceedings of the 4th IEEE International Conference on Collaboration and Internet Computing, CIC 2018, Philadelphia, PA, USA. IEEE (2018)
8. Sallam, A., Bertino, E.: Detection of temporal insider threats to relational databases. In: 2017 IEEE 3rd International Conference on Collaboration and Internet Computing (CIC), pp. 406–415 (2017)
9. Sallam, A., Bertino, E.: Result-based detection of insider threats to relational databases. In: Proceedings of the 9th ACM Conference on Data and Application Security and Privacy, CODASPY 2019, pp. 25–35. ACM (2015)
10. Mazzawi, H., Dalal, G., Rozenblatz, D., Ein-Dorx, L., Niniox, M., Lavi, O.: Anomaly detection in large databases using behavioral patterning. In: 2017 IEEE 33rd International Conference on Data Engineering (ICDE), April 2017, pp. 1140–1149 (2017)
11. Yao, Q., An, A., Huang, X.: Finding and analyzing database user sessions. In: Zhou, L., Ooi, B.C., Meng, X. (eds.) DASFAA 2005. LNCS, vol. 3453, pp. 851–862. Springer, Heidelberg (2005). https://doi.org/10.1007/11408079_77
12. Sallam, A., Bertino, E., Hussain, S.R., Landers, D., Lefler, R.M., Steiner, D.: DBSAFE - an anomaly detection system to protect databases from exfiltration attempts. IEEE Syst. J. **11**(2), 483–493 (2017)
13. Difallah, D.E., Pavlo, A., Curino, C., Cudre-Mauroux, P.: OLTP-Bench: an extensible testbed for benchmarking relational databases. Proc. VLDB Endow. **7**(4), 277–288 (2013)

14. Fonseca, J., Vieira, M., Madeira, H.: Integrated intrusion detection in databases. In: Bondavalli, A., Brasileiro, F., Rajsbaum, S. (eds.) LADC 2007. LNCS, vol. 4746, pp. 198–211. Springer, Heidelberg (2007). https://doi.org/10.1007/978-3-540-75294-3_15

15. Bossi, L., Bertino, E., Hussain, S.: A system for profiling and monitoring database access patterns by application programs for anomaly detection. IEEE Trans. Softw. Eng. **PP**(99), 1 (2016)

16. Hussain, S.R., Sallam, A.M., Bertino, E.: DetAnom: detecting anomalous database transactions by insiders. In: Proceedings of the 5th ACM Conference on Data and Application Security and Privacy, CODASPY 2015, pp. 25–35. ACM (2015)

17. Valeur, F., Mutz, D., Vigna, G.: A learning-based approach to the detection of SQL attacks. In: Julisch, K., Kruegel, C. (eds.) DIMVA 2005. LNCS, vol. 3548, pp. 123–140. Springer, Heidelberg (2005). https://doi.org/10.1007/11506881_8

18. Costante, E., Vavilis, S., Etalle, S., den Hartog, J., Petković, M., Zannone, N.: A white-box anomaly-based framework for database leakage detection. J. Inf. Secur. Appl. **32**, 27–46 (2017)

# Policies and Autonomy in Federated and Distributed Environments

# Towards Enabling Trusted Artificial Intelligence via Blockchain

Kanthi Sarpatwar, Roman Vaculin$^{(\boxtimes)}$, Hong Min, Gong Su, Terry Heath, Giridhar Ganapavarapu, and Donna Dillenberger

IBM Research, Yorktown Heights, NY, USA
{sarpatwa,vaculin,hongmin,gongsu,theath,engd}@us.ibm.com,
giridhar.ganapavarapu@ibm.com

**Abstract.** Machine Learning and Artificial Intelligence models are created, trained and used by different entities. The entity that curates data used for the model is frequently different from the entity that trains the model, which is different yet again from the end user of the trained model. The end user needs to trust the received AI model, and this requires having the provenance information about how the model was trained, and the data the model was trained on. This chapter describes how blockchain can be used to track the provenance of training models, leading to better trusted Artificial Intelligence.

## 1 Introduction

At the present time, Machine Learning and Artificial Intelligence models are seldom written from scratch. Most data scientists start their exploration by selecting one or more pre-existing models from a library of models. The data used to train the models is frequently provided by third parties. Once the models have been trained, they can be provided to application architects within the same corporate entity, or provided to a public marketplace where others can buy and use those trained models.

When models are used without knowing what data they were trained with, they can produce erroneous results. A lack of attention to the training data used for a model can lead to vulnerabilities that can be exploited in different types of attacks on AI models. For example, in 2017, MIT tricked Google's Artificial Intelligence (AI) classification services to classify a 3-D printed turtle as a rifle [2]. Models that are trained as SPAM filters can be sent training data that misspells known SPAM signatures to cause misclassifications [3]. Models that have been trained to detect malware can be injected with poisoned data to allow malware to pass through without being recognized [11]. Fake biometric features can be sent identity recognition models to mislead them, resulting in impersonation [5] and fraud.

It is not easy to read the code of models, or interpret the parameters of a model, in order to determine if they have been corrupted with poisoned training data. Similarly, it is difficult to determine if a model has been unintentionally

S. Calo et al. (Eds.): PADG 2018, LNCS 11550, pp. 137–153, 2019.
https://doi.org/10.1007/978-3-030-17277-0_8

trained with biased data. Training on biased data will result in a biased model that can provide results dependent on a specific population's age range, geography, or gender [9]. This leads to a wide variety of false and biased results from models [4, 6, 13, 15, 30].

In order to protect AI models against these pitfalls, a mechanism to keep track of a model's history – ranging from its creation, the training data used for it, and the process used for training it, is needed. This history is the *provenance* of the model.

The provenance of a model would describe how the model was trained, with what data, what group or person provided the data and the effect on the accuracy of the model when trained with each data set. The provenance of models would have to be protected from corruption, false changes and tampering. Many models evolve after their creation due to additional training by different participants over time, which requires that provenance information should be sharable, and a history of trusted updates to provenance ought to be maintained.

While the provenance of models can be stored in a shared document, file or database, such a solution suffers from the drawback that participants can change the provenance of models after the original record has been created. This allows unscrupulous entities to falsify the provenance data, and even honest entities can unintentionally corrupt the provenance data.

Several trust related issues arise in any typical distributed learning environment. Data must be protected for privacy reasons (e.g., sensitive information such as age, gender, zip code, etc., are often subject to regulatory restrictions) as well as for maintaining ownership. Direct sharing of raw data could immediately result in the loss of ownership. Another issue is fairness in attributing credit to the various entities that provide data to help train a model, since those need to be based on the quality of data and its value to the overall training process.

Blockchain is a technology that enables multiple participants to share data in a trusted way. A blockchain network is composed of multiple copies of blockchain datastores. Blockchain records are hashed with each other so it is very difficult to change blockchain data once it is written to the blockchain.

This chapter will describe how blockchain technology can be used to tackle various aspects of trust in the AI training process, including auditable provenance of data and models, data privacy and fairness. Blockchain data can include: the history of model creation, a hash of the data used to train the models, origin of the model and, potentially, the contribution of various participants in the creation of the model.

Models can then be passed to different groups in the same organization or to other organizations, and each organization can read the historical provenance of the model from a blockchain and choose to retrain the model with additional data, e.g., to compensate for lack of diversity in previous training sets. Organizations can also read from a blockchain the results of prior training iterations of the model that were done by a different group, to see if some of the previous training data skewed the results adversely.

The rest of the chapter is organized in the following way. In Sect. 2, we discuss some of the prior work that is related to ours. Section 3 introduces the notion of trusted AI, the definition of provenance that we use and the scenarios that need trusted AI, and why a centralized approach for trusted AI is not adequate in many cases. Section 4.1 details our vision and requirements for blockchain to enable trust in AI processes. Section 4.2 discusses various constructs in our blockchain design and Sect. 4.3 exemplifies the ideas using a popular distributed learning algorithm known as federated learning. Section 4.4 highlights some of the implementation details, and we conclude in Sect. 5.

## 2   Related Work

Many important aspects need to be addressed for trusted AI, for example, reinforcing moral disciplines, reducing bias, providing transparency, and increasing explainability of AI models. Providing data and model provenance in AI practice is only the first but a signification step towards enabling trusted AI.

In computer science, the notion of provenance originated in information management [8]. Data provenance is the ability to provide the origins of data and a tracking history of how entities, systems, and workflows influence data. The generated evidence can be used in various business and management activities including, but not limited to, security management, auditing, and compliance analysis. The problem of computing data provenance in the relational model was first considered by Woodruff and Stonebraker [28]. With a database modeling and query approach, Buneman, Khanna and Wang-Chiew [8] address the distinction between "why" provenance (refers to the source data that had some influence on the existence of the data) and "where" provenance (refers to the location(s) in the source databases from which the data was extracted). The work of Loo et al. [17] extends provenance to distributed systems by modeling the distributed system as a giant database where information about the nodes is stored in tables and the programs are modeled as a set of declarative rules. Jabal and Bertino [14] propose a provenance framework which includes an expressive provenance model able to represent the provenance of any data object captured with various granularities. The model is represented per relational and graph specifications. From a system perspective, McDaniel et al. [19] study the performance and security aspects of an end-to-end provenance system. Wylot et al. [29] study provenance techniques used in linked data modeled via Resource Description Framework (RDF) for application domains such as social networks. Chen et al. [10], with the experience learned in network provenance, assert that the system architecture and runtime need to address the new data provenance challenges at the network scale to provide data provenance at the internet level.

To support trusted Machine Learning, Baracaldo et al. [3] apply a method that uses data provenance to identify groups of data whose likelihood of being poisoned are highly correlated, as well as a provenance-based defense for cases when datasets are only partially trusted or fully untrusted. The work of Ma et al. [18] proposes LAMP, a provenance computation system for graph based Machine Learning (GML) algorithms. LAMP quantifies the importance of an input for an output by computing the partial derivative to address the challenging problem of ripple effects in GML algorithms, where a vertex can affect other vertexes many edges away due to the iterative nature of the algorithms. Schelter et al. [24] present a system design and a database schema for modeling and storing the corresponding metadata across a variety of Machine Learning frameworks such as pipelines and computational graphs of neural networks.

The rapid growth of blockchain technology offers opportunities for decentralized solutions for distributed trusted computing. Research has been done in applying this technology to data and workflow provenance. In a recent work by Liang et al. [16], an architecture named ProvChain is designed and implemented to collect and verify Cloud data provenance, by embedding the provenance data into blockchain transactions. It provides security features including tamper-proof provenance, user privacy and reliability with low overhead for Cloud storage applications. Ramachandran and Kantarcioglu [22] propose SmartProvenance, a secure and immutable scientific data provenance management framework based on blockchain. It utilizes smart contracts and an open provenance model (OPM) to record immutable data trails, which guarantees the validity of provenance data against malicious modifications if most of the participants are honest.

## 3 Trusted Artificial Intelligence

We refer to an environment in which the end user of an AI model can trust its predictions as one supporting trusted AI. Building the mechanism for trusted AI requires establishing the provenance of the AI model. In this section, we first discuss the scenarios for trusted AI, followed by a discussion of the provenance model that is needed for trusted AI to be supported in those scenarios.

### 3.1 Scenarios for Trusted AI

The first scenario for trusted AI is the case for a model marketplace [1]. In the AI model marketplace, users of the AI models purchase them from the marketplace, whereas providers of the models offer those for sale on the marketplace. The marketplace provides a convenient location for the users to avoid the laborious process of training a model, but they require provenance information to be able to understand whether or not they would be able to trust the model in their environment.

Another scenario requiring trusted AI is that of AI enabled operations in the context of coalition operations [21,25]. In coalition operations, training data and Machine Learning models may be acquired from different organizations that make up a coalition. Not all members of the coalition are equally trusted, which requires the need for model provenance when training data may have come from many different sources and may have been used in a variety of ways for creating a Machine Learning model.

When different agencies in a government organization are cooperating together, they may have limited trust among each other. Like coalition operations, different agencies would need to share training data and AI models with each other [26] in a collaborative manner and would benefit from provenance information attached to the training data and models they obtain from other partners.

Edge Computing [23] is an emerging paradigm in current IT systems. When AI enabled operations are conducted in the context of edge computing, AI models are computed at powerful servers in the Cloud and cached at potentially weaker edge devices [27]. When caches at the edge may belong to an organization different from the one that controls the Cloud, provenance information may need to be attached to the models as they are retrieved from the Cloud based sources.

Federated learning [20] is a scenario where Machine Learning models are built using data from many different sources. When building such models, provenance data about the source of data, as well as how the training model has evolved needs to be captured, to get assurances about the nature and capabilities of the training data and the model built from such information.

As AI models get adopted in more complex environments, get modified, adapted and adjusted for new types of training data, and reused in different ways, the need for provenance information to maintain trusted AI will be required in several other contexts.

## 3.2 Provenance Data for AI Model

In order to support trust in the model being retrieved in these various situations, we need to work with a model for provenance that would be applicable for AI models. While there has been some work towards defining provenance for AI models [3,18,24], as mentioned in Sect. 2, we need to formalize the definition of an AI model so that it is useful in the myriad situations in which AI models may be used.

The provenance information for AI models can be viewed as meta-data associated with the model, which can be provided by any entity that distributed the AI model such as an AI market-place or a Cloud-based AI model distributor. The provenance data for an AI model includes the following information:

- Details about the training data that was used for training the AI model;
- Details about the model pipeline that was used for training, since many models are formed from a pipeline containing basic training steps;
- Details about the training process that was used for training the AI model;
- Details about any adaptation or modifications that may have been done to the AI model; and,
- Details about any tests that may have been done using the AI model, and the results from those tests.

For each of these details, provenance information needs to be stored, so that the details are maintained in a way by which they can be verified even in cases where they may be modified after the fact. The details need to be provided with a set of attestations that can be verified and cross-checked by any user of the AI model.

When models are built from a distributed set of training data across multiple organizations as in federated learning [18,21,25,26], the provenance information needs to be further augmented with the contribution made from each of the data sources. It must capture the evolution of the AI model as it progresses through the different stages of federated learning and different parts of the model are created and updated.

The provenance data can be represented in a concrete manner using a schema like the one described in [24], expressed in a specific format like XML [7], or expressed visually as a UML model [12]. The provenance data needs to be provided and distributed in a manner that will be acceptable to the user of the model.

### 3.3   Provenance Distribution Architectures

Provenance data, which provides the basic foundation for creating trusted AI, can be distributed in many different ways. One way is to store the provenance data in a file which is maintained by some party with the choice of the party depending on the scenario, e.g., by the AI market-place in the market-place scenario [1] or by the Cloud service distributing models to edge sites in the edge-caching scenario [27] described in Sect. 3.1. However, such a file can easily be tampered with, and does not provide a convenient way for the recipient of a model to validate the provenance information.

An alternate option is to use a trusted provenance data repository, e.g., a site like openprovenance.org, which provides provenance information, translation among provenance data, and tools for validating the provenance information. However, this solution requires all entities to trust the operator of the provenance site. In many business ecosystems, it is difficult to find an organization whose provenance information would be trusted by all involved parties – the groups providing training data, the ones providing trained models, those running validation tests of the models, etc.

An alternative approach to a central trusted system is to use a distributed system which can store provenance information without requiring a trusted central entity. Blockchain provides such an approach. A blockchain based approach provides a good solution to maintain provenance information that can be created, validated and cross-checked by a diverse set of entities. This approach is described in the next section.

## 4   Blockchain Solution for Provenance of Data and AI Models

Similar to the approaches described in [16] and [22], we leverage blockchain technology to provide the foundational layer capable of capturing immutable provenance in a distributed manner. However, our focus is not strictly on provenance of data alone, but instead we intend to model and capture provenance of the overall AI process. The goal is to provide an immutable provenance of how, and by which participants or organizations the models were created and trained, what data and compute capabilities were leveraged, etc. This in turn leads to a more verifiable and, therefore, a more trusted Artificial Intelligence. As mentioned in the previous section, we assume that there is no single organization that the participating entities fully trust. Instead, there is a need for a distributed system based on blockchain to provide a mechanisms for maintaining the provenance in a trusted way by a diverse set of entities.

In this section, we start by stating some key requirements, followed by a description of the design and implementation of a prototype system. Finally, we present an illustrative AI scenario. Specifically, we will use a well-known setting of federated learning in which several distributed participants (e.g., organizations or geographically distributed divisions of the same organization) jointly train a Machine Learning model leveraging their own data without actually sharing it. Although we illustrate the use of blockchain to instill trust in this setting, the presented capability and its design are generic and applicable to broad range of settings as described in the previous section.

## 4.1    Requirements of Blockchain for Trusted AI

In this section, we briefly discuss requirements that need to be satisfied in order to enable trusted AI via blockchain. Typically, trust comes into play when multiple parties are involved, as in federated learning [20] or, in general, any other collaborative learning framework. The ultimate goal in the collaborative learning setting is to share and reuse AI assets such as data and AI models. Oftentimes, parties involved may be reluctant to share data directly for privacy (e.g., in case where sensitive data is involved) or ownership reasons (ownership is lost as soon as the data is shared). Hence, the assets must be shared in a confidential fashion. An integral part of enabling trust is ensuring fairness in assigning value to assets based upon their contribution in model creation. As AI assets can be composed to create more complex assets, it is crucial to trace the ownership and provenance of different models, data and their relationships. Further, it is important to ensure that the entire AI process is auditable by an independent third party. Finally, our goal is to build a generic system that can support several different types of AI scenarios and different types of datasets. We elaborate on these key aspects needed to enable trust in AI processes.

1. **Reuse of models, AI assets:** As AI became one of the key and pervasive technologies, the need arose to reuse and share AI assets in a trusted manner. With the advent of AI, issues of model reuse, underlying trust and guarantees of ownership, origin, and the process of creation and tracking of use, have become important.
2. **Confidential sharing:** Unlike many other digital assets, AI assets are often created using sensitive, confidential and highly valuable data.

3. **Auditability, verification, assurance/attestation of results and the AI process:** This may apply to the final results (e.g., trained models) or to partial or intermediate results. For instance, in the case of long running or distributed computations, it may be required to provide auditability of which participant contributed towards what part of the computation and what was the outcome (ideally without the need to completely re-run the entire process).
4. **Provenance, traceability of ownership, usage:** Need to record and trace in an immutable and tamper-proof manner origin, ownership, use and the entire AI process across possibly complex provenance chains and AI pipelines.
5. **Fairness and bias:** This is becoming a critical requirement for any AI system. Blockchain can record, in an authoritative way, details of data used, types of data processing, and manipulations; and, in turn, enable fairness guarantees.

In addition to the above requirements, we also target the following design principles:

1. **Support for a variety of AI scenarios and workloads:** While our illustration scenario is based on federated learning, we target a broad range of AI settings including collaborative learning, transfer learning, long running learning/simulation/optimization processes, AI asset catalogs, marketplaces, etc.
2. **Support for a variety of organizational settings:** Here, we primarily discuss multi-organization set up, but the objective is to enable both inter or intra-organizational use cases.
3. **Different/varying granularity:** In some cases, it may be satisfactory to trace only the "end results" of the AI process (e.g., trained models), whereas in other situations fine granularity of the entire process needs to be traced (e.g., including relationships between data and models used or exchanged, operations applied, intermediate results, etc.)

### 4.2 Key Blockchain Constructs and Provenance Model

In this section, we describe the modeling constructs we use to represent the AI assets and the AI process on blockchain. As a principle, we do not tightly integrate the AI compute platforms with blockchain, neither do we try to bring some of the AI compute capabilities to blockchain itself. Instead, we treat blockchain as a mechanism that records important aspects of the AI process in an immutable and verifiable way. As another principle, we only record, on blockchain, elements of the process that are critical for the purposes of increasing trust as described in the requirements in the previous subsection. In particular, in most of the cases, we do not store large datasets on blockchain, since such data typically resides in dedicated storage or compute platforms, and typically there is no need to replicate the data on blockchain. Instead, in order to achieve verifiability, we store, on blockchain, only a reference to the AI asset, along with its unique cryptographic "fingerprint" computed using standard cryptographic hash functions. This way, we do not need to store large data objects on blockchain directly, but we still provide guarantees of data integrity and authenticity.

We now define the key blockchain constructs in our design. Broadly, there are the following classes of constructs involved in our blockchain schema: Participants, Datasets (or just Data, for short), Models, Operations, and Compute Pipelines (or Projects). Each AI process (say training of a particular model) is recorded on blockchain in the form of blockchain transactions, where each transaction is an instance of one of the classes described below.

- *Participant:* Participant instances represent the actual participating entities of the learning processes. Participants can be organizations or individuals with a unique identity on blockchain. Participants can play different roles, e.g., be data owners, providers of a learning service, model consumers, etc. Every instance of the other classes (data, model, etc.) is always associated with at least one participant (e.g., owner of the dataset, consumer of the model, etc.).
- *Dataset (or Data for short):* These constructs store the reference to the actual real dataset objects along with the digital crypto hash of the dataset. Additional metadata can be recorded as optional attributes.
- *Model:* This construct includes information about the model including who created it and how. It also stores a unique fingerprint (crypto hash) of the actual model. Optionally, the model parameters and hyper-parameters corresponding to the model, and additional metadata (e.g., accuracy) can be recorded as well.
- *Operation:* This construct represents any action that can be performed by a participant. There can be many types of operations, e.g., learning, transform, fuse, use, reuse, etc., operations corresponding to different functions, scripts or computations in typical AI compute platforms. Importantly, the operation construct captures the inputs and outputs to represent relationships between all other constructs. For example, a particular blockchain transaction, capturing a learning operation, can represent the actual training that has a particular dataset as one input, a model initialization as another input and a trained model as its output.
- *Compute Pipeline (or Project):* The compute pipeline construct is simply a container object that represents a group of other related objects. For example, a particular compute pipeline instance can represent a learning project in which multiple participants use several datasets to work towards creating a trained model.

The above constructs are meant to be rather generic to provide the modeling flexibility needed to capture a variety of use cases. They achieve the requirements defined in Sect. 4.1 by leveraging the inherent properties of blockchain, such as immutability, strong connection between participant identities and blockchain transactions, and by explicitly modeling important aspects of the AI process and the relationships among the objects.

Finally, we describe the provenance model used in this work. Similar to existing work in the area
of provenance [14, 22, 24], we use
directed acyclic graphs as the underlying structure to represent the provenance graph. The provenance graph is
an annotated directed acyclic graph
whose nodes can represent one of the
following constructs (defined above):

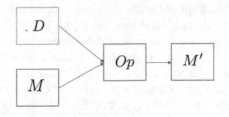

**Fig. 1.** Illustration of the provenance model

*Dataset, Operation* or *Model*. The directed arcs from node $A$ to node $B$ represents the relationship that $A$ is required in the creation of $B$. For illustration,
consider a simple scenario where we wish to record the fact that a dataset $D$ is
used by a training operation $Op$ to update a model $M$ to obtain another model
$M'$. Figure 1 shows how we capture this in our provenance model.

### 4.3   Illustration: Trusted Federated AI

In this section, we use federated learning, as an illustrative example, to demonstrate how the blockchain constructs (defined in Sect. 4.2) can be used to represent provenance in a typical AI process.

The basic setting of federated learning, as depicted in Fig. 2, is described in
the following. Multiple parties, referred to as learning agents, may possess their
own datasets. These datasets are private and cannot be shared with other participants. The goal is to create a model that is trained using these private datasets,
without naively combining them in their raw form. Instead of combining the
datasets, the learning agents are allowed to share their incremental models. A
system component, referred to as the fusion manager or fuser, is responsible for
combining the models created by individual learning agents.

Federated learning is an iterative learning algorithm, where each participant
trains and maintains a learning model. In each iteration, the participants internally train the model using their own private data, and upon completion, submit
their model parameters to the fusion manager. The fusion manager, in turn, fuses
the model parameters and sends the updated model back to the participants.

As Fig. 2 illustrates, each participant of this process runs its compute platform to train models locally, and each compute platform is connected to
blockchain (via API calls). During the computations, the agents record on
blockchain the log of their computations in the form of the blockchain constructs
defined in Sect. 4.2.

Figure 3, shows a subset of the provenance graph, for a single iteration of
the federated learning process involving participants Learner A, Learner B and
Fuser. Each box in Fig. 3 represents one blockchain transaction. As can be seen,
one iteration of the overall learning process is captured as an instance (transaction) of the Compute Pipeline container called Learning Project 1. In this case,
we chose to represent the provenance graph with a relatively fine granularity,
to capture transactions representing (a) the input data (instances $D_A$, $D_B$),

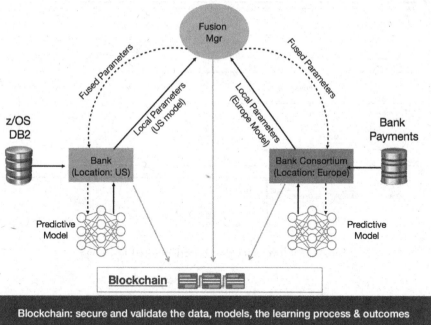

**Fig. 2.** Trusted federated learning: the basic setting

(b) final trained model (instance Trained Model), and (c) intermediate training operations (e.g., transactions $train_{A1}$, $train_{A2}$, etc.), fusion operations ($fuse_1$, $fuse_2$, etc.), and models (e.g., $M_{A1}$, $M_{A2}$, etc.). Importantly, the arrows in Fig. 3 represent the input/output relationships among the objects, which allows us to capture the complete provenance. Figure 3 also indicates that the final Trained Model produced in Learning Project 1 was further reused in Learning Project 2.

As mentioned in Sect. 3, provenance information needs to be tracked at different stages during the process of federated learning. Figure 4 shows an intermediary step during the process of training data in the federated learning process. During different iterations of the learning process, the information that is transferred by each of the parties is maintained and the relative increase in the fidelity of the model captured. The attributes of the training model at each site, the attributes of the training data that is provided, and the attributes of the fused model are all maintained in the blockchain to provide a trace of how the data was trained and the impact of each data set on the attributes of the fused model.

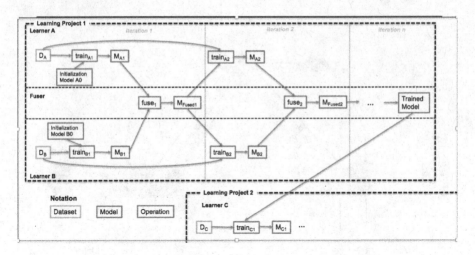

**Fig. 3.** A provenance graph for federated learning

## 4.4   Implementation

We have implemented a blockchain library that supports the constructs described in Sect. 4.2, thereby capturing the entire distributed AI training process: data, intermediate and final models, flow and dependencies, participants, operations and relevant metadata. Our design is independent of any specific ML/AI library, algorithms or model. While primarily implemented and tested in PyTorch, any other popular AI library, such as TensorFlow or IBM's Watson Studio/Data Science Experience (DSX), may be used. We have exposed our library as a set of REST or Python APIs. These APIs support immutable recording of the AI process, querying for traceability and audit, fair value attribution, etc.

We now provide a more detailed description of the key implemented blockchain constructs following the conceptual design defined in Sect. 4.2. Figure 5 shows our design in the form of a class diagram which are going to explain in the context of federated learning.

- PARTICIPANT: As mentioned before, this class defines the various entities involved in a learning task. We recall that in the federated learning setting there are two primary participants, namely *learner* and *fuser* (or *fusion manager*). Accordingly, in our design, we have two participant classes derived from the base PARTICIPANT class, namely LEARNER and FUSER (See Fig. 5).
- DATASET: This class defines the private datasets owned by different learners. Since typical datasets involved in the training processes are massive, we only store their cryptographic signatures on the blockchain.
- OPERATION: This class captures different actions performed by the learners and the fuser. Specifically, it captures the model updates performed by the learners over their respective datasets and the fusion operation performed by

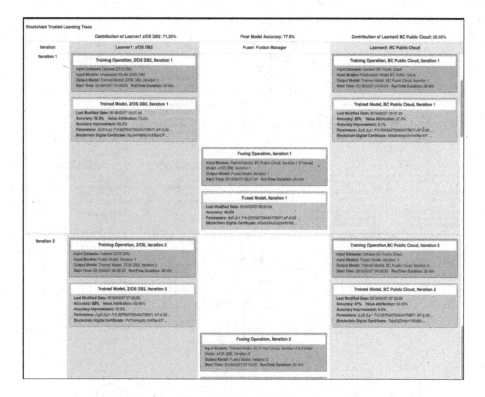

**Fig. 4.** Trace of provenance data during training

the fuser. In our design, we have two classes derived from the base class OPER-ATION, i.e., LEARNINGOPERATION and FUSINGOPERATION. The LEARNING-OPERATION contains, as its members, the model (or its signature) created by the fuser in the previous iteration, its private datasets, and the updated model (or its signature). Among the members of the FUSINGOPERATION are the models created by different learners and the resulting fused model.

- MODEL: This class defines the various attributes of models created by different participants over various iterations. For the purpose of attributing value to different participants, it may optionally contain other meta information such as accuracy improvements achieved, etc.
- LEARNINGPROJECT: As mentioned before, this class represents the learning task. As evident from the Fig. 5, all other constructs store a reference to the LEARNINGPROJECT class to accurately capture the provenance graph.

Now we describe the various APIs that manipulate the objects corresponding to the above constructs.

- LAUNCHLEARNINGPROJECT: This API call records, on blockchain, the start of a learning task. It creates an object of the class LEARNINGPROJECT and stores it on the blockchain.

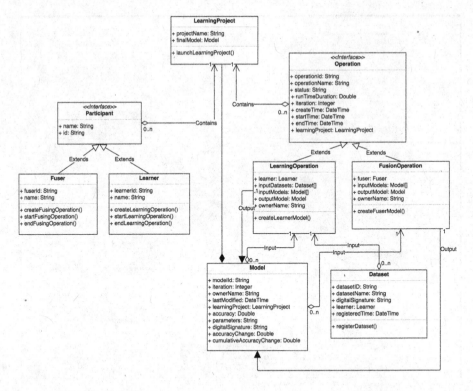

**Fig. 5.** Class diagram with key constructs of the blockchain library

- REGISTERDATASET: This API call registers various learner datasets, or their signatures, on the blockchain by creating and storing an object of type DATASET.
- CREATEOPERATION: The purpose of this API call is to create and record an object of type OPERATION. Depending on the participant involved, there are two possible invocations, namely:
  - CREATELEARNINGOPERATION, that initializes an object of LEARNING-OPERATION. The payload for this API should include the learner identification, current iteration, previous model from the fuser and learner dataset (or its signature).
  - CREATEFUSINGOPERATION, that initializes an instance of FUSINGOPER-ATION. The inputs to be supplied are fuser identification, current iteration, and updated models from different learners from the previous iteration.
- STARTOPERATION: This API can be used to record the actual start of an operation.
- ENDOPERATION: This API can be used to record the end of an operation. It takes in the final output model from different participants and internally calls the CREATEMODEL API to generate an object of type MODEL. Finally, it updates the corresponding OPERATION objects with the output model. Again,

depending on the participant, there are two types of invocations possible: ENDLEARNINGOPERATION and ENDFUSINGOPERATION.

- CREATEMODEL: This can either be used internally by the ENDOPERATION API or as a standalone call to create a MODEL object. It takes, as input, the parameters of the model and, optionally, the accuracy achieved on a test dataset. If the accuracy is provided, it computes, and stores, the improvement in accuracy from the previous iteration.

In conclusion, while our blockchain library is primarily intended for distributed/collaborative learning settings, it can also be used to trace a non-distributed learning process. However, in the non-distributed settings, it may be sufficient to record only input data and the final model. On the other hand, in the distributed case it is crucial to record various snapshots, from the perspective of different participants, in order to enable trust in the learning process.

## 5 Conclusion

In this chapter, we present our vision to build a generic blockchain library to enable trust in distributed AI applications and processes. We discuss one such use case of a collaborative AI application, namely federated learning, that has become popular recently. Our future work will be focused on supporting diverse AI applications. In parallel, we will work towards natively supporting AI on blockchain, tightly coupled with our notions of trust and auditability.

These capabilities will provide the trust and fairness characteristics needed to encourage the use of AI components in distributed, collaborative, autonomous systems. Along with generative policies and the other mechanisms described in the chapters of this book, this work is meant to contribute to the creation of a base of fundamental technologies to support the advancement of autonomic computing.

## References

1. Mehri, V.A., Tutschku, K.: Flexible privacy and high trust in the next generation internet-the use case of a cloud-based marketplace for AI. In: Swedish National Computer Networking Workshop (2017)
2. Athalye, A., Sutskever, I.: Synthesizing robust adversarial examples. arXiv preprint arXiv:1707.07397 (2017)
3. Baracaldo, N., Chen, B., Ludwig, H., Safavi, J.A.: Mitigating poisoning attacks on machine learning models: a data provenance based approach. In: Proceedings of the 10th ACM Workshop on Artificial Intelligence and Security, pp. 103–110. ACM (2017)
4. Barreno, M., Nelson, B., Sears, R., Joseph, A.D., Tygar, J.D.: Can machine learning be secure? In: Proceedings of the 2006 ACM Symposium on Information, Computer and Communications Security, pp. 16–25. ACM (2006)
5. Biggio, B., Didaci, L., Fumera, G., Roli, F.: Poisoning attacks to compromise face templates. In: 2013 International Conference on Biometrics (ICB), pp. 1–7. IEEE (2013)

6. Biggio, B., Fumera, G., Roli, F.: Security evaluation of pattern classifiers under attack. IEEE Trans. Knowl. Data Eng. **26**(4), 984–996 (2014)

7. Bray, T., Paoli, J., Sperberg-McQueen, C.M., Maler, E., Yergeau, F.: Extensible markup language (XML). World Wide Web J. **2**(4), 27–66 (1997)

8. Buneman, P., Khanna, S., Wang-Chiew, T.: Why and where: a characterization of data provenance. In: Van den Bussche, J., Vianu, V. (eds.) ICDT 2001. LNCS, vol. 1973, pp. 316–330. Springer, Heidelberg (2001). https://doi.org/10.1007/3-540-44503-X_20

9. Calders, T., Kamiran, F.: Classification with no discrimination by preferential sampling. In: Proceedings of 19th Machine Learning Conference. Belgium and The Netherlands (2010)

10. Chen, A., Wu, Y., Haeberlen, A., Loo, B.T., Zhou, W.: Architecture, experiences, and the road ahead. In: CIDR, Data Provenance at Internet Scale (2017)

11. Cretu, G.F., Stavrou, A., Locasto, M.E., Stolfo, S.J., Keromytis, A.D.: Casting out demons: sanitizing training data for anomaly sensors. In: IEEE Symposium on Security and Privacy, SP 2008, pp. 81–95. IEEE (2008)

12. Fowler, M., Kobryn, C., Scott, K.: UML Distilled: A Brief Guide to the Standard Object Modeling Language. Addison-Wesley Professional, Boston (2004)

13. Huang, L., Joseph, A.D., Nelson, B., Rubinstein, B.I., Tygar, J.D.: Adversarial machine learning. In Proceedings of the 4th ACM Workshop on Security and Artificial Intelligence, pp. 43–58. ACM (2011)

14. Jabal, A.A., Bertino, E.: SimP: secure interoperable multi-granular provenance framework. In: 2016 IEEE 12th International Conference on e-Science (e-Science), pp. 270–275. IEEE (2016)

15. Li, B., Vorobeychik, Y.: Feature cross-substitution in adversarial classification. In: Advances in Neural Information Processing Systems, pp. 2087–2095 (2014)

16. Liang, X., Shetty, S., Tosh, D., Kamhoua, C., Kwiat, K., Njilla, L.: Provchain: a blockchain-based data provenance architecture in cloud environment with enhanced privacy and availability. In: Proceedings of the 17th IEEE/ACM International Symposium on Cluster, Cloud and Grid Computing, pp. 468–477. IEEE Press (2017)

17. Loo, B.T., et al.: Declarative networking: language, execution and optimization. In: Proceedings of the 2006 ACM SIGMOD International Conference on Management of Data, pp. 97–108. ACM (2006)

18. Ma, S., et al.: LAMP: data provenance for graph based machine learning algorithms through derivative computation. In Proceedings of the 2017 11th Joint Meeting on Foundations of Software Engineering, pp. 786–797. ACM (2017)

19. McDaniel, P.D., Butler, K.R.B., McLaughlin, S.E., Sion, R., Zadok, E., Winslett, M.: Towards a Secure and efficient system for end-to-end provenance. In: TaPP (2010)

20. McMahan, H.B., Moore, E., Ramage, D., Hampson, S., et al.: Communication-efficient learning of deep networks from decentralized data. arXiv preprint arXiv:1602.05629 (2016)

21. Pham, T., Solomon, L., Ciricionne, G., Henz, B.: Prevailing in a complex world: ARL's essential research area on AI & ML. NATO IST-160 (2018)

22. Ramachandran, A., Kantarcioglu, M.: SmartProvenance: a distributed, blockchain based dataprovenance system. In: Proceedings of the Eighth ACM Conference on Data and Application Security and Privacy, pp. 35–42. ACM (2018)

23. Satyanarayanan, M.: The emergence of edge computing. Computer **50**(1), 30–39 (2017)

24. Schelter, S., Böse, J.-H., Kirschnick, J., Klein, T., Seufert, S.: Automatically tracking metadata and provenance of machine learning experiments. In: Machine Learning Systems Workshop at NIPS (2017)
25. Verma, D., Cirincione, G., Pham, T., Ko, B.J.: Generation and management of training data for AI-based algorithms targeted at coalition operations. In Ground/Air Multisensor Interoperability, Integration, and Networking for Persistent ISR IX, vol. 10635, p. 106350U. International Society for Optics and Photonics (2018)
26. Verma, D., Julier, S., Cirincione, G.: Federated AI for building AI solutions across multiple agencies. arXiv preprint arXiv:1809.10036 (2018)
27. Verma, D.C., Bent, G.: Policy enabled caching for distributed AI. In: 2017 IEEE International Conference on Big Data (Big Data), pp. 3017–3023. IEEE (2017)
28. Woodruff, A., Stonebraker, M.: Supporting fine-grained data lineage in a database visualization environment. In: Proceedings of 13th International Conference on Data Engineering, pp. 91–102. IEEE (1997)
29. Wylot, M., Cudré-Mauroux, P., Hauswirth, M., Groth, P.: Storing, tracking, and querying provenance in linked data. IEEE Trans. Knowl. Data Eng. **29**(8), 1751–1764 (2017)
30. Xiao, H., Xiao, H., Eckert, C.: Adversarial label flips attack on support vector machines. In: ECAI, pp. 870–875 (2012)

# Secure Model Fusion for Distributed Learning Using Partial Homomorphic Encryption

Changchang Liu[✉], Supriyo Chakraborty, and Dinesh Verma

Distributed AI Department, IBM T J Watson Research Center,
Yorktown Heights, NY 10598, USA
Changchang.Liu33@ibm.com, {supriyo,dverma}@us.ibm.com

**Abstract.** Distributed learning has emerged as a useful tool for analyzing data stored in multiple geographic locations, especially when the distributed data sets are large and hard to move around, or the data owner is reluctant to put data into the Cloud due to privacy concerns. In distributed learning, only the locally computed models are uploaded to the fusion server, which however may still cause privacy issues since the fusion server could implement various inference attacks from its observations. To address this problem, we propose a secure distributed learning system that aims to utilize the *additive* property of partial homomorphic encryption to prevent direct exposure of the computed models to the fusion server. Furthermore, we propose two optimization mechanisms for applying partial homomorphic encryption to model parameters in order to improve the overall efficiency. Through experimental analysis, we demonstrate the effectiveness of our proposed mechanisms in practical distributed learning systems. Furthermore, we analyze the relationship between the computational time in the training process and several important system parameters, which can serve as a useful guide for selecting proper parameters for balancing the trade-off among model accuracy, model security and system overhead.

## 1 Introduction

Today, massive amounts of data are distributed across multiple geographic locations. To mine the data for useful analytics, the commonly used approach is to collect all the data in a centralized location and train an AI model on the aggregated data. However, there are many situations where this approach may not be feasible. In particular, sharing data across national or organizational boundaries may not always be permitted.

In order to address these situations, approaches for federated learning [1–5] have been proposed. Federated learning enables models to be built at different locations and then brought together by a fusion operation to create a single model that captures the patterns present at all the different locations. Many flavors of federated learning can be used, depending on the nature of the relationship that exists between different sites hosting the distributed data.

© Springer Nature Switzerland AG 2019
S. Calo et al. (Eds.): PADG 2018, LNCS 11550, pp. 154–179, 2019.
https://doi.org/10.1007/978-3-030-17277-0_9

Federated learning shares some methodologies with distributed machine learning [6–8] which aims to handle complicated models computed over big training datasets. However, the main difference is that federated learning needs to deal with a system where different participating sites are not able to communicate over a high bandwidth, low latency and high reliability network, a typical situation when going across multiple organizations.

Since federated learning typically deals with the training of models across multiple organizations, its basic approach is to share model parameters instead of sharing the training data itself. By migrating models instead of migrating data for training, it can integrate the artificial intelligence insights from data found in different systems and locations.

While existing approaches for federated learning tend to focus on performance metrics such as the time required to train a model optimally over bandwidth-constrained networks [4] or achieving model accuracy metrics comparable to centralized learning [1,5], a key aspect of federated learning across multiple organizations is that of trust. Current work assumes complete trust among different sites, and that each site is comfortable sharing model parameters with each other. However, the organizations involved may not completely trust each other.

Trust and regulatory compliance is one of the motivating drivers for federated learning. By sharing only model parameters instead of training data, the privacy of individual data elements can be protected. However, even when local training data is not directly exposed to build models, the models and even the local training data are still susceptible to various inference attacks [9,10]. This leads to a need to protect and encrypt model parameters when building models. In this paper, we present an approach for federated learning which enables model building without exchanging model parameters in the clear.

Our approach uses partial homomorphic encryption to enable federated learning in an environment where model movement outside of the location can not be done in the clear. We also provide two optimization mechanisms to mitigate the performance hit that arises in distributed applications with the use of encryption schemes by: (1) constructing encryption/decryption lookup tables based on model parameter quantization; and, (2) leveraging batch encryption.

By enabling distributed fusion in this manner, we are increasing the autonomy of the distributed systems. Specifically, we are providing schemes that can address some of the privacy and data protection constraints that arise due to organizational policies, and provide a mechanism to enable learning in the presence of such restrictive policies.

We begin this paper with a discussion of the high-level federated learning architecture and the use-cases that motivate the use of partial homomorphic encryption. This is followed by a description of our approach, a discussion of issues associated with the performance aspects of using encryption for federated learning, followed by evaluation of some performance optimization mechanisms. We also provide an overview of related work, and conclude with a discussion of the limitations of our technique and open areas of investigation.

## 2   Architecture and Use Cases

We assume that federated learning happens in the environment shown in Fig. 1. There are multiple sites, each site with its share of training data, and an ability to create a neural network model from such data. Each site has an additional component, the federation agent, which is responsible for working with a federation server that performs model fusion. The federation agent takes the model resulting from the training process, provides it to the federation server, retrieves the fused model from the federation server, and interfaces with the learning mechanism present locally.

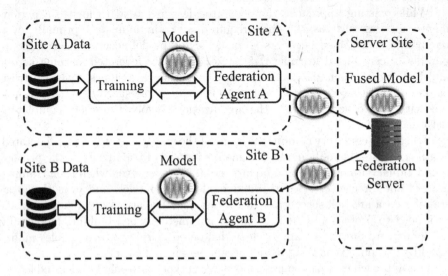

**Fig. 1.** Machine learning with data from partners

When the federation agents and federation server trust each other, the approach for federated learning is addressed by the algorithms and papers published previously [1–5]. Those algorithms exchange model parameters with each other in the clear to attain the goal of a common model trained over all of the data. However, there are many situations where the agents and the server may be running at sites which may not completely trust each other. In those cases, the model parameters can not be shared in the clear. In the following subsections, we discuss some of the common use-cases in which the exchange of model parameters may be problematic.

Depending on the trust relationship among different agents and servers, the system may be divided into one or more trust zones. Entities belonging to the same trust zone can share data and/or model parameters with each other. However, entities belonging to different trust zones should not get access to the raw data or the model parameters in the clear when the model parameters deal with the results of training performed on data in another trust zone.

## 2.1   Cloud Based Federation

One case of federated learning consists of the situation where the Federation Server is run and operated as a cloud-hosted service, while the data is present within different branches of a company. As an example, a bank may have its local data warehouses at three different locations, and would like to build a common AI model across the three data warehouses. It can leverage the federation server hosted at a cloud provider site, but may not be willing or able to send either the local data or the model parameters resulting from training a local model to the federation server in the cloud.

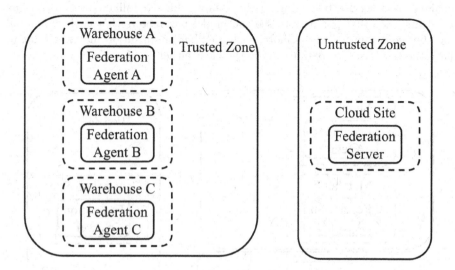

**Fig. 2.** Cloud based federation scenario

The situation is shown in Fig. 2. The trust relationship among the different federation agents, which operate in environments belonging to the same organization, is that of complete trust. However, there is limited trust between the agents and the federation server. The agents can not trust the federation server with the model parameters that are being sent to it.

In this case, one can argue that the federation server should be set up in a trust zone which can be trusted by the agents, e.g., a private Federation Server owned by the financial company. However, setting up a private service is a slow and time-consuming process, whereas using the ready-made services on an active already-running federation service in the cloud could accelerate the task of model building substantially.

This challenge of cloud based federation can arise in any industry which is subject to strict regulatory restrictions, including but not limited to financial companies, health-care companies, public sector companies, and military organizations.

## 2.2  Consortium and Alliances

In many industries, consortia are formed to enable sharing of knowledge and information among different organizations. As an example, it is not uncommon for health-care organizations of different countries to form an alliance to share information about health-care data with each other. Several joint organizations have been formed to share information about agriculture, social issues, and demographics among member organizations. While some information can be shared with each other, portions of the data may contain sensitive details which different consortia members may not feel comfortable sharing with each other. In these cases, sharing of models among the alliance members may be permitted, or even enabled by a service belonging to the alliance, but the alliance members may not want the other partners to see the model parameters that each individual member contributes. Furthermore, each member organization may not want to have the server see its parameters in the clear either.

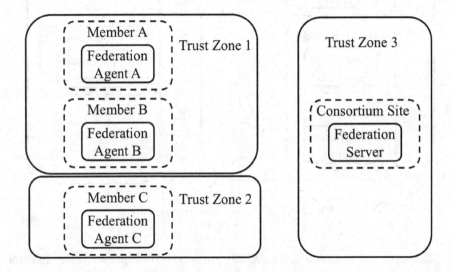

**Fig. 3.** Consortium scenario

In this scenario, each of the alliance members is in its own separate trust zone. Some of the alliance members may trust each other, but not all members are trusted equally. Such a trust zone relationship is shown in Fig. 3, where two of the agents belong to the same trust zone, while a third agent and the federation server belong to separate trust zones.

## 2.3  Military Coalitions

Modern military operations are frequently conducted within coalitions, where more than one country joins forces to conduct missions in a collaborative manner. Such coalition operations are a common occurrence in peace-keeping, where multiple countries work together to maintain peace in a region subject to conflict. They are also used for humanitarian operations in cases of natural disasters.

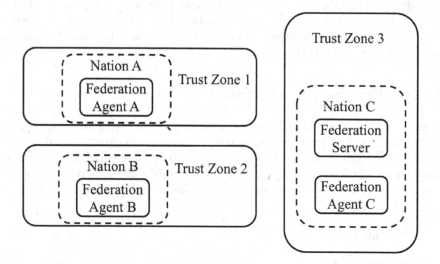

**Fig. 4.** Military coalition scenario

As coalitions work together, almost every member nation collects data from its operations. Such data may consist of video footage from surveillance, audio recordings and seismic readings from sensors, or tabular data that is maintained manually by the personnel involved in the joint effort. Much of this data can be shared among coalition members to improve their operations. As an example, the video footage of insurgents collected by the member nations can be shared to improve the AI models used to detect insurgency and to alert the peace-keepers.

Coalition members may not be able to share raw data, but may be able to share model parameters with each other. One specific case in which that may arise in shown in Fig. 4, where one of the coalition members is training its model but using the information available from all of the coalition partners. Each coalition partner would be willing to share the models, but not if the model parameters are sent in the clear. The trust zone for federation server includes the federation agent that belongs to the same nation, but each of the other agents are in their own trust zones.

A situation analogous to coalition operations can also arise in other emergency situations where different government agencies are cooperating together in any joint operation, e.g., reacting to a natural disaster, or planning for a special event. Different types of regulations may prevent complete sharing of raw data or unprotected model parameters among the agencies, but they would be able to train models and share the models with each other, especially if the model parameters can be encrypted during the fusion process.

We assume that in each of the above scenarios, the model parameters cannot be shared in the clear among entities that are not in the same trust zone. Thus, two federation agents in different trust zones should not be able to see the individual model parameters that are trained from any of the agents in the other trust zones. If the federation agent and the federation server are in different trust zones, the federation server should not be able to see the model parameters provided by the federation agent.

## 3   Our Proposed Mechanism

Although there are many different methods to perform distributed learning, we present our method for secure fusion in terms of a synchronized online approach described in papers such as [1] and [4]. While these form only one of the many flavors of distributed learning that are possible, as enumerated in [3], the approach proposed in this paper can be extended to other flavors as well.

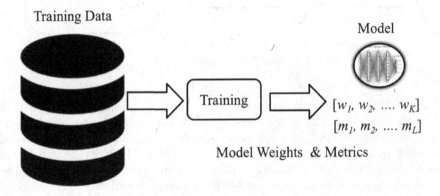

**Fig. 5.** Abstract representation of machine learning

We focus on the task of training a neural network for classification to illustrate our approach to distributed learning. The typical process of supervised machine learning for a neural network takes as an input training data, and tries to determine the weights on the neural network which can best estimate the patterns that are present within the training data. Although there are many different types of machine learning algorithms, and many different types of neural networks with different interconnections among different nodes, we can model the machine learning process as a black box which takes as an input the training data, and outputs a list of numeric weights which best represent the function/pattern present in the training data. The simplified model of training the machine learning model is shown in Fig. 5. The training process produces some $K$ weights $[w_1, w_2, \ldots w_K]$ from the input data. Additionally, it might also produce some $L$ metrics $[m_1, m_2, \ldots m_L]$ which may represent attributes such as the

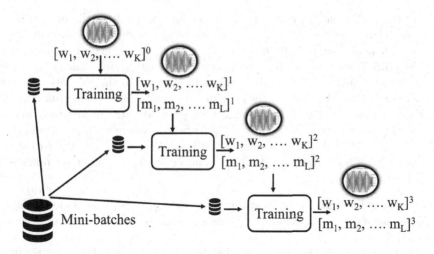

**Fig. 6.** Machine learning with mini-batches

accuracy of the model, the loss metric associated with the training process, or other metrics such as the count of the number of samples in the training data.

In neural network training, the training process usually takes the training data and divides it into several mini-batches as illustrated in Fig. 6. The big data set shown in Fig. 6 on the lower left side is divided into multiple smaller data sets, or mini-batches. The machine learning process is usually initiated with a random set of weights, and the error in prediction over the mini-batch estimated using a network with the specified weights. The error is then used to determine how to adjust the weights to come up with a new set of weights that can reduce this error. The process is then repeated with the next mini-batch. These cycles are repeated until all the data is examined one or more times, and the weights eventually converge. This mechanism is leveraged during the federated learning process.

## 3.1 Federated Learning Model

We first present the approach for federated learning described in [1,2] and [4], which all follow the mini-batch oriented process outlined in Fig. 6. In federated learning, the approach is to have each of the different sites start with a neural network with the same set of weights that are initialized randomly. The Federation Server may provide the agents with the initial set of weights.

Each mini-batch training step at each agent is modified somewhat. Once the agent finishes calculating the new weights over a mini-batch, it sends these new weights and associated metrics to the federation server. The federation server then computes a function over these weights. The function could be an average across the different weights provided by the agents, or it could be a weighted average where different priorities are given to different sites, and the priorities are used as coefficients to compute the weighted average (i.e., the priorities are used as weights for averaging). We use the term priority to reduce confusion with the elements being sent which are the weights on the neural network.

The process is shown in Fig. 7 with three participating sites. Each of the sites computes its weights and metrics locally and sends it to the federation server. The federation server combines the weights, and sends the resulting fused model back to each of the sites. The sites can then proceed with the training process for the next mini-batch. We consider a distributed system with $N$ agents, each with access to a local dataset consisting of labeled samples, i.e., the $i$-th agent has access to a local data set $d_i$. The pseudo-code for the training process is given below:

- 1: Each agent contacts the fusion server to get hyper-parameters for training. Note that each agent will train the same type of model (such as a neural network).
- 2: Each agent trains its model on a local mini-batch of the data. For instance, each model can be characterized by a weight vector.
- 3: Each agent sends the weights to the fusion server, which computes a function of the weight values provided by the agents. This function could be an average of the values supplied by the agents. In other cases, agents may be given different priorities in the computation of the average. If agent $i$ has a priority $p_i$, the function could be $\hat{w} = \sum_i p_i w_i$.
- The steps 2 through 3 are repeated until convergence.

In some cases, the function $f$ shown in Fig. 7 would be simple averaging, while in other cases it may be averaging with priorities at the end of each mini-batch. In some other cases, e.g., using flavor 2 of federated learning as described in [3], the function $f$ would be the identity function, and the federation server sends the results of the function computation back to the participating nodes using a random sequence.

Our main challenge is to enable the federation server to continue to perform these functions while not being able to see the model parameters in the clear. The agents at each site would be sending the model parameters to the federation server after encryption.

## 3.2   Secure Model Fusion

It has been shown [1,4] that the above process leads to the same model at the fused location as would be produced by using all the data from the distributed sites to train a model at a single site, for loss functions that are additive, which are the most common types of loss functions that are used. However, this federated learning mechanism still faces the challenge of revealing the weights of the model to the federation server which may not be trusted.

To counter this situation, we can use fully homomorphic encryption or FHE [11] to completely perform the fusion for the encrypted local models at the fusion server. However, FHE causes a significant degradation in performance, with each

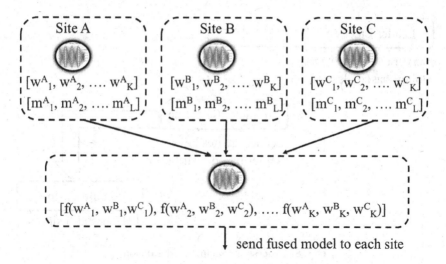

**Fig. 7.** Federated learning synchronization step

operation running several orders of magnitude slower than the unencrypted operation, which makes its use in a real-world situation difficult. Instead of FHE, we will use partial homomorphic encryption or PHE to only send encrypted parameters for fusion to the model fusion server.

Since any PHE operation can only perform one of the mathematical operations, multiplication or addition, on encrypted information and still preserve the homomorphy, we will need to restructure the operations at the agents and the federation server so that they only use one type of operation. Each of the local sites performs the other operation needed for the fusion process, with the fusion server helping with the coordination aspects. We can use any PHE mechanism (such as Paillier [12] and El Gamal [13]) for encryption, each of which are homomorphic with respect to addition.

In order for PHE operations to work properly, each of the agents ought to be using the same parameters. Thus, a key generation and parameter exchange process needs to be in place for the agents to use consistent keys. The shared keys cannot be created by the federation server, since it can possibly use the knowledge of the key to decrypt the model parameters. One of the agents will have to take over the task of generating the shared keys and ensuring that it reaches the other agents in the system. We call this agent the leader agent.

In order to select the leader, a distributed leader election protocol [14] can be followed. However, distributed leader election protocols are complex, and it will be easier to use a client-server centric approach for electing the leader. This simplified leader election can be enabled by the federation server.

The resulting mechanism follows a three stage process as shown in Fig. 8. In the first stage, the federation server acts as the central location where the federation agents can register and indicate their presence along with their attributes. A set of policies are used by the federation server to determine one of the agents as

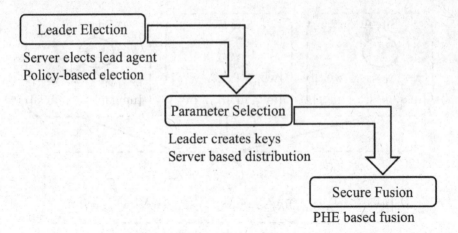

**Fig. 8.** Process for secure model fusion

the leader. While the federation server and the federation agents are in different trust zones, each of them can check whether the federation server had done the selection in accordance with the specified policies. Using a centralized federation server for this election would be more efficient than a distributed leader election process among the different agents.

In the second stage, the elected leader selects the common keys that can be used for partial homomorphic encryption. These keys are shared securely among all the agents using public key cryptography. The server can assist in the dissemination of the keys but never gets to see the keys itself. In the third stage, the different agents work together with the federation server using the commonly selected keys for partial homomorphic encryption.

Looking at the process in more detail, the agents all register with the fusion server in the first stage. Each agent generates a public/private pair of keys, with agent $i$ creating a pair $(Pk_i, Sk_i)$ for secure communication. The agent then provides its public key/certificate to the fusion server. The fusion server can send the public keys to any agents that join the fusion session. These public keys are used to establish secure communication between the agents and the fusion server, and for agents to communicate with each other securely.

The fusion server keeps track of the fusion session (i.e., counts the number of agents in the fusion process, keeps track of their public keys) and it also selects one of the agents as the leader for the fusion process. Based on the set of policies provided to the federation server, the elected leader could be the first agent that joined a federation session, or it could be the agent with the best possible computational resources, or the agent with the maximum amount of data.

In the second stage, the leader agent selects the hyper-parameters for the federated model learning. It uses the public key of other agents to send this information securely to each of the agents via the fusion server. It also selects

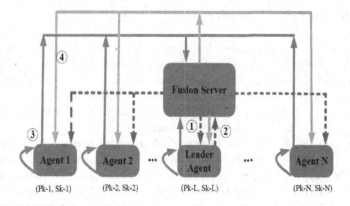

**Fig. 9.** Information exchange in secure model fusion

the type of the PHE algorithm to be used, and the parameters required for it. This information is distributed securely to other agents via the fusion server.

During each step of the training process, the agents use the same homomorphic encryption algorithm and the same parameters to encrypt the weights before sending them over to the fusion server. If required, each agent would locally compute the product of its priority $p_i$ and each of the entries in the model weight vector $w_i = [w_{i1}, w_{i2}, \cdots, w_{ik}]$. Each of these entries are then encrypted and sent to the fusion server.

The fusion server performs an element-wise multiplication on the weights of the encrypted model that it gets from each of the agents, and then sends the vector of this multiplication back to the agents. Each agent decrypts the results and then recreates the model parameters of the fused model system.

By using this strategy, the fusion server never sees the raw model parameters, and can utilize the additive homomorphic property of PHE to fuse the models together.

We show the whole process for secure model fusion in Fig. 9. In step 1, the public/private key registration is computed between each agent and the fusion server. The fusion server selects a leader agent for coordinating parameter setup between agents and fusion server. In step 2, the leader agent selects the hyper-parameters of the learning including the types and parameters of the PHE method and the priority for each agent, which are then distributed securely (encrypted with each agent's public key) to each participating agent by the fusion server. In step 3, each agent computes its local model and sends the encrypted local model (with priorities) to the fusion server. In step 4, the fusion server performs multiplication over the encrypted models and sends the encrypted model back to each participating agent. The process from Step 3 to Step 4 would repeat until convergence.

## 4    Performance Considerations

While the accuracy of federated learning is comparable to that of centralized learning, the use of partial homomorphic encryption raises concerns about the performance of the system. One specific concern is the increase in the training time that the system would incur. This increase in the training time depends on the relative ratio of the time it takes to encrypt the weights of the model, versus the time it takes for the unencrypted training.

Figure 10 illustrates the time-line by which federated learning happens. Each of the agents trains a pre-negotiated neural network over a mini-batch of the data that it has. After each mini-batch, the different sites exchange information with each other for synchronization and to average the weights that they have computed. After this synchronization, they move on to the next mini-batch of training data.

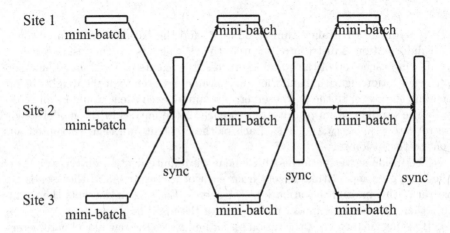

**Fig. 10.** Steps in federated learning

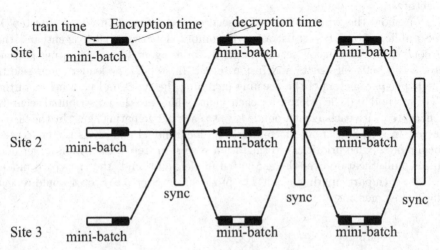

**Fig. 11.** Steps in secure federated learning

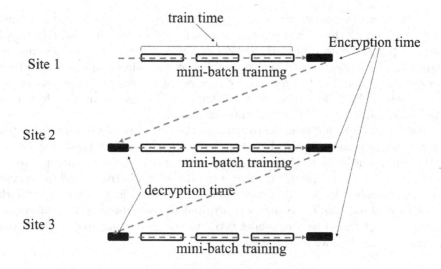

**Fig. 12.** Steps in secure federated learning using model movement approach

When PHE is employed, an encryption of the weights is done prior to the synchronization. This adds an additional overhead. The process is illustrated in Fig. 11, and the encryption time is shown as a dark shaded area after the white training period. After the synchronization happens, each site receives the fused model and has to decrypt the weights before proceeding to training on the next mini-batch. This results in an increase in the overall time taken for the model to execute.

The degradation in performance depends on the ratio of the time it takes to train on a mini-batch compared to the time it takes to encrypt the parameters and decrypt them on receipt. This ratio depends on several factors, the size of the mini-batch, the number of parameters in the model, and the network synchronization latency. The training time increases according to the ratio, with the network synchronization time remaining unchanged. A larger network synchronization time mitigates against the increase caused by the encryption.

There are several flavors of federated learning, and the overhead of partial homomorphic encryption would be different depending on the flavor used. In addition to the synchronized model for federated learning, another flavor can be used in which the training is done over all the mini-batches [3], and the model moved over to another site once the training is done. The encryption overhead in this case is negligible compared to the time taken to train the model at each site, and it results in very little overhead. This process with encryption added in is shown in Fig. 12. The dashed gray line in the figure shows how the training happens over the mini-batches distributed over different sites, interspersed with the encryption of the parameters and the decryption at the next site. The encryption step happens after the training finishes at each site, while the decryption step happens at the beginning of the training of each site.

With model migration, the homomorphic encryption needs to be performed only once after all the data at any site has been used for training the model, and the parameters are decrypted at the next site after it is moved there. In another variation, the models are trained in parallel at each site, and the weights are averaged together after the models are received at the federation server. When trained for multiple such rounds, this approach also results in a performance that is comparable to that of the centralized model.

We can create a simple model to compare the performance of secure federated learning to the standard model based on the steps shown in Fig. 11. If we define $T_l$ as the time spent in the machine learning process at a site between encryptions, $E$ as the time to encrypt a single number using the PHE algorithm, and to decrypt the same number back, $W$ as the number of weights in the neural network being trained on, and $T_n$ as the time involved in the network synchronization, the amount of time a secure model takes to complete compared to federated learning in the clear would equal

$$(T_l + E \cdot W + T_n)/(T_l + T_n),$$

which is equal to

$$1 + E \cdot W/(T_l + T_n).$$

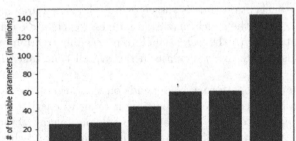

**Fig. 13.** The number of parameters for 6 models (ResNet-50, Inception-v3, ResNet-101, ResNet-151, AlexNet, VGG-19).

The amount of overhead incurred depends on the number of parameters that are included in the neural network model. For models built on relational data, which usually consists of less than 100 weights, the overhead may be relatively minor. An increase in the size of the mini-batches will result in improving the overall performance.

On the other hand, in the domain of image classification, where convolutional neural networks can easily have thousands of weights, the overhead may be substantially higher. Figure 13 shows the number of parameters for 6 popular

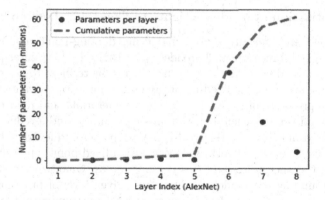

**Fig. 14.** The number of trainable parameters per layer of the AlexNet model.

models for image processing (ResNet-50, Inception-v3, ResNet-101, ResNet-151, AlexNet, and VGG-19). Figure 14 shows the number of trainable parameters per layer of the AlexNet model. From both figures, we know that the models for image classification are usually associated with large numbers of weights, thus making the element-wise encryption/decryption time-consuming. If we need to use secure federated learning with images, we need to develop techniques that can reduce the overhead of PHE encryption.

In the next couple of sections, we discuss some of the techniques that can reduce the overhead to make the scheme practical for networks with large numbers of weights.

## 5 Optimization for Practical Realization of Secure Distributed Systems

Depending on the number of weights in the neural network model (e.g., a multilayer network with dense connections will have more weights), the computation time taken for encrypting and decrypting the weights can dominate the training time of the secure federated learning system. To reduce the overall training time for large models, we propose two optimization strategies representing different trade-off regimes between model accuracy and encryption/decryption speed. The first strategy is *quantization of model weights*. By limiting the precision of model weights, we can construct two lookup tables (for encryption and decryption respectively) of the pre-computed encryption/decryption pairs for each possible model weight. In the training process, we encrypt each locally computed model weight by looking up its encrypted value in the encryption table. The fused model weights securely computed by the server can be similarly decrypted by each agent by use of the decryption table. The second strategy is *batch encryption/decryption of model weights*, i.e., implementing encryption/decryption for a series of model weights by batching them together. Next, we discuss these two optimization strategies in detail and evaluate their effectiveness using experiments.

## 5.1    Quantization of Model Weights to Construct Lookup Tables

Model weights are typically represented using floating-point numbers (which allows for greater precision and broader range). However, training algorithms used for deep neural networks have been shown to be resilient to the error introduced by using low precision fixed-point representations [15]. Advantages of using fixed point representations are faster hardware operations and reduced memory footprint. Disadvantages include loss in model accuracy, and a reduced range of the represented numbers. Motivated by [15], we propose to leverage the natural resilience of deep neural networks to low-precision fixed-point representations for speeding up the encryption and decryption process. Quantization can be performed by rounding the model weights. For a given level of precision, one can pre-compute the encryption/decryption pairs for every number in the range and construct the encryption/decryption lookup tables accordingly. During model training, constant time encryption and decryption can be performed using the look-up tables.

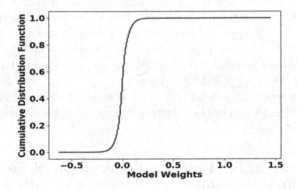

**Fig. 15.** CDF of model parameters in the training process.

**Experimental Setup:** We conduct experiments to validate the effectiveness of this optimization mechanism. In our experiments, we consider a scenario where 2 agents aim to train a neural network for digit recognition using the MNIST dataset [16], which has 60,000 training data elements and 10,000 testing data elements. The training dataset is randomly distributed among the two agents and the size of each training sample is $28 \times 28$. We set the initial learning rate as 0.003 and the learning rate decay as 0.9, and aim to minimize the cross-entropy loss. Furthermore, we consider two models representing a complicated model and a simple model, respectively. The first model has one hidden layer with 784 neurons (Model I), i.e., fully connected network, and the second model also has one hidden layer with 20 neurons (Model II). In the optimization process, we quantize each model weight to a fixed level of precision (with a limited number of decimal places) and construct the lookup tables for the encryption/decryption pairs using the El Gamal algorithm [13]. Our experiments were conducted in the

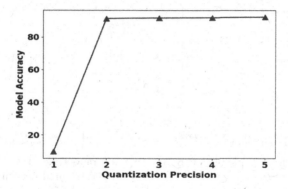

**Fig. 16.** Model accuracy under different precision of model weights ($x$-axis represents the number of decimal places in the model weights).

Python programming language on a PC with a 2.9 GHz Intel Core i7 processor and 16 GB of memory.

**Intuition of Constructing Lookup Tables:** We first show the cumulative distribution function (CDF) of the model weights in the distributed learning process in Fig. 15, where we set the size of each mini-batch as 50 and the number of epochs as 2 under Model I. From Fig. 15, we observe that most weights are concentrated within $[-0.25, 0.25]$, which provides the foundation for our optimization scheme through weight quantization.

**Influence of Model Weight Quantization:** To construct the lookup table, we aim to limit the precision of the model weights by rounding them to a fixed number of decimal places. In Fig. 16, we show the model accuracy under different precision levels (by rounding model weights to $1, 2, 3, 4, 5$ decimal places). From Fig. 16, we observe that rounding model weights to 2 decimal places is enough to maintain high model accuracy. Therefore, in our following experiments, we construct the encryption/decryption lookup table by pre-computing the encrypted values for all numbers $\in [-1, 1]$ with 2 decimal places.

**Trade-off Between Model Accuracy and Training Time with Varying Sizes of Mini-batch:** In Fig. 17, we show the performance of our secure distributed learning and the unencrypted distributed learning with varying sizes of mini-batches under Model I. Specifically, we set the number of epochs as 1 and quantize each model weight to 2 decimal places. Similarly, we show the trade-off between model accuracy and training time under Model II in Fig. 18. From Figs. 17 and 18, we have the following important observations: (1) a smaller size of mini-batch would result in a higher accuracy while at the cost of a longer training time; (2) comparing Fig. 17(a) and (b) (also Fig. 18(a) and (b)), we know that the quantization of model weights would degrade the model accuracy

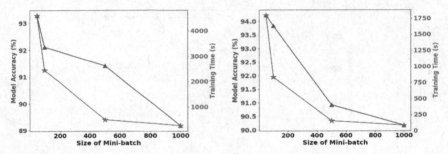

(a) Accuracy-Time Trade-off of Secure Distributed Learning

(b) Accuracy-Time Trade-off of Unencrypted Distributed Learning

**Fig. 17.** The trade-off between accuracy and training time of secure distributed learning and unencrypted distributed learning with varying sizes of mini-batch under Model I.

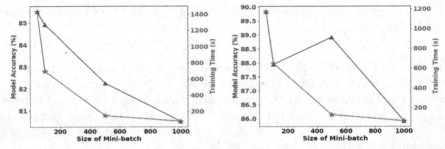

(a) Accuracy-Time Trade-off of Secure Distributed Learning

(b) Accuracy-Time Trade-off of Unencrypted Distributed Learning

**Fig. 18.** The trade-off between accuracy and training time of secure distributed learning and unencrypted distributed learning with varying sizes of mini-batch under Model II.

and the encryption/decryption implementation would increase the training time; (3) comparing Figs. 17 and 18, we know that different models have various influence on balancing model accuracy and training time. For instance, the accuracy degradation under Model II ($\approx$5%) is much more serious than that of Model I ($\approx$1%), indicating that the influence of model weight quantization has a more significant effect on this simpler model.

In Fig. 19(a) and (b), we show the accuracy degradation ratio and training time increase ratio of our secure distributed learning system compared to the unencrypted learning system for Model I and Model II, respectively. From Fig. 19(a), we observe that the encryption/decryption implementation incurs up to $3x$ overhead in training time while there is negligible accuracy degradation under Model I, validating the effectiveness of this optimization strategy. From Fig. 19(b), we observe that the additional training time under Model II is much lower than that of Model I.

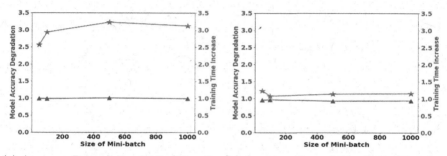

(a) Accuracy Degradation Ratio/Time Increase Ratio under Model I     (b) Accuracy Degradation Ratio/Time Increase Ratio under Model II

**Fig. 19.** Accuracy degradation ratio and training time increase ratio with varying sizes of mini-batch under Model I and Model II.

For a secure federated learning system, where the agent models are fused after every mini-batch, increasing the size of the mini-batch can reduce the number of encryption and decryption cycles improving training time (shown in Figs. 17(a) and 18(a)). However, a very large mini-batch size have been shown to adversely effect the training accuracy of the model. Therefore, depending on the training data and the model parameters, an appropriate mini-batch size needs to be selected. One can employ a separate search algorithm to obtain the right mini-batch size such as grid search or Bayesian optimization [17].

**Trade-off Between Model Accuracy and Training Time with Varying Number of Epochs:** The number of training epochs also has a direct effect on the training time and accuracy of the model. Figure 20 shows the trade-off between model accuracy and training time of our secure distributed learning system with different number of training epochs under Model I (the size of mini-batch is set to 500). From Fig. 20, We observe that the accuracy improves a bit with more epochs, while the computational time is almost linearly increasing with the number of epochs. A proper number of training epochs needs to be selected to obtain a desired trade-off between model accuracy and training time.

**Limitation:** Although this optimization mechanism has shown effectiveness in experiments (Fig. 19), there still exist scenarios where the construction of lookup tables may not be feasible. There is *randomness* in the PHE mechanisms and we exploit the same randomness in each training process (which could vary in the next training process). In this manner, the security of such encryption/decryption processes may not be that strong as scenarios where the randomness varies for each message. For instance, the same randomness in the training process (which allows for constructing the lookup table) may make the training model/data suffer from the *chosen ciphertext attack*. How to construct the lookup table while enhancing the security of the PHE mechanism (e.g., with arbitrary randomness per message) is an interesting problem for future research.

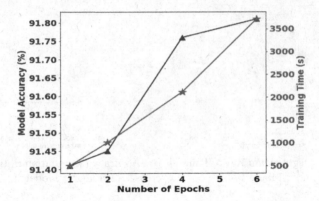

**Fig. 20.** The trade-off between accuracy and training time of secure distributed learning and unencrypted distributed learning with varying sizes of mini-batch under Model I.

## 5.2   Batch Encryption of Model Weights

Most existing PHE methods [12, 13] encrypt only a single scalar at a time. Therefore, an intuitive approach for secure model fusion by applying PHE to each element in the local model vector is computationally expensive. We propose another optimization strategy by leveraging batch encryption that can encrypt/decrypt a group of weights in one operation. Our batch encryption algorithm combines quantization and zero-padding techniques to enhance computational efficiency without degrading the learning accuracy. To adopt PHE to work with batches of model weights at one time, we need to concatenate multiple weights together prior to the encryption process and then separate them apart after the decryption process.

For a locally trained model $p_i\boldsymbol{w}_i$, we first quantize the precision for each element to only keep $r$ numbers of decimal places. Next, we pad zeros prior to the quantized element to keep its overall length as $l$. Then, we concatenate all the weights into one value and then apply PHE for one-time encryption of the weighted local model, i.e., $Enc_{batch}(p_i\boldsymbol{w}_i)$. The fusion server then applies multiplication over all the local models as $\prod_i Enc_{batch}(p_i\boldsymbol{w}_i)$. Next, the encrypted fused model is transmitted to each agent for decryption as $Dec(\prod_i Enc_{batch}(p_i\boldsymbol{w}_i))$, which would be divided into multiple $l$-digit scalars corresponding to each fused model weight. Based on the decrypted model weights, each agent will update its own local model and repeat the whole process until convergence.

**Advantage of Batch Encryption:** In this section, we aim to first show the advantage of our proposed batch encryption mechanism over the baseline element-wise approach. Specifically, we consider the Paillier method [12] and evaluate the computational time with respect to the size of model weights while fixing the size of key pairs as $KeySize = 2048$ in Fig. 21(a). We can observe that the computational time of the baseline approach increases linearly with the num-

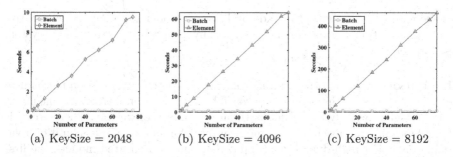

(a) KeySize = 2048        (b) KeySize = 4096        (c) KeySize = 8192

**Fig. 21.** Computational complexity of our proposed batch encryption and the baseline element-wise encryption

ber of the model weights. In comparison, our proposed batch encryption method ($r = 5$, $l = 8$) causes negligible additional computation with a larger number of model weights, which shows the superiority of this optimization strategy. For safely storing the integer and detecting integer overflow, we only consider to concatenate every 75 weights into one value as shown in Fig. 21(a). Therefore, we can conclude that this batch encryption mechanism can achieve up to $75x$ improvement in computational complexity over the baseline approach.

To evaluate the performance under different lengths of the key in Paillier, we show the results under $KeySize = 4096$ and $KeySize = 8192$ in Fig. 21(b) and (c), respectively. We observe that a longer key would incur more computations, which at the same time is more secure to defend against key inference attacks. In practice, it is important to select a proper key size for achieving balance between model security and training time.

**Training Time Estimation for Batch Encryption:** Next, we analyze the overall complexity for using this batch-encryption optimization mechanism. We assume that there are $N_{train}$ data in the model training process, $N_{agent}$ agents each with $N_{train}/N_{agent}$ training data, the number of model weights is $N_{model}$, the size of mini-batch is $S_{batch}$ and the number of epochs is $N_{epoch}$. Therefore, the gradient fusion process for each epoch is repeated for $N_{train}/N_{agent}/S_{batch}$ times. Then, we have the overall operations of implementing PHE encryption and decryption process as $N_{epoch} \times N_{model} \times N_{train}/N_{agent}/S_{batch}$ and $N_{epoch} \times N_{model} \times N_{train}/N_{agent}/S_{batch}/75$ for the baseline approach and the batch encryption approach, respectively. Denote the computational time for one-time encryption and decryption process in PHE frameworks under a given $KeySize$ as $T_{KeySize}$. Therefore, the additional computational time incurred by the baseline approach and our batch encryption approach can be computed as

$$\begin{aligned} T_{baseline} &= N_{epoch} \times N_{model} \times N_{train}/N_{agent}/S_{batch} \times T_{KeySize} \\ T_{batch} &= N_{epoch} \times N_{model} \times N_{train}/N_{agent}/S_{batch}/75 \times T_{KeySize} \end{aligned} \tag{1}$$

Since the $N_{epoch}, N_{model}, N_{train}, N_{agent}, S_{batch}$ would significantly affect the accuracy of the training model and $T_{KeySize}$ determines the security performance of the model, we know that a trade-off between model accuracy, model security and computational time can be achieved by properly selecting these system parameters.

**Limitation:** Although the training time for this batch optimization mechanism can decrease that of the baseline approach by $75x$, the overall training time might still be high especially for models with large numbers of weights. Therefore, this batch optimization mechanism is more suitable for shallow models built on relational data. For high-dimensional input data and complicated models, the first optimization mechanism using encryption/decryption lookup tables (Sect. 5.1) is likely to achieve better performance.

### 5.3 Discussion on Practical Implementation

- The first optimization strategy of leveraging encryption/decryption lookup tables can greatly reduce the time consumed in encrypting/decrypting each model parameter. For instance, our experiments demonstrate that the training time of secure distributed learning is only increased by $3x$ compared to that of unencrypted distributed learning, while the accuracy of the training model is not seriously degraded.
- The second optimization strategy of leveraging batch encryption can greatly reduce the training time without affecting model accuracy. Our experiments demonstrates that the batch-encryption optimization mechanism can achieve up to $75x$ improvement in training time over the baseline approach.
- In practice, we need to select a proper optimization method by comprehensively analyzing the training process and carefully selecting appropriate values of system parameters including the size of mini-batch, the number of training epochs, etc. These provide interesting opportunities for practical design of secure distributed learning systems.

## 6 Related Work and Threat Model

In this section, we first briefly discuss the frameworks of distributed learning and partial homomorphic encryption, as well as related works regarding these two topics. Then, we describe the threat model considered in our work.

### 6.1 Distribution Learning

The proliferation of big data has boosted the development of distributed machine learning [1,2,4–8]. Distributed machine learning aggregate the computational capability of multiple agents to achieve accurate model training performance. Specifically, each agent trains a learning model locally which is then transmitted to the central server for aggregation, and this process is repeated at each training step. Within distributed machine learning, Federated learning [1,2] aims to enable a collaborative learning among different agents using their local training data without the need to store user data in the cloud. Therefore, the models can be learnt from each other without exposing private data sources.

## 6.2  Partial Homomorphic Encryption

Homomorphic encryption scheme enables computation (addition and multiplication) in the encrypted domain. Fully homomorphic encryption (FHE) [11] is capable of encrypting a value that can be added and multiplied by another encrypted value. Partially homomorphic encryption (PHE) [12,13], on the other hand, can only perform either addition or multiplication. The Paillier cryptosystem [12] is one of the most popular PHE mechanism which utilizes public key encryption scheme while preserving the *additive* property. Therefore, the product of two ciphertexts will decrypt to the sum of their corresponding plaintexts, i.e., $Dec(Enc(m_1) \times Enc(m_2)) = m_1 + m_2$ for any two plaintexts $m_1, m_2$. Both FHE and PHE can be applied in the distributed learning setting to protect privacy of the computed model and the locally stored data. However, FHE mechanisms are usually computationally complicated making it difficult to be applicable for reality. Therefore, we consider to apply PHE for secure model fusion in distributed learning in order to achieve a better balance between security and usability.

## 6.3  Privacy-Preserving Distributed Machine Learning

**Threat Model:** In our setting, we consider all the other agents and the fusion server as potential adversaries that are honest-but-curious. Our mechanism aims to protect both the computed models and the locally stored data which are sensitive information of the users.

Previous work in [18] encrypted the locally computed models to protect the individual data from the server while the server can still access the aggregated model, based on their assumption that the aggregate model does not disclose any sensitive information about individual data. However, recently proposed model inversion attacks [19] and membership inference attacks [9], have shown that individual data can be inferred from the aggregate model. That is to say, the direct exposure of the aggregate model to the server would put the privacy of individual data into risk. Therefore, the protection for the computed model should also be taken into consideration in the design of secure model fusion system as in our setting.

Secure multi-party computation (SMC) [20] aims to obtain correct output computed over multiple agents even if some agents may misbehave. In SMC, if one agent learns the output then all honest parties can learn the output. Therefore, it is different from our setting where we only consider honest-but-curious agents in distributed learning and the fused model can not be exposed directly to these agents for security reasons.

# 7  Conclusion

In this paper, we have proposed a secure model fusion mechanism in federated learning systems, in order to protect the computed models and the corresponding training data. By leveraging the *additive* property of PHE mechanisms, we convert fusion operation into portions where the fusion server can update the model over the encrypted local models. We further propose two optimization mechanism that can decrease the computational overhead and make the scheme practical even for networks with large number of model weights.

Although we have presented our work using El Gamal [13] and Paillier [12], it can be generally applied to other PHE/HE methods in a straightforward manner. Our future work includes balancing model accuracy, model security and computational time by properly selecting system parameters.

# References

1. McMahan, H.B., Moore, E., Ramage, D., Hampson, S.: Communication-efficient learning of deep networks from decentralized data. arXiv preprint arXiv:1602.05629 (2016)
2. Bonawitz, K., et al.: Practical secure aggregation for federated learning on user-held data. arXiv preprint arXiv:1611.04482 (2016)
3. Verma, D., Julier, S., Cirincione, G.: Federated AI for building AI solutions across multiple agencies. In: AAAI FSS-18: Artificial Intelligence in Government and Public Sector, Arlington, VA, USA (2018)
4. Wang, S., et al.: When edge meets learning: adaptive control for resource-constrained distributed machine learning. In: IEEE International Conference on Computer Communications (2018)
5. Verma, D., Chakraborty, S., Calo, S., Julier, S., Pasteris, S.: An algorithm for model fusion for distributed learning. In: Ground/Air Multisensor Interoperability, Integration, and Networking for Persistent ISR IX, vol. 10635, p. 106350O. International Society for Optics and Photonics (2018)
6. Li, M., et al.: Scaling distributed machine learning with the parameter server. In: USENIX Symposium on Operating Systems Design and Implementation (OSDI), vol. 14, pp. 583–598 (2014)
7. Kraska, T., Talwalkar, A., Duchi, J.: MLbase: a distributed machine-learning system. In: 6th Biennial Conference on Innovative Data Systems Research (CIDR 2013) (2013)
8. Dean, J., et al.: Large scale distributed deep networks. In: Advances in Neural Information Processing Systems, pp. 1223–1231 (2012)
9. Shokri, R., Stronati, M., Song, C., Shmatikov, V.: Membership inference attacks against machine learning models. In: 2017 IEEE Symposium on Security and Privacy (SP), pp. 3–18. IEEE (2017)
10. Long, Y., et al.: Understanding membership inferences on well-generalized learning models. arXiv preprint arXiv:1802.04889 (2018)
11. Gentry, C.: A fully homomorphic encryption scheme. Stanford University (2009)
12. Paillier, P.: Public-key cryptosystems based on composite degree residuosity classes. In: Stern, J. (ed.) EUROCRYPT 1999. LNCS, vol. 1592, pp. 223–238. Springer, Heidelberg (1999). https://doi.org/10.1007/3-540-48910-X_16
13. ElGamal, T.: A public key cryptosystem and a signature scheme based on discrete logarithms. IEEE Trans. Inf. Theory 31(4), 469–472 (1985)
14. Nakano, K., Olariu, S.: A survey on leader election protocols for radio networks. In: Proceedings. International Symposium on Parallel Architectures, Algorithms and Networks, I-SPAN 2002, pp. 71–76. IEEE (2002)

15. Gupta, S., Agrawal, A., Gopalakrishnan, K., Narayanan, P.: Deep learning with limited numerical precision. In: International Conference on Machine Learning, pp. 1737–1746 (2015)
16. LeCun, Y., Bottou, L., Bengio, Y., Haffner, P.: Gradient-based learning applied to document recognition. Proc. IEEE 86(11), 2278–2324 (1998)
17. Snoek, J., Larochelle, H., Adams, R.P.: Practical Bayesian optimization of machine learning algorithms. In: Advances in Neural Information Processing Systems, pp. 2951–2959 (2012)
18. https://blog.n1analytics.com/distributed-machine-learning-and-partially-homomorphic-encryption-1/
19. Fredrikson, M., Jha, S., Ristenpart, T.: Model inversion attacks that exploit confidence information and basic countermeasures. In: Proceedings of the 22nd ACM SIGSAC Conference on Computer and Communications Security, pp. 1322–1333. ACM (2015)
20. Goldreich, O.: Secure multi-party computation. Manuscript. Preliminary version 78 (1998)

# Policy-Based Identification of IoT Devices' Vendor and Type by DNS Traffic Analysis

Franck Le[1](✉), Jorge Ortiz[2], Dinesh Verma[1], and Dilip Kandlur[3]

[1] Distributed AI Department, IBM TJ Watson Research Center,
Yorktown Heights, NY 10549, USA
{fle,dverma}@us.ibm.com
[2] ECE Department, Rutgers, The State University of New Jersey,
Piscataway, NJ 08854, USA
jorge.ortiz@rutgers.edu
[3] Google, 1600 Amphitheatre Parkway, Mountain View, CA 94043, USA
dkandlur@gmail.com

**Abstract.** The explosive growth of IoT devices and the weak security protection in some types of devices makes them an attractive target for attackers. IoT devices can become a vulnerable weak link for penetrating a secure IT infrastructure. The risks are exacerbated by the Bring-Your-Own-Device trend that allows employees to connect their own personal devices into an enterprise network. Currently, network administrators lack adequate tools to discover and manage IoT devices in their environments. A good tool to address this requirement can be created by adapting and applying natural language interpretation algorithms to network traffic. In this paper, we show that an application of algorithms like Term Frequency - Inverse Document Frequency (TF-IDF) to the domain name resolution process, a required first step in every Internet based communication, can be highly effective to determine IoT devices, their manufacturers and their type. By treating the domain names being resolved as words, and the set of domain names queried by a device as a document, then comparing these synthetic documents from a reference data set to real traffic results in a very effective approach for IoT discovery. Evaluation of our approach on a traffic data set shows that the approach can identify 84% of the instances, with an accuracy of 91% for the IoT devices' vendor, and 100% of the instances with an accuracy of 94% for the IoT devices' type. We believe that this is the first attempt to apply natural language processing algorithms for traffic analysis, and the promising results could open new venues for securing and understanding computer networks through natural language processing algorithms. These and other techniques require policies to determine how the large volume of data will be handled efficiently. By assisting in detecting potential malicious devices, this paper contributes to the topic of safe autonomy.

© Springer Nature Switzerland AG 2019
S. Calo et al. (Eds.): PADG 2018, LNCS 11550, pp. 180–201, 2019.
https://doi.org/10.1007/978-3-030-17277-0_10

# 1   Introduction

The Internet of Things (IoT) extends Internet connectivity beyond standard devices (e.g., servers, laptops, and smartphones), to physical devices that were traditionally not Internet enabled (e.g., doorbells, refrigerators, cameras, speakers). Today, there are an estimated 8.4 Billion Internet-of-Things (IoT) devices in active use. That is up from 4 Billion just three years ago and is expected to more than double in the next three years [1]. As such, they have become a prime target for attackers. Insight into these devices is required for the safety and security of the devices themselves, and understanding which devices are present in an environment is a pre-requisite for safe autonomy.

In October 2016, more than 100,000 DVRs and cameras from XiongMai Technologies were hacked into botnets [2]. More recently, in July 2017, researchers revealed that more than 175,000 cameras from Shenzhen Neo Electronics could easily be hacked and used for remote execution [3]. Many other examples have been recorded in the literature [4–8]. This trend is raising major concerns about the ability to mitigate and protect against such attacks.

With enterprises allowing employees to "bring their own devices" and connect to internal networks, mitigation approaches have started to focus on *internal perimeter* security instead of *outside perimeter* security. Outside perimeter security like firewalls and gateways prevent external intruders. Internal perimeter security aims to secure the network from within by allowing administrators to learn about and manage devices that are plugged into the network. Broadly, these tools provide two primary functions: *visibility* into the network and *control* of devices on the network. Visibility is the harder problem of the two. A popular example of commercial internal security tools is Cisco's Identity Service Engine (ISE) [9].

Tools like ISE come with a set of predefined profiles which are rules mapping traffic sources to devices and/or device types. Network administrators can augment the set of profiles, and define policies limiting access to parts of the network. Vendor identification is done by comparing physical network addresses which embed a 24-bit Organizationally Unique Identifier (OUI) assigned by the IEEE Registration Authority [10], the assignments being available publicly. A set of manually defined rules are used to map the OUI to classify the device. Policies to quarantine devices that are most vulnerable or potentially dangerous [7,11] can subsequently be triggered.

Given the continuous growth of the IoT device market – with new companies, devices and functionality introduced into the market every few months – and the increasing demand from employees and clients to use them, static profile based approaches will not scale. When new IoT devices connect to the network and there is no profile to match, administrators are at a loss. In addition, profiles may become deprecated as device protocol and software versions change. Manual management of profiles and devices is just not a viable long-term approach. In this paper, we propose new algorithms that automatically create profiles and identify devices by their *vendor* and *type*, inferring these two properties using only the traffic generated on the network by a device. Our algorithm can answer questions like: "*Is any camera from Shenzhen Neo Electronics present in my network?*", without requiring a predefined profile for Shenzhen Neo. The proposed algorithms can then be composed with additional policies, e.g., to restrict network access of devices that are most vulnerable.

We show that existing text processing algorithms, such as Term Frequency-Inverse Document Frequency (TF-IDF) [12], can be used to effectively learn and identify IoT devices. We also show how it can be used to compare never-seen-before devices with devices that have been observed in the past. This allows administrators to learn about new devices and provides useful feedback to help them determine what kind of device it is. To the best of our knowledge, this is the first attempt to apply natural language processing algorithms to traffic classification, and more broadly, this study can help us better understand how the rich body of work in natural language processing is surprisingly effective in this context.

We focus on the Domain Name System (DNS) [13] queries that an IoT device issues. DNS queries are a required part of network communication. They translate a server name (e.g, *myhost.mydomain.org*) into an IP addresses (e.g., 192.168.1.1), and they precede the establishment of communication channels between the device and the server. A DNS name, more specifically termed a fully qualified domain name, consists of a host name (e.g., *myhost*) concatenated with the domain name suffix (e.g., *mydomain.org*). We treat each fully qualified domain name (e.g., *myhost.mydomain.org*) as a word, and the list of words observed during a specified observation period (e.g., 24 h) as a document. We use this document to infer the vendor/manufacturer of the IoT device. As part of preparing this document, we remove DNS names of commonly used services, which can be viewed as analogous to removal of stop words in a document. An analysis of the remaining words provides a good insight into the vendor of the device. Then, we apply TF-IDF to compare each document from an observed IoT device with other documents representing devices from the same vendor (reference set), and can identify the device type closest to the device being observed. Our proposed approach can also handle new IoT device classes that are not present in the reference data set. Intuitively, documents from new classes of IoT devices that are not present in the reference set should exhibit low similarity scores with all documents in the reference set. As such, documents with a similarity scores below a threshold can be classified as "*unseen*", and be brought up to the network administrator's attention (e.g., for labeling).

Examining DNS traffic has several advantages compared to analyzing physical network addresses used in current network visibility tools. Physical network addresses disappear after the fist router in the network, and require a complex infrastructure to capture them from servers that assign them (e.g., DHCP servers [14]) and correlate them to addresses visible in the Internet Protocol layer. In addition, physical network addresses can reveal the vendor of a device (e.g., Amazon), but do not provide any information regarding the type of the device (e.g., Echo). In contrast, DNS analysis can be used in any environment where DNS queries can be collected. These are possible in many types of network environments. In a typical enterprise network, the DNS queries can be parsed out from network traffic filters, or from systems deployed for network intrusion detection or network intrusion prevention, both of which collect packet traces. They can be collected as logs from Domain Name Servers or their proxies, which are deployed and owned by the enterprise networks. Some enterprise networks outsource their domain name services to cloud based service providers (e.g., NeuStar [15], or EasyDNS [16]) and these services can provide IoT discovery as a service to their clients. Similarly the network ISP that is supporting an enterprise network can collect DNS queries flowing on its network, and use them to discover IoT devices. Also, some traffic analysis schemes become ineffective because of prevalent and growing use of encryption on network packets. DNS based analysis is impervious to the use of encrypted traffic because it is required prior to actual traffic commencement, and is carried in cleartext.

There are many natural language interpretation algorithms for comparing documents. However, the idiosyncrasies of DNS make many of them less attractive. DNS services use the concept of caching at the device to reduce the number of queries being made, which effectively masks any order or proximity information in the sequence of queries made by a device. IoT devices may cache the latest DNS domain to IP address mapping received from a DNS server, and use this cached record for subsequent queries. The time-to-live (TTL) for every DNS record, i.e., the number of seconds the record can be cached by a DNS client, is set by the authoritative name server. However, some caching DNS nameservers set their own TTLs regardless of the authoritative records. As a result, the observed order of queried DNS names and how close they appear to each other may differ in each environment. Proximity information is a key driver in the effectiveness of Paragraph Vector schemes [17], with order (distributed memory scheme) or without order (distributed Bag of Words) approaches. Therefore, we opted to choose TF-IDF instead of paragraph vector schemes.

In this paper, we more specifically make the following contributions:

- First, we propose an algorithm IoT-VEN to infer the vendor of an IoT device based on DNS query information.
- Second, we propose another algorithm IoT-TYP to infer the type of an IoT device using TF-IDF after IoT-VEN has identified the vendor
- Third, we evaluate IoT-VEN on two independent datasets $D_1, D_2$ consisting of DNS queries captured over 30, and 21 days for 72, and 22 IoT devices, respectively.
- Fourth, we compare IoT-VEN with the OUI-based query lookup. While the DNS based mechanism works better, we find that combining the two as complementary, rather than competing, schemes in environments where both are feasible leads to a more accurate approach.
- Fifth, we validate IoT-TYP using out-of-sample testing, showing that it is a highly effective scheme with an accuracy of 0.94; more specifically, IoT-TYP identifies known device types with an accuracy of 0.99, and detects instances belonging to unknown device types with an accuracy of 0.92.
- Finally, we propose a mechanism to use policies to guide the operation of different algorithms for vendor and device type identification.

The rest of the paper is organized as follows. Section 2 discusses the related work, and Sect. 3 describes the TF-IDF text processing approach. Section 4 presents a detailed overview of our system, and introduces the two algorithms IoT-VEN, and IoT-TYP that automatically learn and identify an IoT device's vendor and type. Section 5 evaluates the proposed algorithms on real network traffic from 94 IoT devices, describing the methodology and presenting the results. Section 6 discusses the role of policies in device identification; and, finally, Sect. 7 concludes.

## 2   Related Work

The discovery of devices within a network is an established problem in the field of systems management [18], and several solutions to discover IT devices (e.g., PCs, servers) exist in the industry. However, they rely on either the ability to probe devices that make management information accessible via standard communication protocols, or the ability to install an agent on the IT systems so that the agents can report their characteristics to a repository. A Protocol like SNMP [19] is supported widely on network devices, and forms the basis of network device and topology discovery tools in enterprise and Internet Service Provider networks [20]. CIM-RS [21] provides a web-based REST protocol [22] to access information stored on devices using the standard DMTF CIM specifications and is supported on servers and PCs, but it is rarely supported on IoT devices. As a result, the most common system management approaches for discovery cannot be used to discover IoT devices. Instead approaches that discover devices based on analysis of traffic patterns and DNS exploration, like the one proposed in this paper, need to be used.

One of the approaches to discover devices using traffic analysis is by examining the MAC addresses that a device has. Some commercial systems create a database of how MAC addresses are assigned to manufacturers using resources such as the IEEE OUI listing [10], and use that database to infer the maker of a device. However, these listings are based on a limited set of assigned entries in the MAC addresses, usually identify the vendor who makes the networking card in the device, and can not infer more details. Approaches have been suggested to learn attributes of other fields in the MAC addresses [23], and use that for a finer grain discovery of devices. That provides the closest work approaching our goals, but relying solely on the MAC address still restricts discovery only to the manufacturer of the networking card, which frequently is different from the manufacturer of the device.

Other types of traffic analysis that can provide useful insights include understanding timing patterns of requests, but timing behavior is significantly erratic when captured in enterprise networks. Nevertheless, in wireless networks where timing information can be captured with a higher degree of fidelity, these approaches can discover attributes such as the Operating System of a device [24]. Other higher level information such as the user-agent field in HTTP headers can also provide useful information to finger-print devices, and has been used in cellular networks [25], and in community source projects such as Finger-bank [26] to create a database to infer the type of device from this protocol information. Such approaches can only be used in networks which do not encrypt communication so that the right fields can be extracted using a network traffic analyzer. The challenges and limitations of such approaches are also well-known, specially in mobile device identification [27]. In contrast, the approach of analyzing domain names is easy to implement in enterprise networks, and more robust than timing analysis.

Machine learning approaches have been proposed as a way to discover IoT devices. One approach is to capture MAC level traffic of different IoT devices, use that as training data to create models that can classify a new traffic pattern into one of the matching device types, where the models could be learning finger-printing rules [7] or use clustering algorithms like random forest [8]. These approaches work well when the training data set contains the device types being monitored, but are unable to identify devices that are not present in the training data set. Our approach overcomes that limitation by detecting new unseen IoT device types. Furthermore, DNS analysis is feasible in more deployment configurations than analysis over a full packet trace. Recently, Guo and Heidemann also proposed a method that analyzes DNS traffic to detect IoT devices, and identify their type [28]. The method is based on the observation that IoT devices regularly exchange traffic with servers run by their manufacturers, and those servers tend to be distinct for each class of IoT device. However, the proposed method requires the prior knowledge acquisition of device servers, a process which can entail significant pre-processing work. In contrast, our solution automatically identifies important domain names thanks to the use of statistical natural language processing.

The use of natural language interpretation algorithms such as TF-IDF is a new contribution for traffic analysis, and we are not aware of it having been used in other studies.

## 3    Background: TF-IDF

This Section provides a brief background on *term-frequency inverse document frequency* (TF–IDF) [12], a popular natural language text processing approach. It is widely used to retrieve documents that are most relevant to a set of keywords from a corpus of documents. Each word in a document is assigned a TF–IDF value which represents the importance of that word in that document. The TF–IDF is the product of the *term frequency* and *inverse document frequency*. The *term frequency* counts how many times a word appears in the document. The more times a word appears, the more important it is likely to be. Not to give more importance to words in longer documents, the *term frequency* is commonly normalized by the total number of words in a document. The *inverse document frequency* counts the number of documents in the corpus in which the word appears. The more documents in which a word appears, the less relevant it may be (e.g., "the","and", etc.). For a word $w$ in a corpus $C$, $IDF(w,C)$ can be computed as

$$IDF(w, C) = log \frac{\text{Number of documents in C}}{\text{Number of documents where w appears}}$$

|         | Document 1 | Document 2 | Document 3 |
|---------|------------|------------|------------|
| Content | The dog is chasing after the cat. | Paris is the capital of France. | What is the next big challenge? |
| TF | (the, 2/8)<br>(dog, 1/8)<br>(is, 1/8)<br>(chasing, 1/8)<br>(after, 1/8)<br>(cat, 1/8)<br>(., 1/8) | (paris, 1/7)<br>(is, 1/7)<br>(the, 1/7)<br>(capital, 1/7)<br>(of, 1/7)<br>(france, 1/7)<br>(., 1/7) | (what, 1/7)<br>(is, 1/7)<br>(the, 1/7)<br>(next, 1/7)<br>(big, 1/7)<br>(challenge, 1/7)<br>(?, 1/7) |
| TF–IDF | (the, 0)<br>(dog, 0.13)<br>(is, 0)<br>(chasing, 0.13)<br>(after, 0.13)<br>(cat, 0.13)<br>(., 0.05) | (paris, 0.15)<br>(is, 0)<br>(the, 0)<br>(capital, 0.15)<br>(of, 0.15)<br>(france, 0.15)<br>(., 0.05) | (what, 0.15)<br>(is, 0)<br>(the, 0)<br>(next, 0.15)<br>(big, 0.15)<br>(challenge, 0.15)<br>(?, 0.15) |

**Fig. 1.** Illustration of TF–IDF

Figure 1 illustrates TF–IDF for a corpus of three documents. Because the words "the" and "is" are present in all documents, their IDF value (and hence, their TF-IDF value) is 0. Contrarily, the word "paris" is unique to the second document, and therefore its TF-IDF value for Document 2 is larger.

As depicted in the last row of Fig. 1, each document is actually converted into a vector of words. The similarity between two documents can then be computed, e.g., using the cosine similarity. For two vectors $U$, $V$, the cosine similarity is defined as (with $U_i$ and $V_i$ being the $i^{th}$ dimension of vectors $U$, $V$):

$$\frac{\sum_{i=1}^{n} U_i V_i}{\sqrt{\sum_{i=1}^{n} U_i^2} \sqrt{\sum_{i=1}^{n} V_i^2}}$$

The cosine similarity ranges from 0 to 1, with 0 meaning no similarity and 1 indicating strong similarity between the vectors. As such, in addition to returning the most relevant document to a keyword, TF-IDF can also be used to find the most similar document in a corpus to an input document.

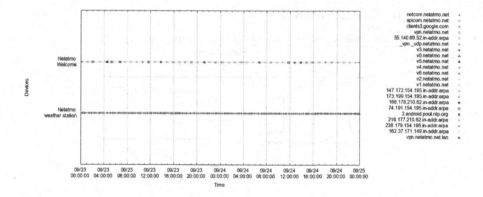

**Fig. 2.** Illustration of IoT devices' DNS traffic

# 4    Identification Algorithms

## 4.1    Overview

To automatically learn and identify an IoT device's vendor and type, we propose two algorithms IoT-VEN, and IoT-TYP respectively, to be used together in a chain. In this section, we present the intuition behind the algorithms, discuss the underlying assumptions, and illustrate the workflow.

Our solution is motivated by two observations about IoT devices' DNS traffic. First, the majority of the DNS names queried by an IoT device belong to the device's vendor. This can be explained by the fact that IoT devices need periodic maintenance and housekeeping functions, such as a check for software updates, a check for firmware updates, report crashes and diagnostic metrics, etc. Second, different IoT devices from a vendor commonly query different DNS names from that vendor. A reason is that devices of different types (e.g., cameras, weather stations) access different services (e.g., facial recognition, weather forecasts) from their vendor, or from the general Internet. To illustrate these two characteristics, Fig. 2 depicts the DNS queries from two IoT devices from the same vendor: a *Netatmo Welcome* (camera), and a *Netatmo weather station*. The x-axis represents the time spanning 48 h. Each dot represents a DNS name queried by one of the devices. First, most queried DNS names (e.g., *netcom.netatmo.net*, *apicom.netatmo.net*) belong to the devices' vendor (e.g., Netatmo). Second, the two devices being of different types (e.g., weather station versus camera) do query different servers from that vendor (e.g., *netcom.netatmo.net* versus *apicom.netatmo.net*). Although Fig. 2 is specific to two IoT devices, we observe that other IoT devices show very similar behaviors. We postulate that these are distinguishing characteristics of IoT devices' DNS traffic, and both IoT-VEN and IoT-TYP exploit them. Section 5.1 analyzes the traffic from 94 IoT devices, and confirms the validity of those assumptions.

Figure 3 depicts the workflow. First, IoT-VEN identifies the vendor of the IoT device: For example, is the IoT device from *Amazon, Netatmo, Google,*

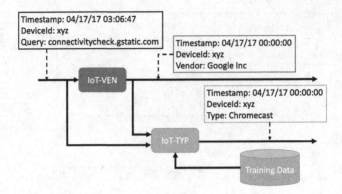

**Fig. 3.** Overview of IoT-VEN and IoT-TYP

*Belkin, Invoxia, LIFX*, etc.? IoT-VEN monitors the DNS queries (e.g., *connectivitycheck.gstatic.com, clients4.google.com*) of an IoT device, and at the end of each observation period (e.g., 24 h), predicts the vendor (e.g., *Google Inc*) of that device. Section 4.2 further describes the step-by-step procedure of IoT-VEN.

Then, IoT-TYP either identifies the device type – for example, given that the device is from *Google Inc*, is it a *Google Home*, a *Google Home Max*, a *Nest camera*, etc.? – or returns *"unseen"* if the instance is estimated to belong to a device type that is not present in the reference set. IoT-TYP takes as inputs (1) the list of DNS queries of a device observed for a configured time period, (2) the output from IoT-VEN (e.g., *Google Inc*), and (3) a reference dataset. Section 4.3 presents IoT-TYP in more details.

## 4.2   IOT-VEN

---

**Algorithm 1.** IoT-VEN

---
**INPUT:** *setDNSnames*
**OUTPUT:** *vendorName, fraction*
1: **for** *name* in *setDNSnames* **do**
2:     **if** filter(*name*) == 0 **then**
3:         *owner* ← lookup(*name*)
4:         *count[owner]*++
5: *sum*=0
6: **for** *owner* in *count* **do**
7:     *sum = sum + count[owner]*
8: **for** *owner* in *count* **do**
9:     *fraction[owner] = count[owner]/sum*
10: Return *argmax count, fraction[argmax count]*

---

| Device | Set of queried DNS names |
|--------|--------------------------|
| Chromecast | ['www.google.com', 'clients3.google.com', 'clients4.google.com', '_googlecast._tcp.local', 'channel.status.request.url', 'tools.google.com', 'pool.ntp.org', 'clients1.google.com', 'connectivitycheck.gstatic.com', 'mtalk.google.com', 'xxxx.local', 'ajax.googleapis.com', 'ssl.gstatic.com', 'fonts.googleapis.com', 'www.gstatic.com', 'fonts.gstatic.com', 'lh3.googleusercontent.com', 'google.com', 'x.x.x.x.in-addr.arpa', 'x.x.x.x.in-addr.arpa', 'x.x.x.x.in-addr.arpa', 'x.x.x.x.in-addr.arpa', 'x.x.x.x.in-addr.arpa', 'x.x.x.x.in-addr.arpa'] |

**Fig. 4.** IoT-VEN example input

The goal of IoT-VEN is to identify the vendor of an IoT device. Algorithm 1 presents the pseudo-code. For a given IoT device, IoT-VEN takes as input the set of DNS names (*setDNSnames*) that the device queries over a time period $T$, and outputs the potential name(s) of the vendor (*vendorName*) as well as the *fraction* of queried DNS names that belong to it. The set of unique queried DNS names can be readily extracted with existing open source tools (e.g., Bro [29]). Figure 4 provides an example of the observed unique queried DNS names over a 24 h period for a Chromecast device. For anonymity, a number of characters (e.g., IP addresses) have been replaced with the character 'x'.

For each DNS name in that set, IoT-VEN performs the following actions:

- Line 2 applies a filter() function to discard a number of domains including local queries (e.g., *\*.local*), and queries to common services (e.g., *\*.ntp.org, \*.arpa*) for two reasons:
  - (i) *\*.local* domains are often employed as part of the automatic discovery of devices. Such domains can help narrow down and better identify the type of IoT devices (e.g., the DNS domain *google-cast.tcp.local* is used by Chromecast devices as part of the Bonjour service [30]). However, the propagation of those DNS *\*.local* domains is restricted to a device's subnet. The packet capture may not be performed on the same subnet as the IoT devices, and such *\*.local* domains may not be visible. We therefore exclude them for generality.
  - (ii) A number of domains are not conducive to determining the vendor of the device. For example, *\*.ntp.org* provides a cluster of timeservers for computer systems to synchronize their clock. The philosophy in filtering out these names is similar to that of removing stop words, names that are extremely common and of little value in discriminating among different vendors.
- Line 3 retrieves the owner of the DNS name. The lookup() function can extract such information from different sources including WHOIS [31], and x509 certificates [32]. WHOIS is a registrar containing the users of the registered DNS domains, and x509 certificates are electronic credentials to certify the identities of individuals, computers, and other entities on the Internet. When used to certify the identity of a DNS domain, we can infer

the organization responsible for that domain. For example, a x509 certificate may include the following attributes ("CN=*.gstatic.com, O=Google Inc, L=Mountain View, ST=California, C=US") allowing DNS names of the form *.gstatic.com to be mapped to *Google Inc*. The mapping from WHOIS or certificates is often imperfect, since variations of names are used sometimes for the same vendor. To eliminate the impact of such changes, the creation of a cleaned-up table mapping raw organizations to the canonical name of the organization was used.

- Line 4 increments the *count* for the owner of that DNS name. Considering the example in Fig. 4, and the previous x509 certificate, each of the DNS name *connectivity-check.gstatic.com*, *fonts.gstatic.com*, *gstatic.com* will increment the *count* corresponding to *Google Inc* by 1.
- Lines 5 to 9 normalize the *count*s. The goal is to derive the fraction of DNS names that belong to each owner.
- Line 10 returns the *owner* and *fraction* that has the largest value. In the event that multiple owners are tied with the largest fraction value, Line 10 returns all of them. Continuing the example from Fig. 4, Line 10 returns ('Google Inc', '1.0'): All the DNS names queried by the device belong to *Google Inc*. The Chromecast is indeed a device from *Google Inc* [33].

### 4.3   IOT-TYP

After IoT-VEN has identified the vendor of the IoT device (e.g., *Google Inc*), the goal of IoT-TYP is to identify the device type (e.g., *Google Chromecast*)). This second algorithm takes three inputs: (1) the output from IoT-VEN, i.e., the name(s) of the device vendor, (2) the list[1] of DNS name that a device queried over a configured period of time $T$, and (3) a reference dataset. A reference set consists of instances, where each instance is a list of DNS names queried over the specified period of time $T$ by a device. An instance is labeled with the device vendor, and the device type.

Figure 5 illustrates an excerpt of a reference set, with $T$ set to 24 h. The first instance consists of the DNS names that a *Chromecast* queried over a day. The instance is therefore labeled with *Chromecast* as the device type, and *Google Inc* as the device's vendor. The second instance represents the DNS names queried by another Chromecast over the same or another day, and is therefore also labeled with *Chromecast* and *Google Inc*. The list of queried DNS names of instances 1 and 2 differs reflecting that a Chromecast may be in different modes of operations (e.g., idle, casting). The third instance depicts the DNS names from a *Withings Aura sleep sensor*.

---

[1] While IoT-VEN takes as input the set of queried DNS names from an IoT device, IoT-TYP takes the list of DNS names. In a list, a DNS name may appear multiple times. The difference comes from the fact that IoT-TYP is based on TF/TF-IDF: the term frequency of each DNS name can reflect how important that domain is to the device type.

| Instance | List of queried DNS names | | | Type | Manufacturer |
|---|---|---|---|---|---|
| 1 | ['www.google.com', | 'www.google.com', | 'clients4.google.com', | Chromecast | Google Inc |
| | 'www.google.com', | 'www.google.com', | 'www.google.com', | | |
| | 'www.google.com', | 'www.google.com', | 'www.google.com', | | |
| | 'clients4.google.com', | 'www.google.com', | 'www.google.com', | | |
| | 'www.google.com', 'channel.status.request.url', ...] | | | | |
| 2 | ['clients1.google.com', | 'connectivitycheck.gstatic.com', | 'mtalk.google.com', | Chromecast | Google Inc |
| | 'clients4.google.com', | 'tools.google.com', | 'tools.google.com', | | |
| | 'clients3.google.com', | 'ajax.googleapis.com', | 'www.gstatic.com', | | |
| | 'ssl.gstatic.com', | 'fonts.googleapis.com', | 'fonts.gstatic.com', | | |
| | 'lh3.googleusercontent.com', ...] | | | | |
| 3 | ['scalews.withings.net', | 'scalews.withings.net', | 'scalews.withings.net', | Aura sleep sensor | Withings |
| | 'scalews.withings.net', | 'scalews.withings.net', | 'scalews.withings.net', | | |
| | 'scalews.withings.net', | 'scalews.withings.net', | 'scalews.withings.net', | | |
| | 'scalews.withings.net', 'scalews.withings.net', 'scalews.withings.net', ...] | | | | |
| ... | ... | | | ... | ... |

**Fig. 5.** IoT-TYP excerpt of reference set

IoT-TYP relies on and adapts TF-IDF to the DNS names[2] that a device queries. Each DNS name is equivalent to a word. The list of DNS names queried by a device over the period of time $T$ (e.g., 24 h) constitutes a document. For the corpus, IoT-TYP retrieves all documents from the reference dataset that are generated by the devices from the same vendor as the one provided as input (i.e., first argument). As an example, if IoT-VEN has identified *Amazon* as the device vendor, IoT-TYP retrieves documents from *Amazon* devices such as *Amazon Echo*, *Amazon Tap*, and *Amazon Fire TV*, from the reference dataset. IoT-TYP then computes the similarity between the provided list of DNS names (second argument) and every document from the corpus. The document with the highest similarity score is selected, and its type is returned. In other words, IoT-TYP compares the DNS names access patterns from the input device with those of the devices from the same vendor in the reference dataset, and returns the type of the most similar device. Figure 6 depicts the flow diagram of IoT-TYP in further details.

First, if there is no instance in the reference set from the identified vendor, the instance is classified as *"unseen"*. Second, IoT-TYP checks if there are instances of at least two different device types from the identified vendor in the reference set. To illustrate the rationale behind it, we consider a reference set with only smart bulbs from LIFX. Those bulbs query one single DNS name *"v2.broker.lifx.co"*. If converting those instances into TF-IDF vectors, all the vectors become NULL since *"v2.broker.lifx.co"* is the only DNS name and is present in all instances. As such, if there are only one device type from a vendor, we consider the term frequencies but ignore the inverse document frequency. IoT-TYP then computes the cosine similarity between the input instance and the instances in the reference set from the same vendor, and selects the reference instance with the largest similarity score. If the similarity score is below a specified threshold, IoT-TYP classifies the input instance as *"unseen"*. Intuitively, results with low

---

[2] Similar to the preprocessing in IoT-VEN, we discard *.local* domains, and queries to common services (e.g., *.ntp.org, *.arpa*).

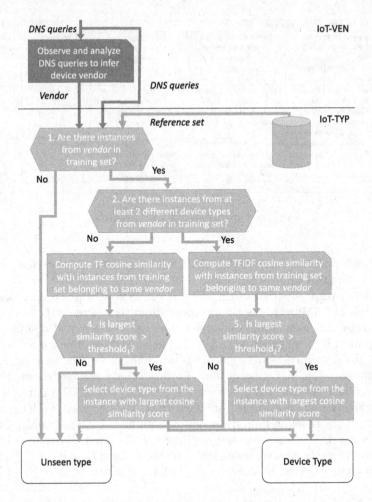

**Fig. 6.** IoT-TYP data flow diagram

scores can indicate new unseen device types and be raised as exceptions. Otherwise, IoT-TYP returns the type of the selected reference instance (with the largest similarity score).

## 5   Evaluation

### 5.1   Datasets

To evaluate our proposed algorithms, we analyze the network traffic from two independent sources (Fig. 7). The first source is a private US lab where commercial IoT devices are continually added, and whose traffic has been captured for two years. We focus on the traffic captured during the month of April 2017. During that time period, we observe and receive the confirmed labels from the lab

| | Dataset 1 | Dataset 2 |
|---|---|---|
| Time | April 2017 | September 2016 |
| Days | 30 | 21 |
| IoT | 72 | 22 |
| Source | Private | UNSW [8] |

**Fig. 7.** Datasets

| | | | |
|---|---|---|---|
| (1, Amazon, Echo) | (1, Google Inc, Chromecast, 3) | (1, Samsung, Refrigerator) | (1, Withings, HomeCamera) |
| (1, Amazon, FireTV, 1) | (1, Google Inc, Chromecast, 4) | (1, Samsung, SmartTV,1) | (2, Amazon, Echo) |
| (1, Amazon, FireTV, 2) | (1, Google Inc, Chromecast, 5) | (1, Samsung, SmartTV,2) | (2, Belkin, Wemo-motion-sensor) |
| (1, Amazon, Tap) | (1, Google Inc, Dropcam) | (1, Samsung, SmartTV,3) | (2, Carematix, Blipcare-Blood-Pressure) |
| (1, Amcrest, NVRNV4108) | (1, Google Inc, NEST-Smoke-alarm) | (1, Samsung, SmartTV,4) | (2, Domainoo, PIX-STAR-Photo-frame) |
| (1, Amcrest, WiFiCamera) | (1, Google Inc, NEST-Thermostat) | (1, Sharp, Aquos80) | (2, Evrythng, iHome) |
| (1, Apple, AppleTV) | (1, Google Inc, NestCam) | (1, SkybellTech, SkybellHD) | (2, Google Inc, Dropcam, 1) |
| (1, Apple, AppleTV4thGen) | (1, GraceDigital, Mondo) | (1, SmartLabs, InsteonHub) | (2, Google Inc, Dropcam, 2) |
| (1, Arcsoft, Simplicam) | (1, Honeywell, Thermostat) | (1, SmartThings, Hub, 1) | (2, Google Inc, NEST-Smoke-alarm) |
| (1, Belkin, InsightSwitch, 1) | (1, IRobot, Roomba) | (1, SmartThings, Hub, 2) | (2, HP, Printer) |
| (1, Belkin, InsightSwitch, 2) | (1, LG, SmartTV, 1) | (1, SmartThings, Hub, 3) | |

**Fig. 8.** Sample of IoT devices in the datasets

owner for 72 IoT devices. The second source is the publicly available dataset from UNSW [8]: it consists of the network traffic from 30 devices, captured over 21 days starting from September 23 2016. The devices are labeled and identified with their MAC address. We extracted the traffic corresponding to the 22 IoT devices. Figure 8 presents a sample of IoT devices in the datasets. Each device is represented with the format *(datasetId, Vendor, Type, [DeviceId])*, where *datasetId* indicates the dataset, *Vendor* is the name of the vendor, *Type* is the name of the device type, and *DeviceId* is optional and only present when there are multiple instances of a same device type in a dataset.

### 5.2 IoT-VEN

**Methodology.** We define an instance as the set of unique DNS names queried by a device over a specified period of time $T$. After listening to the DNS traffic from a device, IoT-VEN predicts its vendor name. This allows a network administrator to identify the vendors of the IoT devices in its network. We apply IoT-VEN to all instances of each dataset. We initially set $T$ to 24 h. Section 5.2 presents the results. Then, in Sect. 5.2, we gradually reduce $T$ from 24 h to 10 min, and analyze the impact on the ratio of instances that can be classified, and the accuracy. The goal is to define an observation epoch that is practical for network administrators (i.e., an observation epoch that allows administrators to detect devices of interest quickly enough), and yet offers a good balance between the ratio of instances that can be classified, and the accuracy.

**Results.** We present two metrics, the ratio of instances that can be classified, and the accuracy, of IoT-VEN.

| Observation Period | 24 hours | 1 hour |
|---|---|---|
| Classification (instances) | 76% | 89% |
| Accuracy (instances) | 90% | 87% |
| Number of devices | 94 | 94 |
| Classification (devices) | 77 (82%) | 79 (84%) |
| Accuracy (devices) | 70 (90%) | 72 (91%) |

**Fig. 9.** IoT-VEN summary of results

**Classification:** IoT-VEN classifies 76% of the instances (Fig. 9). For the instances that cannot be classified, we look at the results more closely, and the failures can be attributed to five main reasons: First, one device – the Movo nt4000b camera – issues no DNS queries. Second, two Sonos play devices make only DNS queries of the form *.sonostime.pool.ntp.org which we ignored since those queries are for timeservers for the devices to synchronize their clock. Third, the information of the domain owner receiving the majority of the DNS names may be kept private. Fourth, we may have no information on the owner of the DNS name queried by a device. For example, we may have no x509 certificate associated with that DNS name, and the WHOIS information may have no Registrant Organization. Finally, the network administrator of the lab where Dataset 1 is captured has the DNS suffix search feature configured in his network: the DNS suffix search feature allows a DNS suffix to be added to DNS name queries. To illustrate this feature, we assume a network with the domain name *domain1.com*. An internal user connecting to an internal server could simply type the command "ssh serverXYZ". Thanks to the DNS suffix search feature, the user machine will attempt to resolve the IP address using the qualified domain name *serverXYZ.domain1.com*. However, as a result of this feature, a number of DNS names initiated from IoT devices were incorrect: For example, a Samsung SmartThings Hub in this lab was querying *dc-na02-useast1.connect.smartthings.com.domain1.com* instead of *dc-na02-useast1.connect.smartthings.com*, and the lookup() function returned the owner of *domain1.com*, instead of *smartthings.com*. As such, to improve the classification rate, we could verify the validity of the DNS names (e.g., removing the DNS suffix list).

**Classification (devices):** Within each dataset, devices are continually added to the environment. As such, not all devices are present from the start to the end of the packet capture time interval, and one may question: *Do most classified instances belong to only a small set of devices?* To answer this question, we analyze how many devices can get classified. A device may be present in the dataset for $N$ days, generating $N$ instances (one for each day). Considering those $N$ instances, can any of them classify the device? If the answer is positive, we say that IoT-VEN is able to classify that device, and we observe that IoT-VEN can classify 77 out of the 94 (82%) devices.

**Accuracy:** IoT-VEN correctly classifies 90% of the instances. A number of instances that are incorrectly classified belong to smart TVs (e.g., *LG SmartTV*, and *Sharp Aquos80LE650U*). Those instances show a very similar behavior. To illustrate it, we present an instance of the *LG SmartTV*: The top owners for the DNS queries are *Nuance Communications, Inc.* (74%), *Google Inc.* (15%), and *LG Electronics Inc* (8%). Nuance Communications, Inc. is a software company that offers provides speech and imaging solutions. If we therefore classify domain owners into one of three possible categories (service provider, device vendor, both), ignore service provider, and give a heavier weight to device vendors, we may be able to correctly classify those instances. Among the incorrectly classified instances, a number of them also belongs to the *SonosInc SonosPlay1* device: The DNS queries are for three names: *legato.radiotime.com*, *17603.live.streamtheworld.com*, and *2.sonostime.pool.ntp.org*. The first two DNS queries go to organizations that offer services, and we ignored DNS queries to NTP servers. However, as the query to *2.sonostime.pool.ntp.org* shows, DNS queries to NTP servers can actually contain information revealing the device's vendor. This is because vendors can get their own zone [34]. As such, rather than ignoring DNS queries to *\*.ntp.org*, we could apply further natural language text processing techniques to extract the vendor names. In summary, some of the incorrect instances point to ways that IoT-VEN can be modified for increased accuracy. However, we note that IoT-VEN already achieves an accuracy of 90%.

**How Low Can We Reduce T?** As we reduce $T$ from 24 to 1 h, the accuracy decreases (Fig. 9). This is according to intuition: as the observation time period gets shorter, the number of queried DNS names gets lower, and the probability for misclassification increases: For example, instances of a Roku 3 device may be classified as *netflix*. More surprisingly, as we decrease $T$, the classification rate increases (Fig. 9). To explain it, we illustrate a behavior we observed: an IoT device may query its vendor's server every 10 min, and three other servers – whose ownership information are kept private – once a day. Consequently, when first considering an observation time period ($T$) of 24 h, 75% of the unique DNS names go to organizations whose ownership is kept private, and the instance cannot get classified. In contrast, with an observation time period ($T$) of one hour, for a majority of the instances, the DNS queries to the vendor's server may be the only DNS queries during those observation time periods. As a result, for those instances, IoT-VEN returns a valid vendor name.

However, as we reduce $T$ below 60 min, the classification rate no longer increases but instead decreases. A closer look at the data reveals that a number of IoT devices query servers from their vendor every hour, and servers from *pubnub.com* at shorter time intervals (e.g., every minute). The servers at *pubnub.com* provide a real time messaging infrastructure, but their domain's owner information is kept private. As a result, for short observation time periods (e.g., epoch lower than 60 min), DNS queries to *pubnub* may be the only DNS queries, and IoT-VEN therefore cannot classify those instances. Both classification rates and accuracy decrease as we reduce $T$ below 60 min.

In conclusion, observation periods of one hour provide the best performance, achieving 89% classification, 87% accuracy. Part of the reason is that IoT devices commonly query their vendor's servers at frequent intervals.

IoT-VEN **Versus OUI-Based Query Lookup.** The goal of IoT-VEN is to identify the vendor of an IoT device. To achieve this goal, existing solutions (e.g., nmap [35], Cisco ISE [9]) rely on OUI-based query lookups. We therefore compare the results of IoT-VEN with those of the OUI-based query lookup approach. This solution is based on the fact that vendors can purchase 24-bit globally unique organizationally unique identifier (OUI) from the IEEE Registration Authority. The OUI is then used as the prefix of identifiers (e.g., MAC addresses) to uniquely identify equipment. For example, the 24 bits "5c:aa:fd" belong to *Sonos Inc.*, and their MAC addresses would start with that prefix. As such, by looking at the MAC addresses of the IoT devices and matching their 24 bits prefix with the OUI, one could attempt to identify the vendor of the devices. However, the vendor name may be kept private [10]. Also, the retrieved vendor name may actually correspond to the vendor of – not the IoT device but – the network card used by the IoT device: For example, matching the MAC addresses of *Chromecast* devices and *iRobot Roomba* with the OUI returned *Azurewav AzureWave Technology Inc.* which is a manufacturer of wireless modules. Despite these limitations, we manually retrieved the MAC addresses of the 94 IoT devices present across $D_1$ and $D_2$, and looked up their OUI. Such approach correctly identifies the vendor of 67 of the 94 devices (71%). In comparison, the previous paragraph showed that with observation of one hour, IoT-VEN correctly identified the vendor of 72 of the 94 devices (77%) (Fig. 9.) IoT-VEN correctly identifies a larger number of vendors. More interestingly, combining the two as complementary, rather than competing, systems achieves even higher results, correctly retrieving the vendor for 92% of the IoT devices.

## 5.3   IoT-TYP

**Methodology.** IoT devices (e.g., Amazon Echo, Smartthings Hub, Withings Aura sleep system) may be configured differently, and be subject to distinct usage patterns in each setting. As such, can we observe an IoT device in one environment and still identify it in another environment? To answer that question, we initially set $T$ to 24 h. We isolate one instance at a time. We designate the instance as $I$. As previously explained, we define an instance as the list of DNS names queried by a device over a specified period of time $T$. Assuming that $I$ belongs to dataset $D_i$, we apply IoT-TYP using the other dataset $D_j$ $(j \neq i)$ as the reference dataset, to predict the type of $I$. IoT-TYP relies on two thresholds: $threshold_1$, $threshold_2$ (Sect. 4.3). To determine their values, we vary those

| Classification (instances) | 100% |
|---|---|
| Accuracy (instances) | 94% |

**Fig. 10.** IoT-TYP summary of results

variables from 0 to 1, and we compute the corresponding accuracy. Based on the observed performance, we set $threshold_1$ to 0.2, and $threshold_2$ to 0.1.

**Results.** As illustrated in Fig. 6, for each instance, `IoT- TYP` should ideally return either (1) "*unseen*" if the device type of the instance is not in the reference set, or (2) the device type (e.g., *Google Chromecast, Netatmo weather station*).

**Classification:** `IoT-TYP` classifies every instance, returning either a device type, or a result "*unseen*". As such, the classification rate is 100%.

**Accuracy (unseen):** `IoT-TYP` identifies instances belonging to a new device class (i.e., device type not present in the reference set) with a accuracy of 92%. Instances that are incorrectly identified as "*unseen*" belong to three devices: *SmartThings Hub, NEST Protect Smoke Alarm,* and *Amazon FireTV.* We observe two main behaviors: First, devices from the same vendor and type may query different DNS names. For example, a *SmartThings Hub* in one dataset may query one single DNS name *fw-update2.smartthings.com,* whereas other *SmartThings Hubs* in the other dataset do not query it. This could be due to the devices being in different modes of operation (e.g., one might be registered, whereas other(s) might not yet be), or having different software or firmware versions. Second, devices from the same vendor and type may query different servers from the same domain or subdomain for load balancing. For example, the *NEST Protect Smoke Alarm* in one dataset queries *transport03.rts18.iad01.production.nest.com* whereas the *NEST Protect Smoke Alarm* in the other dataset queries *transport02.rts08.iad01.production.nest.com.* Similarly, a *SmartThings Hub* in one dataset queries *dc-na02-useast1.connect.-smartthings.com,* while other *SmartThings Hub(s)* in the other dataset query *dc.connect.smartthings.com.* To address these cases, we could prune the DNS names and preserve only the subdomains (e.g., *iad01.production.nest.com, connect.smartthings.com*).

**Accuracy (Device Type):** `IoT-TYP` identifies the device type of the instances with a accuracy of 99%. These results confirm that devices from different types but from a same vendor exhibit a set of consistent and distinct DNS frequency distributions. Instances that are missclassified have a DNS distribution that is very similar or identical to an instance of a different device type from the same vendor. For example, we observe that an instance of *Belkin Wemo Motion Sensor*, an instance of a *Belkin Wemo Switch*, and an instance of a *Belkin Netcam HD Plus* all have identical distributions over the DNS names *www.belkin.com, d3gjecg2uu2eaq.cloudfront.net.* Those instances may correspond to a common mode of operation (e.g., registration) for those devices.

In conclusion, considering all instances that are classified either with a device type, or as *unseen*, `IoT-TYP` achieves an accuracy of 94% (Fig. 10).

**How Low Can We Reduce T?** As we reduce the observation time $T$ from 24 h to 1 h, we observe that the accuracy decreases. This is according to intuition: With shorter observation epochs, devices from different types but from the same vendor may query the same servers with similar frequencies. As such, IoT-TYP cannot differentiate the device types. Longer observation periods (e.g., 24 h) provide better performance.

## 6  Policies for Identification

In the previous sections, we have identified two algorithms, IoT-VEN and IoT-TYP, and identified that they can deliver a high degree of accuracy in identifying the vendor and type of the device that is present in the system. However, each of these vendor identification and type identification algorithms come with a set of implicit assumptions. If those assumptions are not satisfied, the algorithms will fail to work properly.

Specifically, the identification of the vendor using the DNS distribution works very effectively when the device is known to be an IoT device. IoT devices have the key characteristic that they tend to address the domain names that are owned by the vendor that manufactured the device. These devices are operating in an unmanned manner to perform a specific task. However, when the device is not an IoT device, but a manner device, e.g. a laptop computer used by a user to surf the web, the access patterns of domain names is not likely to reflect sites that are owned by the manufacturing vendor.

To be used in any system, the algorithms need to be certain that their prerequisites are satisfied. Policies can play an important role in determining how the different algorithms are composed together.

The policy to be used with each algorithm needs to ensure that the algorithm is only invoked in conditions under which it makes sense. Thus, the IoT-VEN algorithm should only be invoked when it is known that the traffic document belongs to a device that is known to be an IoT device. Similarly, IoT-TYP should only be invoked if IoT-VEN has been successful in identifying a vendor field. If the vendor field is not provided, the IoT-VEN algorithm may produce strange values.

Policies thus act as protectors around the invocation of the algorithms, and help ensure that the algorithms are not misused, or used in the wrong context.

## 7  Discussion and Conclusion

This study reveals two surprising insights into the identification of devices through network traffic analysis. First, we can treat elements of network traffic as words. This view allows the rich body of work in natural language text processing to be applied towards device identification and classification. In this study, we focus on DNS requests, consider each DNS name as a word, and model the set of words observed during a specified time interval as a document. By mapping each word to an owner, i.e. the organization owing the device, we can identify the vendor of a IoT device. Second, we observe that each IoT device type queries a set of DNS names according to a consistent distinct frequency distribution. This characteristic allows us to recognize IoT device types, and to detect new unseen classes of IoT device types with high accuracy.

We have evaluated the proposed approach on the network traffic of 94 IoT devices. Previous studies [7,8] considered only 20 s of devices. For identifying the vendor of the devices, we have shown that our approach (IoT-VEN) can obtain an accuracy over 90%, and there are several enhancements that can further improve the accuracy. It has better accuracy than the state of the art OUI based methods, but the surprising result is that when we combined IoT-VEN with OUI based schemes, we can perform better than either of the two approaches. This indicates that the use of multiple methods and combining them would be the best approach for identifying devices.

We have also proposed the scheme of IoT-TYP which works in conjunction with IoT-VEN and used TF-(IDF) to recognize IoT device types. One noteworthy feature of IoT-TYP is its ability to detect instances pertaining to new unseen classes, and raise those instances as exceptions for a human to provide the correct label. We have also demonstrated that IoT-TYP is very effective in identifying IoT device types (accuracy of 0.99), as well as detecting new classes of IoT devices that are not present in the training corpus (accuracy of 0.92).

We have explored how long the traffic needs to be observed to obtain good results for vendor identification and type identification. For an observation period of 24 h, the classification rate and accuracy of IoT-VEN are 76% and 90%, respectively, across the 94 devices. With observation periods of one hour, we can achieve 89% classification rate, and 87% accuracy. These allow for a scheme which can recognize vendors within an hour. For type identification, we found that an hour results in poor accuracy, and 24 h of observations are required.

We are currently in the process of deploying the system in a large enterprise network with thousands of employees. That network also deploys Cisco ISE to identify IoT devices, providing us the opportunity to compare the results of proposed system with those of existing commercial solutions.

# References

1. Gartner Research: Gartner Says 8.4 Billion Connected "Things" Will Be in Use in 2017, Up 31 Percent From 2016 (2017). http://www.gartner.com/newsroom/id/3598917
2. Hautala, L.: Why it was so easy to hack the cameras that took down the web. In: CNET Security (2016)
3. Palmer, D.: 175,000 IoT cameras can be remotely hacked thanks to flaw, says security researcher. In: ZDNet (2017)
4. Yu, T., Sekar, V., Seshan, S., Agarwal, Y., Xu, C.: Handling a trillion (unfixable) flaws on a billion devices: rethinking network security for the internet-of-things. In: ACM Workshop on Hot Topics in Networks (2015)
5. Apthorpe, N., Reissman, D., Feamster, N.: A smart home is no castle: privacy vulnerabilities of encrypted IoT traffic. In: Workshop on Data and Algorithmic Transparency (DAT) (2016)

6. Sivanathan, A., Sherratt, D., Gharakheili, H.H., Vishwanath, A., Sivaraman, V.: Low-cost flow-based security solutions for smart-home IoT devices. In: Advanced Networks and Telecommunications Systems (2016)

7. Miettinen, M., et al.: IoT sentinel demo: automated device-type identification for security enforcement in IoT. In: IEEE International Conference on Distributed Computing Systems (2017)

8. Sivanathan, A., et al.: Characterizing and classifying IoT traffic in smart cities and campuses. In: IEEE INFOCOM Workshop Smart Cities and Urban Computing (SmartCity 2017) (2017)

9. Cisco identity services engine. https://www.cisco.com/c/en/us/products/security/identity-services-engine/

10. IEEE: OUI Public Listing. http://standards.ieee.org/develop/regauth/oui/oui.txt. Accessed 18 Jan 2018

11. Markowsky, L., Markowsky, G.: Scanning for vulnerable devices in the internet of things. In: Intelligent Data Acquisition and Advanced Computing Systems: Technology and Applications (IDAACS) (2015)

12. Ramos, J.: Using TF-IDF to determine word relevance in document queries. Department of Computer Science, Rutgers University (1999)

13. Mockapetris, P.: Domain names - implementation and specification. RFC 1035, Internet Engineering Task Force (1987)

14. Droms, R., Lemon, T.: The DHCP Handbook: Understanding, Deploying, and Managing Automated Configuration Services. New Riders Publishing, Thousand Oaks (1999)

15. Neustar security - DNS services. https://www.security.neustar/dns-services. Accessed 18 Jan 2018

16. easyDNS technologies inc. domains - register, transfer domains. https://www.easydns.com/. Accessed 18 Jan 2018

17. Le, Q., Mikolov, T.: Distributed representations of sentences and documents. In: International Conference on International Conference on Machine Learning (2014)

18. Verma, D.: Principles of Computer Systems and Network Management. Springer, New York (2009)

19. Stallings, W.: SNMP, SNMPv2, SNMPv3, and RMON 1 and 2. Addison-Wesley Longman Publishing Co., Inc., Boston (1998)

20. Breitbart, Y., Garofalakis, M., Martin, C., Rastogi, R., Seshadri, S., Silberschatz, A.: Topology discovery in heterogeneous IP networks. In: IEEE INFOCOM (2000)

21. DMTF: Desktop management task force CIM-RS. https://www.dmtf.org/standards/cimrs. Accessed 18 Jan 2018

22. Pautasso, C., Zimmermann, O., Leymann, F.: Restful web services vs. big'web services: making the right architectural decision. In: Proceedings of the 17th International Conference on World Wide Web, pp. 805–814. ACM (2008)

23. Martin, J., Rye, E., Beverly, R.: Decomposition of MAC address structure for granular device inference. In: Proceedings of the 32nd Annual Conference on Computer Security Applications. ACM (2016)

24. Franklin, J., McCoy, D., Tabriz, P., Neagoe, V., Randwyk, J.V., Sicker, D.: Passive data link layer 802.11 wireless device driver fingerprinting. In: USENIX Security Symposium, vol. 3, pp. 16–89 (2006)

25. Martin, J., Rhame, D., Beverly, R., McEachen, J.: Correlating GSM and 802.11 hardware identifiers. In: Military Communications Conference, MILCOM 2013–2013 IEEE, pp. 1398–1403. IEEE (2013)

26. Fingerbank device fingerprints. https://fingerbank.org/. Accessed 18 Jan 2018

27. Hupperich, T., Maiorca, D., Kührer, M., Holz, T., Giacinto, G.: On the robustness of mobile device fingerprinting: can mobile users escape modern web-tracking mechanisms? In: Proceedings of the 31st Annual Computer Security Applications Conference, pp. 191–200. ACM (2015)

28. Guo, H., Heidemann, J.: IP-based IoT device detection. In: Proceedings of the 2018 Workshop on IoT Security and Privacy. ACM (2018)

29. Paxson, V.: Bro: a system for detecting network intruders in real-time. Comput. Netw. **31**, 2435–2463 (1999)

30. Cisco: Chromecast as mDNS service in order to cast screen configuration on WLC. https://www.cisco.com/c/en/us/support/docs/wireless-mobility/wireless-mobility/119017-config-chromecast-mdns-wlc-00.html. Accessed 18 Jan 2018

31. ICANN: WHOIS. https://whois.icann.org/en

32. Chokhani, S., Ford, W., Sabett, R., Merrill, C., Wu, S.: Internet x.509 public key infrastructure certificate policy and certification practices framework (2003)

33. Google: Chromecast. https://store.google.com/us/product/chromecast_2015? hl=en-US/. Accessed 11 Oct 2017

34. NTP pool project. http://www.pool.ntp.org/en/. Accessed 18 Jan 2018

35. Lyon, G.F.: Nmap Network Scanning: The Official Nmap Project Guide to Network Discovery and Security Scanning. Insecure, USA (2009)

# Redundancy as a Measure of Fault-Tolerance for the Internet of Things: A Review

Antonino Rullo[1], Edoardo Serra[2], and Jorge Lobo[3(✉)]

[1] DIMES Department, University of Calabria, 87036 Rende, Italy
n.rullo@dimes.unical.it
[2] Department of Computer Science, Boise State University, Boise, ID 83725, USA
edoardoserra@boisestate.edu
[3] ICREA and Department of Information and Communication Technologies,
Universitat Pompeu Fabra, 08018 Barcelona, Spain
jorge.lobo@upf.edu

**Abstract.** In this paper we review and analyze redundancy-based fault-tolerant techniques for the IoT as a paradigm to support two of the main goals of computer security: availability and integrity. We organized the presentation in terms of the three main tasks performed by the nodes of an IoT network: *sensing*, *routing*, and *control*. We first discuss how the implementation of fault-tolerance in the three areas is primary for the correct operation of an entire system. We provide an overview of the different approaches that have been used to address failures in sensing and routing. Control devices typically implement state machines that take decisions based on the measurement of sensors and may also ask actuators to execute actions. Traditionally state-machine replication for fault-tolerance is realized through consensus protocols. Most protocols were developed in the 80's and 90's. We will review the properties of such protocols in detail and discuss their limitations for the IoT. Since 2008, consensus algorithms took a new direction with the introduction of the concept of blockchain. Standard blockchain based protocols cannot be applied without modifications to support fault-tolerance in the IoT. We will review some recent results in this new class of algorithms, and show how they can provide the flexibility required to support fault-tolerance in control devices, and thus overcome some of the limitations of the traditional consensus protocols.

**Keywords:** Internet of Things · Availability · Redundancy · Fault-tolerant · Sensors · State machine · Distributed consensus

Jorge Lobo was partially supported by the Spanish Ministry of Economy and Competitiveness under Grant Numbers: TIN-2016-81032-P, MDM-2015-0502.

© Springer Nature Switzerland AG 2019
S. Calo et al. (Eds.): PADG 2018, LNCS 11550, pp. 202–226, 2019.
https://doi.org/10.1007/978-3-030-17277-0_11

# 1   Introduction

In this paper we present a general overview at security in the Internet of Things (IoT) from the point of view of integrity and availability. In particular, we look at mechanisms to make an IoT network tolerant to component failures. Tolerance describes the ability of containing the effects of faults so that a system can avoid failures and continue working properly. Faults must be compensated in such a way that they not lead to a global system failure. The most common way to instrument fault-tolerance is through redundancy, i.e. the physical or logical replication of services. The intuition behind redundancy is that replication of the same service along multiple processing units confers the system the property of being resilient, that is, the ability to withstand the failure of some of its components when the number of healthy components far exceeds that of faulty ones. However, redundancy makes a system more complex and, consequently, more difficult to operate and manage.

Almost all fault-tolerant schemes proposed in the literature give systems the ability of re-configuring themselves to handle components failures and recoveries. Autonomic fault managements typically come in two flavors. In the first one, management is carried in two phases: a *detection* phase, where the faulty components are detected, and a *re-configuration* phase, where the faulty components are excluded and possibly replaced by healthy ones. The ability to agree on the state of the system allows the fault-free replicas to make correct and consistent progress. Alternatively, replicas go without identifying faulty components, as they operate by masking their effects. This management approach may be more efficient, as it does not need to perform additional detection and re-configuration tasks by giving up certainty. Implementations often rely on probabilistic methods, or only guarantee the computation of approximate results.

The implementation of fault-tolerance in the IoT may get more complicated when compared to traditional computer systems for many reasons. First, the IoT is characterized by high heterogeneity in many of its aspects: smart devices may differ from each other both in hardware and software; they can be either static or mobile; they can be used for many different human activities, each with particular critical issues; network topologies are application-dependent, and as such, may present different criticalities and points of failure. Second, the environment where devices are deployed can also impact the reliability of the system: it may negatively affects sensed values, it could also cause intermittent connectivity, or it can even cause the devices to crash; furthermore, most of times devices are unattended, thus more prone to tampering. Finally, IoT devices typically communicate through wireless channels, which is more unreliable than wired communication. Wireless communication can be affected by potential interference caused by a harsh environment or by cyber attackers.

In this paper we review and analyze redundancy-based fault-tolerant techniques proposed so far for the IoT. We identify three complementary areas corresponding to the three main tasks performed by the nodes of an IoT network, that are *sensing, routing,* and *control.* We discuss how the implementation of fault-tolerance in each of these areas is primary for the correct operation of an entire system. We present an overview of the approaches used in sensing and routing. These two areas have fairly developed techniques. The area of control is less developed. Control devices can be seen as state machines and replication of the state machine as the redundancy for fault-tolerance [69]. Traditionally state-machine replication for fault-tolerance is realized through consensus protocols. Most of these protocols were developed in the 80's and 90's, and they are embedded in many distributed systems [13,56]. We will present an overview of such protocols and discuss which are appropriate to support fault-tolerance within IoT. These algorithms though were not developed for environments where nodes participating in the protocol come in and go out of the network and will not cover very dynamic IoT scenarios. They could also take quadratic time with respect to the number of participants to terminate, limiting their scalability. We are, however, witnessing the emergence of a new class of consensus algorithms initially developed to support crypto-currencies [55,76] and later extended to the more general abstraction of distributed ledgers [15] where contracts and other type of transactions can be implemented. We will review some recent results in these new class of algorithms and show how they can provide some of the flexibility required to support implementations of fault-tolerance in control devices in dynamic IoT scenarios.

## 2    Preliminaries

### 2.1    The Autonomic Computing Paradigm

Autonomic systems (AS) are able to manage errors and failures, and dynamically adapt themselves to changes, without the need of human intervention. These features are increasingly important as the size and complexity of systems grow.

IoT systems are complex for their very nature as they are characterized by a high degree of heterogeneity and large number of components. Such heterogeneity raises the sources of errors and faults, expanding the attack surface, as well as increasing the difficulty of deploying all-encompassing security solutions. Hence, they should strive to attain safe autonomic governance.

The autonomic computing initiative promoted by IBM since the early 2000s [40] outlines four basic principles that characterize an autonomic system:

- **self-configuring:** self-configuring features allow a system for adapting dynamically to changes that occur into the environment where the system operates.
- **self-healing:** discovery, diagnosis, and reconfiguration are key tasks that help a system to be aware of the existence of faulty components in order to re-establish a coherent state after errors and components failures.
- **self-optimizing:** tuning resources and balancing workloads to maximize use of IT resources;
- **self-protecting:** anticipating, detecting, identifying, and protecting against attacks.

As we will see in the following sections, the satisfaction of one or more of above principles permits IoT systems to implement reliable routing, sensing, and control. Typically, fault-tolerant techniques are all self-protecting by definition, however most of them also implement one or more of the other three properties to be more robust against failures and attacks. In the next sections we will use these three tenets (self-configuring/healing/optimizing) as categories to classify the most significant fault-tolerant techniques found in the literature.

## 2.2  Network Model

We consider a network model made of three different types of devices:

- **sensor device:** streams measurements to other devices;
- **communication device:** performs routing tasks, i.e. receives/forwards data packets from/to other devices, according to a routing protocol;
- **control device:** it takes decisions based on the measurement of sensors, it also may asks actuators to execute specific actions if required;

These three entities, along with actuators, are at the basis of the operation of various IoT scenarios, like cyber physical systems (CPS), industry 4.0, smart homes, smart cities, health care applications, etc. Sensors monitor physical phenomena and send sensed values to control devices directly or through communication devices; control devices take decisions on the basis of the received data. In many cases a single physical device may play multiple roles, e.g., a device can act as a sensor and as a router simultaneously. An example of an IoT application built according to our network model is depicted in Fig. 1. In this scenario sensor devices detect the presence of cars and pedestrian, and send their readings to the control devices mounted on the semaphore to control its functioning. Notice that, sensor devices also work as communication devices.

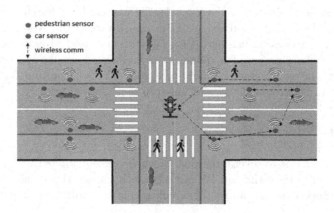

**Fig. 1.** A smart city application to control semaphores.

The accuracy of individual sensors' readings is crucial in applications like surveillance network or health care IoT applications where the readings of sensors must be accurate to avoid false alarms and missed detection of important events. Fault-tolerance is achieved by (and its effectiveness is proportional to) the replication of the sensors, coupled with a fault detection task, or a sensor fusion algorithm (Sect. 3). In large scale networks, reliable routing is equally important as data travels along multi-hop routes. Fault-tolerant routing protocols replicate either the data or the path from the source to the destination (or both) to give data more chances to get to the destination (Sect. 4). Control devices deserve particular attention as if compromised they can take bad decisions that can lead to the crash of the system. Control devices can be replicated according to a state machine paradigm [69], where the replicas take decisions by running a distributed consensus algorithm [2] (Sect. 5). For each of these cases it's important to guarantee that faulty behavior of individual devices do not affect the overall operation of the system.[1]

We do not assume any particular network topology, network size, or IoT application, as we discuss the fault-tolerant techniques.

### 2.3   Failure Classes

Knowing how a device fails allows us to make realistic assumptions for implementing or choosing the most adequate algorithm to detect and handle failures. In the literature several classes of faults have been identified in relation with the device behavior. These classes fall into two general categories: *fail-stop*, that occurs when *"in response to a failure, the component changes to a state that permits other components to detect that a failure has occurred and then stops"* [68]; and *byzantine*, that occurs when *"a component exhibits arbitrary or malicious behavior, perhaps involving collusion with other faulty components"* [46].

Both fail-stop and byzantine faults may be caused by the actions of malicious users, that compromise a device to make it stop working, or to inject false data into the system. Fail-stop faults can also be caused by a harsh environment, by the total depletion of batteries, or by a hardware crash. However, it is not always possible to distinguish between a fail-stop fault and a byzantine behavior, especially in the absence of a diagnosis procedure. Thus, as byzantine faults do not put any constraints on how processes fail, a byzantine fault-tolerant algorithm can be extended to cover fail-stop faults.

## 3   Fault-Tolerant Sensing

Sensors may fail due to several reasons: the environment where they are deployed may negatively affect the sensed value or even causes the crash of a sensor; their unattended nature make them vulnerable to tampering; battery driven

---

[1] Although IoT applications may comprise actuator devices also, we do not take them into account as the management of multiple actuators requires notions of electronics, a topic which fall out of the scope of this paper.

sensors may also stop working because they run out of energy supply. In such conditions, sensors are likely to not perform their work (fail-stop), or report unreliable readings (byzantine behavior) which would not reflect the true state of environmental phenomenon or events under monitoring. Sensor failures have been mainly addressed by means of *redundancy*, i.e., the replication of a service provided by a single device.

## 3.1   Main Approaches

A basic approach to tolerate faulty sensors is to have several of them performing the same task and a *centralized* collector making multiple readings to decide the correct value by means of a fault-tolerant aggregation algorithm. One of the earliest results on how to deal with sensor failures was made by Marzullo [50]. The insight of his solution is the distinction the author makes between *abstract* and *physical* sensors. A *physical sensor* is a device used by a computer or controller to sample a physical variable; an *abstract sensor* is a piece-wise continuous function from a physical variable to a dense interval of physical values. In other words, an abstract sensor is an abstraction of a physical one. An abstract sensor is called *correct* if the interval estimate contains the actual value of the parameter being measured, otherwise it is called *faulty*. The abstraction of physical sensors in terms of intervals allows the interpolation of successive sensor readings (i.e., sensed values can be compared with each other) with known accuracy. In a situation where at most $f$ out of $n$ sensors are faulty, Marzullo considers all possible nonempty $(n - f)$ intersections of the $n$ sensors. A sensor which does not belong to any of the $(n - f)$ cliques is faulty since a correct sensor overlaps with at least $(n - f - 1)$ other correct sensors. One and only one of the $(n - f)$ intersections contains the physical value. But since it is not possible to decide which intersection has the physical value, and since the output is required to be a connected interval, the smallest connected interval containing all the $(n - f)$ intersections is taken to be the output of the algorithm. The accuracy depends on the number of sensor replicas involved. Redundancy also provides protection against byzantine faults. The degree of sensor replication $n$ would be determined by the maximum number of tolerated faulty sensors $f$, and depending on the failure model we have: ($i$) in applications where there exists a limit on the inaccuracy of a sensor (i.e., the width of the abstract sensor interval is finite), the system can tolerate at most $f = (n - 1)/2$ *byzantine* faults; ($ii$) in applications where the inaccuracy of a sensor is unbounded, the system can tolerate at most $f = (n - 1)/3$ byzantine faults; ($iii$) in case of *fail-stop* faults only, the system can tolerate up to $f = n - 1$ faulty nodes. These results are lifted from comparable results first obtained for consensus algorithms. We will present these results when we present replication of controllers in Sect. 5.1. From the point of view of autonomic management, Marzullos' approach results in *self-protecting* systems that can tolerate misbehaving sensors and can compute correct values without identifying the faulty sensors. However, if each interval is associated with a sensor identifier, a server may localize the source of the faults based on information such as the differences of physical intervals (sensors) values from the intersection chosen as the output interval and then use this new derived information to develop tools for *self-healing* capabilities.

Since determining $n$ and, therefore, $f$ in advance might not be possible with full certainty, effort has been directed to doing more sophisticated analysis of historical sensor data, that can be used to get better correlation among the replicas as well as better detection of faulty sensors. Typically, *iterative filtering* (IF) algorithms are used to estimate some level of *trustworthiness* of a sensor based on the distance of its readings from the estimate of the correct values obtained in the previous iteration by some form of aggregation (usually a weighted average) of the readings of all sensors. Sensors whose readings significantly differ from such estimate are less trusted and, consequently, in the aggregation process of the current iteration their readings are given a lower weight. The performance of IF algorithms in the presence of different types of faults and false data injection attacks has been extensively studied showing significant improvements over simple averaging of values. The reader can find details of the basic approach in [20], and work addressing collusion attacks in [36] and [64].

These domain-independent approach can be extended with semantic information to improve the detection of faults. One type of semantic information is the relation between the geographical location of sensors and their readings. For example, sensing readings of acoustic volume and thermal radiation in sensor networks attenuate over distance. Such a piece of information can be used to differentiate between faulty readings and correct data. The authors of [29] leverage this concept and propose a fault-tolerant technique where faults are detected by assuming a mismatch between the distance rank and sensor data rank, i.e., a mismatch between the distance from the event and the sensed data.

An alternative approach to cope with faulty sensors is to make the collection of sensors that have been replicated to collect and report the same data agree in the sensing data to report. In other words, the sensors may implement a majority voting mechanism to decide what are the readings coming from faulty sensors, in order to avoid sending them to the collector. Two examples of such a distributed approach are [44] and [77]. In [44] the authors introduce the concept of *spatial correlation*, a piece of semantic information according to which readings from non-faulty sensors in close proximity are spatially correlated, i.e., similar because they are coming from adjacent places. With this in mind, a sensor can autonomously decide whether a neighbor is faulty or not. The author of [77] improved this mechanism by introducing a trustworthiness value for each sensor, such that the voting mechanisms is enhanced with the use of votes weighted according to the trust of sensor values. These techniques confer systems the property of being *self-healing*, as they would be able to autonomously detect and isolate faulty devices.

Another complementary approach to sensor replication is to have several sensors of different modalities be deployed to provide backup services for each other. More specifically, devices of different types may be deployed in order to have independent readings that can substitute each others in case of faults.

For example, passive infrared sensors are often used to detect human presence. However, human presence can also be inferred by other types of sensors such as graphical monitors and sound sensors. This approach is discussed in [81], where the authors propose a *self-healing* technique which strength is directly proportional to the heterogeneity degree of the deployed devices.

Researchers have also looked at the problem of how many sensors to use and where best to locate them. The typical approach is to set the problem as an optimization problem that minimizes the number of sensors guaranteeing some minimal level of sensing coverage, so as if some sensor stops working, the sensing task continues to be performed correctly by its neighbors. Two examples of this line of work are [11] and [35], where the concept of *k-coverage* is used for ensuring a minimum quality of service. *k-coverage* is defined as any location in the network being monitored by at least $k$ nodes. The parameter $k$ measures the amount of fault-tolerance inherent in the sensors deployment scheme. These techniques only provide the *self-protecting* property, as the deployment of sensors is static, and no dynamic adjustments are expected in case of faults.

# 4 Fault-Tolerant Routing Protocols

Data transmission in IoT is inherently faulty and unpredictable due to two main reasons. The first one is related to the brittle nature of wireless communication: links may fail when blocked by an external object or environmental condition, causing network partitions and changes in network topology. The second cause is linked to the failure of routers, that may stop working due to the harsh environment where they are deployed, or because of the depletion of batteries.

To these sources of faults we need to add malicious users compromising the communication channels and routers showing byzantine behavior as sources of faults. The action of an attacker aimed at preventing the use of a communication channel by interfering with the radio frequencies is known as *jamming attack* [54]. A router shows a byzantine behavior if it does not comply with the routing protocol rules. This typically happens when an attacker compromises a device by injecting malicious code by means of a malware. In literature, different types of byzantine behaviors have been identified in the field of wireless sensor networks [39], those that aim at disrupting the routing task are:

- *dropping attack:* malicious nodes do not forward part of (*selective forwarding* attack) or all (*black hole* attack) the received messages.
- *replay attack:* malicious nodes store received packets to forward them successively. This may be the cause of multiple issues: routing loops, extended or shortened source routes, generation of false error messages, network partition.
- *delay attack:* malicious nodes delay the forwarding of received packets so as to fail the time synchronization process, causing the production of excessive amount of routing control traffic.
- *sybil attack:* a malicious node presents multiple identities to other nodes in the network.

– *sinkhole attack:* malicious nodes lure network traffic by advertising better communication performance than their neighbors, thus creating a sinkhole with them in the center. The sinkhole attack occurs in protocols that use advertised information such as remaining energy or an estimate of end-to-end reliability to construct a routing topology.

### 4.1 Main Approaches

Fault-tolerance in routing schemes is achieved by means of redundancy, which in turn, is implemented in various ways depending on the characteristics of the network. An effective and well established approach comes from the concept of *dispersity routing* introduced by Maxemchuk [51]. In dispersity routing mechanisms a source node divides the message and sends its components and possibly replicas of its components on different paths. This mechanism provides the ability of tolerating a large number of transmission errors before requiring the messages to be re-transmitted. This is the foundation of what is now referred to as *multi-path protocols*. Multi-path approaches are mainly adopted in *flat* networks, i.e. where nodes are not organized hierarchically because all of them have more or less the same computing and communication capabilities, thus playing the same role. Dispersity based systems are classified as *redundant* or *non-redundant*. In a non-redundant system, a message is divided into a number of chunks equal to the number of paths between the source and the destination. Each chunk is sent on a different path and the message is then reconstructed at the destination. Fault-tolerance is partially achieved since in case of link failure just a fraction of the original message has to be re-transmitted. In a redundant system the number of chunks is less than the number of paths. Additional chunks are formed as a linear combination of the bits in the message divisions, and each of the redundant and original chunks is transmitted along a different path. With an appropriate choice of linear combinations the message can be reconstructed without receiving all of the chunks. Intermittently connected networks, like mobile ad-hoc networks, vehicular ad-hoc networks and IoT applications deployed in harsh environments, have characteristics that made dispersity routing attractive. Messages routed over different paths whose nodes are completely disjoint withstand well dropping and sink hole attacks, as attackers should break at least one node for each path in order to be effective. However, completely disjoint paths may be difficult to create, especially in networks with a sparse topology. Braided paths (paths sharing some nodes but with no links in common) may be a viable alternative to provide probabilistic protection. For example, Ganesan et al. [27] proved that their braided multi-path scheme is a viable alternative for energy-efficient recovery from isolated and geographically correlated failures. Braided multi-paths require lower maintenance overhead than disjoint ones, and increasing the level of path disjointedness only provides modest gains in resilience gain with larger cost. Multi-paths have been used to extended standard protocols such as TCP [26] as well as bringing novel ideas for doing routing. For example, in the GRAB protocol proposed in [79], each node keeps the cost of forwarding a packet to the sink, such that nodes closer to the sink have smaller costs. Instead of a node choosing specific neighbors, each neighbor decides whether to forward a received packet by comparing its own cost to that of the sender. This way, data follow the direction of descending cost to reach the sink through multiple paths. Notice that the originality of this work lies in its ability to maintain multiple paths from the sources to the sink without the need to store them in routing tables.

Multi-path based approaches can also be implemented in a probabilistic way. In *probabilistic* broadcast approaches, called gossip protocols, a node randomly forwards packets to all its neighbors with a certain probability. Messages, then, follow multiple paths toward the destination, but unlike non-probabilistic protocols, such paths are not fixed but rather they are selected hop-by-hop. Since traffic is routed towards a physical location over multiple paths, it is difficult to create a sink hole type of attacks. Moreover, allowing nodes to choose the next hop using some probabilistic distribution, it reduces the chances of adversaries to successfully perform dropping attacks. The authors of [12] propose *Anonymous Gossip*, a probabilistic protocol that works in two concurrent phases. In the first phase a message is multicast, while in the second concurrent phase the gossip protocol recovers lost messages. Nodes need not know other nodes identity for gossip to be successful. This is extremely desirable for mobile nodes, that have limited resources, and where the knowledge of group membership is difficult to obtain. In contrast to the classical gossip algorithm where the same probability distribution to select the next hop is the same across all the nodes, the use of variable gossiping probabilities has been a common choice of many researchers, as it makes the work of an attacker more difficult. For example, in [4] the gossiping probability of a node is determined by the difference between its proximity to the destination and the proximity to the destination of the node from which the message was received. A comprehensive analysis on the choice of probabilities and protocols on the basis of the network topology can be found in [30]. The topologies considered are: *(i)* non-sparse networks (e.g. grids or dense topologies); *(ii)* sparse networks; *(iii)* sparse networks with the possibility to specify the gossip probability for a node having a number of neighbors under a certain threshold; and *(iv)* several topologies with the possibility for a node to know whether a message is dying out, so as to introduce a further copy of the message in the network (*self-healing* property).

Although multi-path approaches withstand well the presence of faulty nodes, they don't account for the energy consumption caused by the high number of messages transmitted. One of the most energy taxing task in many wireless devices is communicating with other devices. For IoT applications where energy saving is a primary maintenance goal, the solution is hierarchical routing. This approach aims to cluster nodes so that cluster heads can do some aggregation and reduction of data transmitted in order to save energy. This pattern is repeated to form a hierarchy of clusters with the uppermost level cluster nodes reporting directly to the sink. When the node density is high, hierarchical routing protocols tend to achieve much better performance because of less overhead, shorter average routing path, and quicker set-up procedures. Cluster heads are typically chosen based on their communication capabilities, or on their strategical location w.r.t. the rest of the network. Since these protocols use advertised information to construct a routing topology they are prone to sink hole attacks, as attackers use to advertise better communication performances to attract network traffic. Furthermore, once a compromised node get all the traffic it can perform black-hole attacks. Two approaches have been suggested to provide fail-tolerance to cluster head nodes: *(i)* by means of redundancy by introducing more than one cluster head; and *(ii)* by changing the set of cluster heads frequently enough to make it difficult for adversaries to choose the right nodes to compromise. Hao et al. [32] investigated the problem of cluster-head placement so that every node can communicate with at least two neighboring cluster heads. Thus, when a cluster head fails, a node can transfer itself to another cluster and transmit to an active cluster-head (*self-healing* property). Kuhn et al. [45] have improved this model by increasing the minimum number of cluster-heads a node can communicate with. They convert the node placement problem into a $k$ minimum dominating set ($k$-MDS) problem. The goal of $k$-MDS is to find the minimal subset of cluster-heads so that every node can communicate with at least $k$ cluster-heads. However, these approaches have a drawback related to the battery depletion of cluster-heads, since their battery is drained much earlier than that of others nodes. Boukerche et al. [5] proposed a method to overcome this issue, according to which cluster-heads are dynamically chosen considering their residual energy (*self-configuring* property). This way, cluster-heads change over time and energy dissipation is uniformly distributed among the nodes. LEACH (Low-Energy Adaptive Clustering Hierarchy) [33], is another clustering-based protocol aimed at distributing energy consumption that utilizes randomized rotation of local cluster-heads. This feature simultaneously provides the model *self-configuring* and *self-optimizing* properties. LEACH is very comprehensive: it builds up clusters of sensor nodes based on their signal strength, uses localized coordination to enable scalability and robustness for dynamic networks, and incorporates data fusion into the routing protocol to reduce the amount of information that must be transmitted to the base station.

For the delay, replay, jamming, and sybil attacks, redundancy is not sufficient to make routing resilient, methods based on attack detection and/or authentication are needed instead. Some of the work in this research area are discussed in Sect. 6.

## 5   Fault-Tolerant Control Devices

Control devices in an IoT network provide stateful services by performing computations as a reaction to interactions with other entities in the network. For example, a control device may receive events from motion detectors which the controller can analyze and then trigger actuators to turn cameras on. The cameras will send images back to the controller that must identify if there is a moving object, authenticate the object, decide whether to provide access to the object to protected areas, and decide to trigger another set of actuators to lock or unlock doors accordingly. Such a central role makes control devices essential for the correct system operation, thus it is paramount to keep them running appropriately.

*State machine replication* can be considered the accepted paradigm to work with to provide fault-tolerance to stateful services [69]. Informally, the state machine replication is a distributed computing paradigm for implementing a fault-tolerant service by replicating a server and make sure that the behavior of the replicas under the same conditions are identical. Hence, if some of the servers fail the correct replicas can continue to provide the service. State machine replication protocols aim to implement a *linearly ordered* log abstraction that represent the trace of execution as if it were a single state machine. For that to happen, there are two properties that must be satisfies: (1) all servers must have the same view of the logs, and (2) whenever an event occurs in the system, it is incorporated quickly in the log. The first property is known as *consistency* and the second as *liveliness*. These protocols are referred as *consensus* protocols or algorithms since consensus must be reached by all replicas as to what to add to the log and when. Consensus protocols are widely used in high-reliability computing systems and are applied in many distributed applications. We have already seen that some fault-tolerant mechanisms for sensor devices rely on consensus algorithms.

There are many situations in which many consensus algorithms can be simply adapted for IoT, but there are also scenarios for which the standard algorithms have limitations. In the next section we present brief overview of the formal characteristics of the different approached of reaching consensus and reflect on their application in the IoT context.

## 5.1 Distributed Consensus Algorithms

Given a group of $n$ processing units, the main property of a fault-tolerant consensus algorithm is the maximum number of processing unit that can fail and still guarantee a correct consensus. It is important to add that a consensus algorithm is expected to be implemented by a group of processing elements that are inherently asynchronous. These processing elements communicate by message passing and the communication channels may or may not be reliable. Therefore, the second property to establish is the total number of message bits needed. The first result that we mention is a well-known impossibility results that says that without synchronization a deterministic consensus is impossible even if only one participant crashes during the protocol [25]. This result, sometimes referred as the FLP impossibility result, means that a deterministic algorithm must include some form of synchronization and that the algorithm will run in rounds of communication. Lamport et al. [46] demonstrated that tolerating $f$ byzantine faults requires at least $n = 3f + 1$ participants, while tolerating $f$ fail-stops requires at least $n = 2f + 1$ participants. Although a few variations exist, basically it is accepted that about $f + O(f)$ rounds are needed and the message bits required are $O(f^2)$. Randomization in the algorithm, where some operations are the result of a random choice, lower the number of the rounds needed to $O(log(n))$. The liveliness property for randomized protocols becomes *"every correct process eventually knows about the log with probability 1"* [8], while the consistency property becomes *"every participant eventually decides a log entry with probability 1"* [73].

For synchronicity, two assumptions are usually made in the algorithms. One is that communication *is reliable* with a fixed delay, and the computation capabilities of the processes are homogeneous. These assumptions limit the applicability in many IoT scenarios where networks might be unreliable and device capabilities heterogeneous. A typical approach to work around the FLP impossibility result is to work with a *partial synchronous* model [23], where upper bounds on message transmission time $\Delta$, and on process response time $\Phi$, can be established and time constraints can be violated only by system failures. According to this model, a system can behave asynchronously for some time interval until it eventually stabilizes and starts to behave in a synchronous manner, i.e. by respecting $\Delta$ or $\Phi$, or both. This time interval is called the *global stabilization time (GST)*, it is unknown to the processors, but it is assumed that after the GST has elapsed the protocol will behave synchronously for a time interval long enough to achieve consensus. Algorithms based on this model are also probabilistic as they guarantee correctness only when these time constraints are satisfied. Various algorithms exist relaxing in different ways the assumptions, but the general result bounds the numbers of rounds to $O(n + \Delta + \Phi)$.

Another common approach to circumvent the FLP result is to extend an asynchronous system with an *oracle*. Oracles are typically failure detectors that detect, or suspect, when a replica crashes or behaves maliciously. The intuition behind oracles is that, having an idea about the failure/crash of a device, helps bypassing the FLP result as the impossibility derives from the impossibility of distinguishing faulty replicas from slow ones. Failure detectors for byzantine processors have the limitation that cannot detect all faults, but only a subset, and that they can not be completely independent of the consensus algorithm [42]. Chandra and Toueg [14] introduced the concept of *unreliable* failure detector, and showed how to use it to solve consensus in asynchronous systems with fail-stops. The term "unreliable" means that the detector can make mistakes, i.e. it can erroneously report that a process has crashed even though it is still running. The resilience of the approach is for $n = f + 1$ processors, and termination happens after in $n - 1$ rounds.

A way to limit the capabilities of byzantine replicas is to use *authentication*. Authentication is the ability of replicas to establish reliable communication channels to exchange messages. This limits the capabilities of faulty participants as: *(i)* a message signed by a fault-free replica is unable to be forged; *(ii)* any corruption of the message is detectable; and *(iii)* the signature can be authenticated by any other replica. As a consequence, authentication provides a system with a higher resilience. Furthermore, in authenticated systems there is no need for point-to-point private channels among replicas, and messages can also be sent through multi-hop paths involving more than one replica (although they can be faulty replicas too). One of the first contributions in this area was from Dolev and Reischuk [22], that proposed a deterministic consensus protocol for synchronous systems, which provides a resilience of $n = f + 1$ processors, with termination happening after $O(f)$ rounds, employing $O(n + f^2)$ messages and $O(nf)$ signatures. An authenticated-byzantine fault detector was proposed by Kihlstrom

**Table 1.** Comparison of the consensus protocols discussed in Sect. 5.1

| Resilience | No. rounds | Time model | Fault | Det/Prob | Method | Ref |
|---|---|---|---|---|---|---|
| $f \le (n-1)/3$ | $\ge f+1$ | synch | byzantine | det | – | [59] |
| $O(f^{1.5})$ | $\ge f+1$ | synch | byzantine | det | – | [18] |
| $f \le (n-1)/3$ | $\ge 2f+2$ | synch | byzantine | det | – | [74] |
| $f \le (n-1)/3$ | $\le f+1$ | asynch | byzantine | prob | randomization | [6] |
| $f \le n/(3+\epsilon)$ | $O(\log n)$ | synch | byzantine | prob | randomization | [7] |
| $f \le (n-1)/3$ | $O(f/\log n)$ | synch | byzantine | prob | randomization | [17] |
| $f < n-1$ | $O(f)$ | synch | auth. byzantine | det | – | [22] |
| $f \le (n-1)/2$ | $GST+O(n+\Delta)$ | asynch comm. & synch proc. | fail-stop & omission | prob | partially synch | [23] |
| $f \le n$ | $GST+O(n+\Delta+\Phi)$ | synch comm. & asynch proc. | fail-stop | prob | partially synch | [23] |
| $f \le (n-1)/2$ | $GST+O(n+\Delta+\Phi)$ | asynch comm. & asynch proc. | fail-stop & omission | prob | partially synch | [23] |
| $f \le (n-1)/3$ | $GST+O(n+\Delta+\Phi)$ | asynch comm. & asynch proc. | byzantine & auth. byzantine | prob | partially synch | [23] |
| $f \in [(n-1)/2, n/2]$ | $GST+O(n+\Delta+\Phi)$ | synch comm. & asynch proc. | omission | prob | partially synch | [23] |
| $f \le (n-1)/3$ | $GST+O(n+\Delta)$ | asynch comm. & synch proc. | byzantine & auth. byzantine | prob | partially synch | [23] |
| $f \le (n-1)/3$ | $GST+O(n+\Delta)$ | synch comm. & asynch proc. | byzantine | prob | partially synch | [23] |
| $f \le (n-1)/2$ | $GST+O(n+\Delta)$ | synch comm. & asynch proc. | auth. byzantine | prob | partially synch | [23] |
| $f \le n-1$ | $\ge n-1$ | asynch | crash | prob | oracle | [14] |
| $f \le (n-1)/3$ | $\ge f+1$ | synch | byzantine | det | oracle | [42] |
| $f \le (n-1)/2$ | $O(n^2)$ | asynch | crash | det | partially synch | [47] |

et al. in [42], where the authors achieve the resilience of $n = 3f + 1$ processors in asynchronous systems, with a deterministic approach that terminates within $f + 1$ rounds employing $(f + 1)(3n + 1)$ messages.

## 5.2   Consensus Protocols for IoT

In IoT, consensus protocols designed with the byzantine fault model in mind (Sect. 2.3), and for systems assumed to be asynchronous, are preferable considered the uncertainty that characterizes IoT scenarios. In fact, these algorithms are able to deal with issues coming from both the faults and time domain, which makes them tolerant to adverse environments and considerable delays. However, there are limitations to these solutions. Table 1 summarizes the work discussed in this section so far. The reader can notice that these are well-established results coming from the 1990's and 80's. There are several limitations that hamper the utilization of these algorithms in IoT scenarios. One is that they all assume that the number of participants $n$ is fixed. This assumption might be reasonable in a smart home scenarios but it starts to create difficulties in more open situations as smart cities. A second limitation is that participants that don't respond to requested messages from the consensus protocols are pessimistically treated as malicious nodes, but in many IoT scenarios, no all honest nodes will be active all the time. Another potential difficulty can come from the number of messages or rounds required to complete the protocol. Most of the algorithms require a quadratic number of rounds or messages with respect to the number of participants. Examples of real cases where consensus has to be achieved among a non-fixed number of participants are in vehicular ad-hoc networks (VANET) [31,34]. Figure 2 shows a VANET scenario where a micro cloud is formed by smart cars, and where computation and decisions are performed among the cars that are in that region in the same time period. Another well fitting example is a set of unmanned air vehicles (UAV) or drones that patrol an area and that have to cooperate in unstable conditions like switching topology and time delay [52].

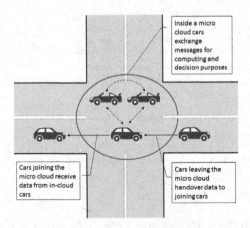

**Fig. 2.** A micro cloud in a vehicular ad-hoc network.

Since 2008, consensus algorithms took a new direction with the introduction of the concept of blockchain [55]. Informally, authentication has been used in consensus protocols to establish some level of trust among honest participants. In blockchain algorithms such trust is not established using cryptographic keys. Instead, trust is established by a "proof-of-work" (PoW) demonstrated through solving some computational puzzle that depends on the current event and the history of events. For that, each participant maintains a *chain* of *blocks* of events.

Each block has a "key-less" signature that is obtained by the PoW. The first important contribution for the IoT is that consensus is reached with no more than a linear number of messages. The second relevant contribution is that by getting a copy of the most recent chain, nodes can enter into the system almost at any point. These consensus algorithms are the basis of all crypto-currencies generating a lot of interest in the research community and industry. There has been a proliferation of blockchain protocols because of their potential impact on publicly verifiable transactions, and yet, able to provide strong privacy guarantees. There have been many suggestions about how blockchain algorithms can be useful to support IoT services focusing on the capabilities of supporting anonymous transactions. These suggestions tend to provide privacy or micro-payments based services [80]. Nevertheless, a fundamental application of consensus algorithms, state machine replication for fault-tolerance has never been mentioned. However, in order to incorporate the concept into consensus protocols for fault-tolerance in IoT the PoW must be replaced since it requires computational capabilities that the IoT devices are unlikely to have. This impediment is not limited to fault-tolerance. Many of the applications summarized in [80] may not be practically realizable for the same reason. Recently though, we have seen technical results that are starting to address this issue. In [58], Pass and Shi propose an algorithm that significantly reduces the PoW by returning to strong authentications but keeping the blockchains. This access control layer allows honest participants to enter and leave the system with very few limitations. The authentication in the protocol requires from the participants some computational capacity, which may be not within the capabilities of all smart devices. However, smart devices computational power is increasing over time, thus in the near future they might be able to afford such heavier tasks. The characteristic of allowing participants to enter and leaving the system could be a key aspect for the implementation of distributed consensus in the IoT, which for some particular applications, it could result in a highly dynamic computing environment. For many consensus protocols the number of participants $n$ is a necessary information for processors to achieve consensus. With some little modification to the protocols, $n$ can be constrained in certain bounds, and the number of candidates participants be larger than $n$, thus leaving the protocol open to whoever holds the credentials to enter. This way, the system is conferred of a higher degree of resilience, as it can replace failed nodes in real time.

Besides PoW, Proof of Stake (PoS) is another mechanism to establish trust in blockchain protocols where the validator of the next transaction is chosen via a combinations of random selection and its reputation based on its performance over time in the system (stake) [41]. Here the "stake" is used as a measure of trust. PoS could be more suited for IoT application as it does not require high computational power to the participants, and can be exploited to model long-lived IoT devices, or devices more resilient to attacks and failures. There is another class of algorithms that can be characterized as combining standard Byzantine consensus with blockcain. In this class we find the *Swirlds hash-graph* consensus algorithm [1] and Algorand [28]. These algorithms are based on gossip protocols. These algorithm can significantly reduce the number of messages exchanged as well as the number of rounds to get consensus. Algorand also randomly selects the $n$ processes that will run the consensus and this set can be replaced in each round of the consensus protocol. The constraint is in the set of $n$ devices at least $2n/3$ are not faulty.

Proving correctness and properties of distributed algorithms is not trivial. Many times the analysis is done under assumptions that are difficult or impossible to implement, and an independent verification and analysis is required [9]. This is the case of the algorithms discussed here: we are not aware of any implementation of the algorithm in [58], there are not publicly available implementations of the algorithm in [28], while the algorithm in [1] has an implementation but no independent validation.

## 5.3  Beyond Self-protecting Autonomic Management of Faults

A state machine as described so far has the characteristic of being self-protecting, a feature conferred by the employment of a consensus protocol which allows to withstand the presence of a minority of fail-stop or byzantine replicas. However it is desirable for a state machine to be self-healing too, so that crashed or compromised replicas can be identified and excluded from the consensus protocol.

As a brief example, let us consider an $f$-fault-tolerant state machine with $n = 19$ participants running a consensus protocol which tolerates $f = (n-1)/3 = 6$ faulty replicas. As long as the number of faulty replicas $t \leq f$ the state machine is capable of producing a correct output. When $t = f$ a non-self-healing state machine can not tolerate any more faults, thus as soon as $t$ exceeds $f$ the state machine might produce incorrect outputs for the next protocol executions. On the contrary, if the state machine is self-healing, i.e., it is able to discover and exclude faulty replicas, when $t$ is approaching $f$, it can update the value of $n$ to $n_{new} \leq n - t$. Let's say $t$ is 4 and $n_{new} = 15$. The value of $f$ can be now $f_{new} = (n_{new} - 1)/3 = 4$. At this point the state machine can run the consensus protocol among the healthy replicas and tolerate 4 more faulty replicas, beside the 4 ones just excluded. Of course, it must be taken into account that a state machine with 14 replicas is less reliable than a state machine with 19 replicas. Removing faulty replicas also reduces both the message complexity and time complexity of the consensus protocols. A further improvement can be achieved if the state machine is able to replace faulty replicas with healthy ones, instead of just excluding them from the consensus protocol.

In blockchain-based consensus protocol, information about the state of the system can be found directly into the blockchain, since it contains the history of the events occurred within the system. The Algorand algorithm uses this to sidestep having to replace faulty replicas by replacing the consensus participants in every step, essentially reconfiguring the system all the time.

An important research direction is to find the most appropriate mechanisms to interleave these consensus protocols with the computation being done by the state machine to decide what part of the computation can be in practice considered atomic and become a block of the blockchain. In any case, the self-healing property requires detecting the faulty controllers and then deciding how to restore their normal behavior. Detection is even more important in situations where the number of devices is not very large to randomly select $n$ controllers with more than $2n/3$ healthy controllers at every step.

The methods for detection of faulty processes have been developed long time ago and it is typically performed by participants testing each others. A test consists of requesting the device to perform a computation and comparing the result with that which is expected. If the result disagrees with the expected answer, then the tested device is considered faulty [3, 43, 62]. An effective method for testing is the *remote attestation*. Remote attestation allows for a tester to establish the absence of malicious changes to the memory contents of the tested replica. One way of performing remote attestation is to include an attestation routine in the replica's kernel that performs a checksum on the memory contents of the replica. As replicas are identical by definition, each replica knows the state of the other replicas' memory, thus each replica would also know the value of such a checksum at every moment [70, 71].

## 6    Other Research Areas

As mentioned in Sect. 4, for delay, replay, sybil, and jamming attacks there is no known redundancy based solution, rather, detection and/or prevention based mechanisms are more suitable. Delay attacks are typically addressed by means of intrusion detection mechanisms. The most common one is the *watchdog*, introduced by Marti et al. in [49]. According to this mechanism a network node is monitored by its neighbors, the watchdogs. Thus, if a node misbehaves it is detected by the watchdogs around it, and a failure tally is incremented. When the tally exceeds a certain threshold, a node is labeled as malicious and excluded from forwarding routes. The same approach has been extended so as watchdogs collaborate each other to investigate the source of intrusions and coordinate responses [37], and to be able to detect a wider range of attacks [72]. Some known protocols also implement security mechanisms against the delay attack, as for the RPL routing protocol for low power and lossy networks [75], which can be set to run in different security modes, each providing protection against different attacks.

For replay and sybil attacks we are aware of very few fault-tolerant technique able to withstand the presence of node showing such malicious behaviors [19, 21, 57]. Rather, for these kind of attacks literature mainly provides prevention methods based on authentication. Authentication can prevent against replay attacks, because messages authenticated with previously disclosed keys are ignored. Many routing protocols also adopt sequence numbers in forwarded packets to protect against replay attacks, so as a packet with sequence number smaller than the last received one can be detected as a replayed packet. Authentication can also prevent sybil attacks, as neighbor nodes can use a cryptographic key to implement an authenticated communication channel, where identities are verified.

The jamming attack differs from the attacks discussed above because it is typically carried by an external attacker who does not need to compromise any network node to perform the attack. Moreover, this attack shows the same symptoms of any casual event that can interfere in the routing task (like changes in the environment), that is the unavailability of communication channels. In [10] the authors identify 12 types of "jammers" and propose two anomaly detection mechanisms to differentiate between legitimate and adversary scenarios. These mechanisms use three metrics to detect and differentiate jamming attacks from each other and from natural causes: the packet delivery ratio (PDR), the ratio of the number of delivered packets compared to the number of sent out packets; the bad packet ratio (BPR), the ratio of the number of erroneous packets compared to the number of received total or preamble packets for a sensor node; and the energy consumption amount (ECA), defined as approximated energy amount consumed in a specified time for a sensor node. The detection algorithms are loaded on network nodes, thus forming a distributed and localized detection system. A totally different approach is the *spreading* technique, whereby resilience to interference is achieved by transmitting information using a bandwidth much larger than its required minimum bandwidth [60]. In this approach, the transmitter redundantly encodes information using a spreading code. Then the receiver decodes the message by correlating the signal with the same code. Without knowing the spreading code used in the communication between two nodes, signals such as jamming or casual interference will appear noise-like upon decoding, and thus can be filtered out. However, if an attacker compromises a node, he/she can discover the spreading code in use and perform the attack successfully. To overcome such a circumstance Chiang et al. [16] proposed to adopt an asymmetric system, i.e. where sender and receiver use different codes, which allows network nodes to cooperatively detect a jamming attack.

In security, there are specialized tools for preventing (i.e., avoiding attacks) and monitoring (i.e., detecting attacks) faults in IoT. One of these tools is Kalis proposed by Midi et al. [53], an autonomic security tool for IoT networks. Kalis is *self-configuring*, as it discovers the features of the monitored network (size, topology, mobility, etc.) and enable the set of detection techniques that best fit with the sensed environment. Rullo et al. proposed PAST [65] a protocol-adaptable security tool for the IoT. Like Kalis, PAST is *self-configuring* as it adapts its detection policy based on the set of communication protocols adopted by the monitored IoT application. PAST is *self-optimizing* too, as it leverages the security mechanisms of the protocols to optimize its detection task. Both Kalis and PAST can be integrated with recovery functions and replicated in order to implement a *self-healing* autonomic security system. A *k-coverage*-based method to compute the optimal replication degree and the optimal placement of security resources in IoT scenarios is presented in [66]. A similar approach for mobile IoT networks is presented in [67].

Fault-tolerance in IoT applications, especially in wireless sensor networks, has also been investigated in the area of the data storage. Not always sensors immediately forward sensed data to the sink, but rather they wait until the sink sends them a query. In this cases, as the failure of a sensor would result in a data loss, researchers have focused in designing failover techniques for data replications in order to optimally distribute sensed data over the entire network. An example of such work with local storage for replications is described in [63]. In this work, storage nodes are specified by hash functions to collect data of certain types. Redundancy is achieved by storing replicas directly on neighbors nodes. In [61], a dynamic replication for local data storage is presented. Here replicas are randomly distributed within a replication range influenced by the replica number and its density.

**Beyond the IoT.** IoT networks normally do not have enough computing power to perform heavy tasks like computations on large amount of sensed data for control or analysis purposes. To this end, these tasks are typically delegated to more powerful computing infrastructures like the cloud and the fog. Fault-tolerance approaches for the back-end support of IoT is beyond the scope of this paper, but there are fault detection and prevention mechanisms specifically addressing the potential harm that failures at the IoT can cause at the back-end. In this context attackers may inject false data so as to compromise the outcome of the computation, or worse, to make issuing wrong control commands. Yan et al. [78] proposed a multi-level DDoS mitigation framework to defend against DDoS attacks for industrial IoT, which includes the fog and the cloud computing levels. Their approach implements firmware security checks, access control, malicious firmware/software detection, vulnerability scanning, intrusion detection, honeypot monitoring, and encryption of exchanged data. Lu et al. [48] proposed a lightweight privacy preserving data aggregation (LPDA) scheme for fog computing-enhanced IoT. With the fog device deployed at the network edge, LPDA supports fault-tolerance by filtering false data injected by external attackers, and by computing mean and variance of the reported data even though some IoT devices are malfunctioning and stop reporting to the control center.

Cyber Physical Systems (CPS) share the same basic architecture with the IoT: they are typically made up of sensing and control components that communicate each other by means of some routing scheme. On the other hand, CPS may combine wired and wireless communication channels, they not necessarily consist of smart devices since they may have powerful computing components as integral part of the system. Controllers can complex and are mainly designed by means of control theory. Nevertheless, some basic principles to address fault-tolerance in CPS are the same as in the IoT. In particular in the area of automatic control, fault detection and diagnosis methods as well as fault tolerant control designs have been developed in order to increase the reliability and maintainability of systems prone to failures. The results again resemble the results from consensus protocols, and similar to the IoT, fault-tolerant control systems have been designed so as to be self-protecting (called *passive*) and self-healing (called *active*). Although a detailed discussion of fault-tolerance in CPS is out of the scope of this paper, we refer the interested readers to [38] for a general overview and to [24] for the results on fault-tolerance in CPS control systems.

# 7    Conclusion

In this paper we have described redundancy-based fault-tolerant techniques for the IoT. We have divided the discussion in three parts, one for each role played by devices in IoT networks, namely, sensor, communication device, and control device. By analyzing the main contributions we have shown that the implementation of fault-tolerance in each of these areas is necessary for a system to be resilient to faults and failures. We have seen how to leverage redundancy to implement fault-tolerance, and what are the consequences in terms of trade-off between resilience and costs: fault-tolerance "is not for free", as redundancy implies more complexity in the operate and, consequently, more energy consumed and maintenance overhead. For sensors and routing protocols several fault-tolerant techniques have been proposed in literature: strategic sensors deployment, sensors fusion algorithms, centralized and distributed fault detection tasks, randomized routing protocols, etc. For control devices, instead, fault-tolerance has received less attention. We reviewed the possibility of implementing fault-tolerance with the state machine replication paradigm, and discussed different consensus protocols focusing on both classical and modern solutions. Thanks to recent proposals in the field of consensus protocols, we envision the possibility of making control in the IoT more dynamic, by allowing devices to implement distributed state machines that can change in size and capabilities over time.

# References

1. Baird, L.: The Swirlds hashgraph consensus algorithm: fair, fast, byzantine fault tolerance. Swirlds, Inc., Technical report SWIRLDS-TR-2016-01 (2016)
2. Barborak, M., Dahbura, A., Malek, M.: The consensus problem in fault-tolerant computing. ACM Comput. Surv. (CSur) **25**(2), 171–220 (1993)
3. Barsi, F., Grandoni, F., Maestrini, P.: A theory of diagnosability of digital systems. IEEE Trans. Comput. **6**, 585–593 (1976)
4. Beraldi, R.: The polarized gossip protocol for path discovery in MANETs. Ad Hoc Netw. **6**(1), 79–91 (2008)
5. Boukerche, A., Pazzi, R.W.N., Araujo, R.B.: Fault-tolerant wireless sensor network routing protocols for the supervision of context-aware physical environments. J. Parallel Distrib. Comput. **66**(4), 586–599 (2006)
6. Bracha, G.: Asynchronous byzantine agreement protocols. Inf. Comput. **75**(2), 130–143 (1987)
7. Bracha, G.: An O(log n) expected rounds randomized byzantine generals protocol. J. ACM (JACM) **34**(4), 910–920 (1987)
8. Bracha, G., Toueg, S.: Resilient consensus protocols. In: Proceedings of the Second Annual ACM Symposium on Principles of Distributed Computing, pp. 12–26. ACM (1983)
9. Cachin, C., Vukolić, M.: Blockchains consensus protocols in the wild. arXiv preprint arXiv:1707.01873 (2017)
10. Çakiroğlu, M., Özcerit, A.T.: Jamming detection mechanisms for wireless sensor networks. In: Proceedings of the 3rd International Conference on Scalable Information Systems, p. 4. ICST (Institute for Computer Sciences, Social-Informatics and Telecommunications Engineering) (2008)

11. Chakrabarty, K., Iyengar, S.S., Qi, H., Cho, E.: Grid coverage for surveillance and target location in distributed sensor networks. IEEE Trans. Comput. **51**(12), 1448–1453 (2002)

12. Chandra, R., Ramasubramanian, V., Birman, K.: Anonymous gossip: improving multicast reliability in mobile ad-hoc networks. In: 21st International Conference on Distributed Computing Systems, pp. 275–283. IEEE (2001)

13. Chandra, T.D., Griesemer, R., Redstone, J.: Paxos made live: an engineering perspective. In: Proceedings of the Twenty-Sixth Annual ACM Symposium on Principles of Distributed Computing, pp. 398–407. ACM (2007)

14. Chandra, T.D., Toueg, S.: Unreliable failure detectors for reliable distributed systems. J. ACM (JACM) **43**(2), 225–267 (1996)

15. Chen, J., Micali, S.: ALGORAND: the efficient and democratic ledger. CoRR abs/1607.01341 (2016)

16. Chiang, J.T., Hu, Y.C.: Cross-layer jamming detection and mitigation in wireless broadcast networks. In: Proceedings of the 13th Annual ACM International Conference on Mobile Computing and Networking, pp. 346–349. ACM (2007)

17. Chor, B., Coan, B.A.: A simple and efficient randomized byzantine agreement algorithm. IEEE Trans. Softw. Eng. **6**, 531–539 (1985)

18. Coan, B.A.: Efficient agreement using fault diagnosis. Distrib. Comput. **7**(2), 87–98 (1993)

19. Conti, M., Di Pietro, R., Mancini, L.V., Mei, A.: A randomized, efficient, and distributed protocol for the detection of node replication attacks in wireless sensor networks. In: Proceedings of the 8th ACM International Symposium on Mobile Ad Hoc Networking and Computing, pp. 80–89. ACM (2007)

20. De Kerchove, C., Van Dooren, P.: Iterative filtering in reputation systems. SIAM J. Matrix Anal. Appl. **31**(4), 1812–1834 (2010)

21. Demirbas, M., Song, Y.: An RSSI-based scheme for sybil attack detection in wireless sensor networks. In: Proceedings of the 2006 International Symposium on World of Wireless, Mobile and Multimedia Networks, pp. 564–570. IEEE Computer Society (2006)

22. Dolev, D., Reischuk, R.: Bounds on information exchange for byzantine agreement. J. ACM (JACM) **32**(1), 191–204 (1985)

23. Dwork, C., Lynch, N., Stockmeyer, L.: Consensus in the presence of partial synchrony. J. ACM (JACM) **35**(2), 288–323 (1988)

24. Fawzi, H., Tabuada, P., Diggavi, S.: Secure estimation and control for cyber-physical systems under adversarial attacks. IEEE Trans. Autom. Control **59**(6), 1454–1467 (2014)

25. Fischer, M.J., Lynch, N.A., Paterson, M.S.: Impossibility of distributed consensus with one faulty process. J. Assoc. Comput. Mach. **32**(2), 374–382 (1985)

26. Ford, A., Raiciu, C., Handley, M., Barre, S., Iyengar, J.: Architectural guidelines for multipath TCP development. Technical report (2011)

27. Ganesan, D., Govindan, R., Shenker, S., Estrin, D.: Highly-resilient, energy-efficient multipath routing in wireless sensor networks. ACM SIGMOBILE Mob. Comput. Commun. Rev. **5**(4), 11–25 (2001)

28. Gilad, Y., Hemo, R., Micali, S., Vlachos, G., Zeldovich, N.: Algorand: scaling byzantine agreements for cryptocurrencies. In: Proceedings of the 26th Symposium on Operating Systems Principles, pp. 51–68. ACM (2017)

29. Guo, S., Zhong, Z., He, T.: FIND: faulty node detection for wireless sensor networks. In: Proceedings of the 7th ACM Conference on Embedded Networked Sensor Systems, pp. 253–266. ACM (2009)

30. Haas, Z.J., Halpern, J.Y., Li, L.: Gossip-based ad hoc routing. IEEE/ACM Trans. Netw. **14**(3), 479–491 (2006)
31. Hagenauer, F., Sommer, C., Higuchi, T., Altintas, O., Dressler, F.: Vehicular micro clouds as virtual edge servers for efficient data collection. In: Proceedings of the 2nd ACM International Workshop on Smart, Autonomous, and Connected Vehicular Systems and Services, pp. 31–35. ACM (2017)
32. Hao, B., Tang, H., Xue, G.: Fault-tolerant relay node placement in wireless sensor networks: formulation and approximation. In: 2004 Workshop on High Performance Switching and Routing, HPSR 2004, pp. 246–250. IEEE (2004)
33. Heinzelman, W.R., Chandrakasan, A., Balakrishnan, H.: Energy-efficient communication protocol for wireless microsensor networks. In: Proceedings of the 33rd Annual Hawaii International Conference on System Sciences, p. 10-pp. IEEE (2000)
34. Higuchi, T., Dressler, F., Altintas, O.: How to keep a vehicular micro cloud intact. In: 2018 IEEE 87th Vehicular Technology Conference (VTC Spring), pp. 1–5. IEEE (2018)
35. Hoblos, G., Staroswiecki, M., Aitouche, A.: Optimal design of fault tolerant sensor networks. In: Proceedings of the 2000 IEEE International Conference on Control Applications, pp. 467–472. IEEE (2000)
36. Hoffman, K., Zage, D., Nita-Rotaru, C.: A survey of attack and defense techniques for reputation systems. ACM Comput. Surv. (CSUR) **42**(1), 1 (2009)
37. Huang, Y., Lee, W.: A cooperative intrusion detection system for ad hoc networks. In: Proceedings of the 1st ACM Workshop on Security of Ad Hoc and Sensor Networks, pp. 135–147. ACM (2003)
38. Isermann, R.: Fault-Diagnosis Systems: An Introduction from Fault Detection to Fault Tolerance. Springer, Heidelberg (2006). https://doi.org/10.1007/3-540-30368-5
39. Karlof, C., Wagner, D.: Secure routing in wireless sensor networks: attacks and countermeasures. In: 2003 IEEE International Workshop on Sensor Network Protocols and Applications, Proceedings of the First IEEE, pp. 113–127. IEEE (2003)
40. Kephart, J.O., Chess, D.M.: The vision of autonomic computing. Computer **1**, 41–50 (2003)
41. Kiayias, A., Russell, A., David, B., Oliynykov, R.: Ouroboros: a provably secure proof-of-stake blockchain protocol. In: Katz, J., Shacham, H. (eds.) CRYPTO 2017. LNCS, vol. 10401, pp. 357–388. Springer, Cham (2017). https://doi.org/10.1007/978-3-319-63688-7_12
42. Kihlstrom, K.P., Moser, L.E., Melliar-Smith, P.M.: Byzantine fault detectors for solving consensus. Comput. J. **46**(1), 16–35 (2003)
43. Kreutzer, S., Hakimi, S.: Adaptive fault identification in two new diagnostic models. In: Proceedings of the 21st Allerton Conference on Communication, Control and Computing, pp. 353–362 (1983)
44. Krishnamachari, B., Iyengar, S.: Distributed Bayesian algorithms for fault-tolerant event region detection in wireless sensor networks. IEEE Trans. Comput. **53**(3), 241–250 (2004)
45. Kuhn, F., Moscibroda, T., Wattenhofer, R.: Fault-tolerant clustering in ad hoc and sensor networks. In: Null, p. 68. IEEE (2006)
46. Lamport, L., Shostak, R., Pease, M.: The byzantine generals problem. ACM Trans. Program. Lang. Syst. (TOPLAS) **4**(3), 382–401 (1982)
47. Lamport, L., et al.: Paxos made simple. ACM SIGACT News **32**(4), 18–25 (2001)
48. Lu, R., Heung, K., Lashkari, A.H., Ghorbani, A.A.: A lightweight privacy-preserving data aggregation scheme for fog computing-enhanced IoT. IEEE Access **5**, 3302–3312 (2017)

49. Marti, S., Giuli, T.J., Lai, K., Baker, M.: Mitigating routing misbehavior in mobile ad hoc networks. In: Proceedings of the 6th Annual International Conference on Mobile Computing and Networking, pp. 255–265. ACM (2000)

50. Marzullo, K.: Tolerating failures of continuous-valued sensors. ACM Trans. Comput. Syst. (TOCS) **8**(4), 284–304 (1990)

51. Maxemchuk, N.F.: Dispersity routing. In: Proceedings of ICC, vol. 75, p. 41-10 (1975)

52. Maza, I., Kondak, K., Bernard, M., Ollero, A.: Multi-UAV cooperation and control for load transportation and deployment. In: Valavanis, K.P., Beard, R., Oh, P., Ollero, A., Piegl, L.A., Shim, H. (eds.) Selected papers from the 2nd International Symposium on UAVs, Reno, Nevada, USA June 8–10, 2009, pp. 417–449. Springer, Dordrecht (2009). https://doi.org/10.1007/978-90-481-8764-5_22

53. Midi, D., Rullo, A., Mudgerikar, A., Bertino, E.: Kalis—a system for knowledge-driven adaptable intrusion detection for the Internet of Things. In: 2017 IEEE 37th International Conference on Distributed Computing Systems (ICDCS), pp. 656–666. IEEE (2017)

54. Mpitziopoulos, A., Gavalas, D., Konstantopoulos, C., Pantziou, G.: A survey on jamming attacks and countermeasures in WSNs. IEEE Commun. Surv. Tutorials **11**(4), 42–56 (2009)

55. Nakamoto, S.: Bitcoin: a peer-to-peer electronic cash system (2008)

56. Ongaro, D., Ousterhout, J.K.: In search of an understandable consensus algorithm. In: USENIX Annual Technical Conference, pp. 305–319 (2014)

57. Parno, B., Perrig, A., Gligor, V.: Distributed detection of node replication attacks in sensor networks. In: 2005 IEEE Symposium on Security and Privacy, pp. 49–63. IEEE (2005)

58. Pass, R., Shi, E.: The sleepy model of consensus. In: Takagi, T., Peyrin, T. (eds.) ASIACRYPT 2017. LNCS, vol. 10625, pp. 380–409. Springer, Cham (2017). https://doi.org/10.1007/978-3-319-70697-9_14

59. Pease, M., Shostak, R., Lamport, L.: Reaching agreement in the presence of faults. J. ACM (JACM) **27**(2), 228–234 (1980)

60. Pickholtz, R., Schilling, D., Milstein, L.: Theory of spread-spectrum communications–a tutorial. IEEE Trans. Commun. **30**(5), 855–884 (1982)

61. Piotrowski, K., Langendoerfer, P., Peter, S.: tinyDSM: a highly reliable cooperative data storage for wireless sensor networks. In: International Symposium on Collaborative Technologies and Systems, CTS 2009, pp. 225–232. IEEE (2009)

62. Preparata, F.P., Metze, G., Chien, R.T.: On the connection assignment problem of diagnosable systems. IEEE Trans. Electron. Comput. **6**, 848–854 (1967)

63. Ratnasamy, S., et al.: GHT: a geographic hash table for data-centric storage. In: Proceedings of the 1st ACM International Workshop on Wireless Sensor Networks and Applications, pp. 78–87. ACM (2002)

64. Rezvani, M., Ignjatovic, A., Bertino, E., Jha, S.: Secure data aggregation technique for wireless sensor networks in the presence of collusion attacks. IEEE Trans. Dependable Secure Comput. **12**(1), 98–110 (2015)

65. Rullo, A., Bertino, E., Saccà, D.: PAST: protocol-adaptable security tool for heterogeneous IoT ecosystems. In: 2018 IEEE Conference on Dependable and Secure Computing, pp. 46–53. IEEE (2018)

66. Rullo, A., Midi, D., Serra, E., Bertino, E.: Pareto optimal security resource allocation for Internet of Things. ACM Trans. Priv. Secur. (TOPS) **20**(4), 15 (2017)

67. Rullo, A., Serra, E., Bertino, E., Lobo, J.: Shortfall-based optimal placement of security resources for mobile IoT scenarios. In: Foley, S.N., Gollmann, D., Snekkenes, E. (eds.) ESORICS 2017. LNCS, vol. 10493, pp. 419–436. Springer, Cham (2017). https://doi.org/10.1007/978-3-319-66399-9_23

68. Schneider, F.B.: Byzantine generals in action: implementing fail-stop processors. Technical report, Cornell University (1983)

69. Schneider, F.B.: Implementing fault-tolerant services using the state machine approach: a tutorial. ACM Comput. Surv. (CSUR) 22(4), 299–319 (1990)

70. Seshadri, A., Perrig, A., Van Doorn, L., Khosla, P.: SWATT: software-based attestation for embedded devices. In: Null, p. 272. IEEE (2004)

71. Shaneck, M., Mahadevan, K., Kher, V., Kim, Y.: Remote software-based attestation for wireless sensors. In: Molva, R., Tsudik, G., Westhoff, D. (eds.) ESAS 2005. LNCS, vol. 3813, pp. 27–41. Springer, Heidelberg (2005). https://doi.org/10.1007/11601494_3

72. da Silva, A.P.R., Martins, M.H., Rocha, B.P., Loureiro, A.A., Ruiz, L.B., Wong, H.C.: Decentralized intrusion detection in wireless sensor networks. In: Proceedings of the 1st ACM International Workshop on Quality of Service & Security in Wireless and Mobile Networks, pp. 16–23. ACM (2005)

73. Toueg, S.: Randomized byzantine agreements. In: Proceedings of the Third Annual ACM Symposium on Principles of Distributed Computing, pp. 163–178. ACM (1984)

74. Toueg, S., Perry, K.J., Srikanth, T.: Fast distributed agreement. SIAM J. Comput. 16(3), 445–457 (1987)

75. Winter, T., et al.: RPL: IPV6 routing protocol for low-power and lossy networks. Technical report (2012)

76. Wood, G.: Ethereum: a secure decentralised generalised transaction ledger. Ethereum Proj. Yellow Pap. 151, 1–32 (2014)

77. Xiao, X.Y., Peng, W.C., Hung, C.C., Lee, W.C.: Using sensorranks for in-network detection of faulty readings in wireless sensor networks. In: Proceedings of the 6th ACM International Workshop on Data Engineering for Wireless and Mobile Access, pp. 1–8. ACM (2007)

78. Yan, Q., Huang, W., Luo, X., Gong, Q., Yu, F.R.: A multi-level DDoS mitigation framework for the industrial Internet of Things. IEEE Commun. Mag. 56(2), 30–36 (2018)

79. Ye, F., Zhong, G., Lu, S., Zhang, L.: Gradient broadcast: a robust data delivery protocol for large scale sensor networks. Wirel. Netw. 11(3), 285–298 (2005)

80. Yeow, K., Gani, A., Ahmad, R.W., Rodrigues, J.J., Ko, K.: Decentralized consensus for edge-centric Internet of Things: a review, taxonomy, and research issues. IEEE Access 6, 1513–1524 (2018)

81. Zhou, S., Lin, K.J., Na, J., Chuang, C.C., Shih, C.S.: Supporting service adaptation in fault tolerant Internet of Things. In: 2015 IEEE 8th International Conference on Service-Oriented Computing and Applications (SOCA), pp. 65–72. IEEE (2015)

# Author Index

Printed in the United States
By Bookmasters